Generation X

AMERICANS BORN 1965 to 1976

6th EDITION

The American
Generations Series

BY THE NEW STRATEGIST EDITORS

New Strategist Publications, Inc.
Ithaca, New York

New Strategist Publications, Inc.
P.O. Box 242, Ithaca, New York 14851
800/848-0842; 607/273-0913
www.newstrategist.com

ISBN 978-1-935114-16-1

Printed in the United States of America

Table of Contents

Chapter 9. Spending

Chapter 10. Time Use

Chapter 11. Wealth

Tables

Illustrations

Introduction

Generation X gained fame simply by following the Baby-Boom generation onto the stage of youth decades ago, a stage Boomers created and made the center of the nation's attention. Generation X was everything Boomers were not—small in number, cynical rather than idealistic, they were expected to make their way easily through life because of the swath Boomers had carved. But it did not turn out that way. Generation Xers have struggled to compete with the masses of Boomers ahead of them and the large Millennial generation that follows at their heels. Perhaps no generation has been hit as hard by the housing crisis as Generation X. Now they face a dismal job market, especially as Boomers postpone retirement. The sixth edition of *Generation X: Americans Born 1965 to 1976* tells the sometimes grim story of the small generation spanning the ages of 32 to 43 in 2009.

Although their numbers are small, lifestage dictates that Generation X is a vital part of the nation's commerce and culture. People in their thirties and forties are in the crowded-nest lifestage. They are supposed to be moving up in their careers, their incomes should grow, and their spending should climb because of the expenses of children. *Generation X: Americans Born 1965 to 1976* shows how Gen Xers are coping with these demands and what to expect in the future.

Generation Xers are a diverse segment of the population, with minorities accounting for a large share of the whole. One issue binds together this diversity: cutthroat competition in the job market. While other generations are facing the same issues, getting ahead is proving more difficult for Generation X because they do not have the power of numbers. Only 16 percent of Americans are Gen Xers, while 25 percent are Boomers and another 25 percent are Millennials (see the Population chapter). Perhaps because they are overshadowed by others, Gen Xers are suffering economically. The percentage of men aged 35 to 44 who have worked for their current employer for 10 or more years has plummeted (see the Labor Force chapter). The median income of men aged 35 to 44 is lower today than it was in 1990, after adjusting for inflation (see the Income chapter).

It is not easy to study Generation Xers. Few government surveys focus on the generation, and the ages spanned by the members of the generation make it difficult to tease them out of the government's traditional five- or ten-year age categories. To analyze Gen X lifestyles, then, most of the tables in *Generation X: Americans Born 1965 to 1976* approximate the generation. Single-year-of-age data are shown when they are available, but five-year age groups are most common. When five-year age categories are shown, Gen Xers can be included in the 30-to-34, 35-to-39, and 40-to-44 age groups depending on the year for which data are presented. In a few tables, data are available only for much broader age groups, forcing a more general analysis of trends among the middle aged.

Whether Generation X age groups are exact or approximate, however, the results are clear. Generation Xers are struggling as they search for financial security. *Generation X: Americans Born 1965 to 1976* is your guide to how well they are doing.

How to use this book

Generation X: Americans Born 1965 to 1976 is designed for easy use. It is divided into 11 chapters, organized alphabetically: Attitudes, Education, Health, Housing, Income, Labor Force, Living Arrangements, Population, Spending, Time Use, and Wealth.

The sixth edition of *Generation X* includes the latest data on the changing demographics of homeownership, based on the Census Bureau's 2008 Housing Vacancies and Homeownership Survey. In the Health chapter, you will find up-to-date statistics on health insurance coverage, as well as new data on the use of alternative medicine. The Income chapter, with statistics from the 2008 Current Population Survey, reveals the struggle of so many Americans to stay afloat. *Generation X* presents labor force data for 2008 and includes the government's labor force projections, which show falling labor force participation rates in the age group as the recession took hold. It contains new data on the health of the population, including updated estimates of the overweight and obese. The Census Bureau's latest population projections are also included in the book, and show the imminent decline in the number of 35-to-54-year-olds as the age group shrinks with Generation X. The Wealth chapter presents estimates of household wealth from the Federal Reserve Board's 2007 Survey of Consumer Finances, and reveals the financial status of households just as the housing bubble burst and the recession began. New to this edition is an Attitudes chapter with data from the 2008 General Social Survey that compare and contrast the perspectives of the generations.

Most of the tables in *Generation X* are based on data collected by the federal government, in particular the Census Bureau, the Bureau of Labor Statistics, the National Center for Education Statistics, the National Center for Health Statistics, and the Federal Reserve Board. The federal government is the best source of up-to-date, reliable information on the changing characteristics of Americans. By having *Generation X* on your bookshelf, you can get the answers to your questions faster than you can online. Even better, visit www.newstrategist.com and download the PDF version of *Generation X*, which includes links to an Excel version of every table in the book, which will enable you to do your own analyses, put together a PowerPoint presentation, etc.

Each chapter of *Generation X* includes the demographic and lifestyle data most important to researchers. Within each chapter, most of the tables are based on data collected by the federal government, but they are not simply reproductions of government spreadsheets—as is the case in many reference books. Instead, each table is individually compiled and created by New Strategist's editors, with calculations designed to reveal the trends. The task of extracting and processing raw data from the government's web sites to create a single table can require hours of effort. New Strategist has done the work for you, each table telling a story about Gen Xers—a story explained by the accompanying text and chart, which analyze the data and highlight future trends. If you need more information than the tables and text provide, you can plumb the original source listed at the bottom of each table.

The book contains a comprehensive table list to help you locate the information you need. For a more detailed search, see the index at the back of the book. Also at the back of the book is the glossary, which defines the terms and describes the many surveys referenced in the tables and text.

With *Generation X: Americans Born 1965 to 1976* on your bookshelf, an in-depth understanding of this influential and struggling generation is at hand.

1

Attitudes

■ Older Americans are the most trusting. Forty-one percent of older Americans say most people can be trusted. In contrast, only 24 percent of Millennials say others can be trusted.

■ Generation Xers are least satisfied with their finances, with 36 percent saying they are not at all satisfied.

■ Boomers are most likely to say that their pay has not kept pace with inflation. Forty-five percent of Boomers feel like they are falling behind.

■ Older Americans are by far most likely to think they are much better off than their parents were at the same age (45 percent). Generation Xers are least likely to agree (24 percent).

■ The percentage of people who think two children is ideal ranges from a high of 55 percent among Baby Boomers to a low of 41 percent among Millennials. A larger 44 percent of Millennials think three or more children is ideal.

■ While only 40 percent of older Americans believe in evolution, the share climbs to 48 percent among Boomers, to 52 percent among Gen Xers, and to 62 percent among Millennials.

■ The 52 percent majority of Millennials sees nothing wrong with sexual relations between adults of the same sex. Support shrinks to 45 percent among Gen Xers, 34 percent among Boomers, and to a mere 19 percent among older Americans.

Older Americans Are the Happiest

Most of the married are very happily married.

When asked how happy they are, only about one in three Americans say they are very happy. The 54 percent majority reports feeling only pretty happy. Older people are happier than middle-aged or younger adults. Forty percent of older Americans say they are very happy compared with 31 percent of Baby Boomers and Generation Xers and just 27 percent of Millennials.

The 62 percent majority of married Americans say they are very happily married. Here, too, older Americans are the happiest group, with 67 of them saying they are very happily married. Only 60 percent of Boomers say the same.

Americans are almost evenly split on whether life is exciting (47 percent) or pretty routine (48 percent). Variations by generation are small, but Generation X is slightly more likely than others to find life exciting.

Few believe most people can be trusted. Only 32 percent of the public says that most people can be trusted, down from 37 percent who felt that way 10 years earlier. Younger generations are far less trusting than older Americans, as only 24 percent of Millennials believe most people can be trusted compared with 41 percent of people aged 63 or older.

■ Younger generations of Americans are struggling with a deteriorating economy, which reduces their happiness and increases their distrust.

Few Millennials trust others

(percent of people aged 18 or older who think most people can be trusted, by generation, 2008)

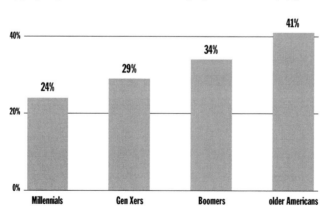

Table 1.1 General Happiness, 2008

"Taken all together, how would you say things are these days—would you say that you are very happy, pretty happy, or not too happy?"

(percent of people aged 18 or older responding by generation, 2008)

	very happy	pretty happy	not too happy
Total people	**31.7%**	**54.4%**	**13.9%**
Millennial generation (aged 18 to 31)	27.4	55.8	16.8
Generation X (aged 32 to 43)	31.0	57.0	12.0
Baby Boom (aged 44 to 62)	30.8	55.6	13.6
Older Americans (aged 63 or older)	39.7	47.2	13.1

Source: Survey Documentation and Analysis, Computer-assisted Survey Methods Program, University of California, Berkeley, General Social Surveys, 1972-2008 Cumulative Data Files, Internet site http://sda.berkeley.edu/cgi-bin32/hsda?harcsda+gss08; calculations by New Strategist

Table 1.2 Happiness of Marriage, 2008

"Taking all things together, how would you describe your marriage?"

(percent of currently married people aged 18 or older responding by generation, 2008)

	very happy	pretty happy	not too happy
Total married people	**62.1%**	**35.3%**	**2.6%**
Millennial generation (aged 18 to 31)	63.7	35.1	1.1
Generation X (aged 32 to 43)	61.5	35.7	2.7
Baby Boom (aged 44 to 62)	60.0	36.7	3.3
Older Americans (aged 63 or older)	66.6	31.7	1.7

Source: Survey Documentation and Analysis, Computer-assisted Survey Methods Program, University of California, Berkeley, General Social Surveys, 1972-2008 Cumulative Data Files, Internet site http://sda.berkeley.edu/cgi-bin32/hsda?harcsda+gss08; calculations by New Strategist

Table 1.3 Is Life Exciting, Routine, or Dull, 2008

"In general, do you find life exciting, pretty routine, or dull?"

(percent of people aged 18 or older responding by generation, 2008)

	exciting	pretty routine	dull
Total people	**47.2%**	**48.1%**	**3.8%**
Millennial generation (aged 18 to 31)	47.4	48.5	3.8
Generation X (aged 32 to 43)	48.6	46.5	3.1
Baby Boom (aged 44 to 62)	46.7	49.0	3.9
Older Americans (aged 63 or older)	46.4	47.7	4.4

Note: Numbers will not sum to total because "don't know" is not shown.
Source: Survey Documentation and Analysis, Computer-assisted Survey Methods Program, University of California, Berkeley, General Social Surveys, 1972-2008 Cumulative Data Files, Internet site http://sda.berkeley.edu/cgi-bin32/hsda?harcsda+gss08; calculations by New Strategist

Table 1.4 Trust in Others, 2008

"Generally speaking, would you say that most people can be trusted or that you can't be too careful in life?"

(percent of people aged 18 or older responding by generation, 2008)

	can trust	cannot trust	depends
Total people	**31.9%**	**63.9%**	**4.3%**
Millennial generation (aged 18 to 31)	24.5	71.1	4.4
Generation X (aged 32 to 43)	29.3	66.7	4.1
Baby Boom (aged 44 to 62)	34.3	61.5	4.2
Older Americans (aged 63 or older)	40.5	55.4	4.1

Source: Survey Documentation and Analysis, Computer-assisted Survey Methods Program, University of California, Berkeley, General Social Surveys, 1972-2008 Cumulative Data Files, Internet site http://sda.berkeley.edu/cgi-bin32/hsda?harcsda+gss08; calculations by New Strategist

Belief in Hard Work Is Strong among Younger Generations

Generation Xers are most likely to own a business.

How do people get ahead? Two-thirds of Americans say it is by hard work. Only 12 percent believe luck alone gets people ahead. Generation Xers (71 percent) and Millennials (70 percent) believe most strongly in hard work to get ahead, whereas Boomers (63 percent) give the least credence to hard work.

Millennials are most likely to live in the same city as they did when they were 16 years old, in part because they have had less time to move than older generations. Boomers are less likely than Gen Xers or older Americans to live in a different state than they did at age 16.

The likelihood of owning a business is greatest among Generation Xers (18 percent) and Boomers (15 percent). Only 8 percent of Millennials own a business, and the share among older Americans is an even smaller 6 percent.

■ The belief in luck as the most important way to get ahead is strongest among older Americans.

Business ownership peaks in middle age

(percent of people aged 18 or older who currently own and help manage a business, by generation, 2008)

	Millennials	Gen Xers	Boomers	older Americans
	8%	18%	15%	6%

Table 1.5 How People Get Ahead, 2008

"Some people say that people get ahead by their own hard work;
others say that lucky breaks or help from other people are more important.
Which do you think is most important?"

(percent of people aged 18 or older responding by generation, 2008)

	hard work	both equally	luck
Total people	**67.1%**	**20.8%**	**12.1%**
Millennial generation (aged 18 to 31)	70.2	18.0	11.8
Generation X (aged 32 to 43)	70.7	20.5	8.9
Baby Boom (aged 44 to 62)	63.4	23.7	12.9
Older Americans (aged 63 or older)	66.2	19.2	14.7

Source: Survey Documentation and Analysis, Computer-assisted Survey Methods Program, University of California, Berkeley, General Social Surveys, 1972-2008 Cumulative Data Files, Internet site http://sda.berkeley.edu/cgi-bin32/hsda?harcsda+gss08; calculations by New Strategist

Table 1.6 Geographic Mobility Since Age 16, 2008

"When you were 16 years old, were you living in this same (city/town/county)?"

(percent of people aged 18 or older responding by generation, 2008)

	same city	same state different city	different state
Total people	**40.0%**	**23.2%**	**36.8%**
Millennial generation (aged 18 to 31)	55.4	16.6	28.0
Generation X (aged 32 to 43)	34.1	22.9	43.0
Baby Boom (aged 44 to 62)	37.0	27.1	35.9
Older Americans (aged 63 or older)	32.9	24.5	42.6

Source: Survey Documentation and Analysis, Computer-assisted Survey Methods Program, University of California, Berkeley, General Social Surveys, 1972-2008 Cumulative Data Files, Internet site http://sda.berkeley.edu/cgi-bin32/hsda?harcsda+gss08; calculations by New Strategist

Table 1.7 **Business Ownership, 2008**

"Are you, alone or with others, currently the owner of a business you help manage, including self-employment or selling any goods or services to others?"

(percent of people aged 18 or older responding by generation, 2008)

	yes	no
Total people	**12.6%**	**87.4%**
Millennial generation (aged 18 to 31)	8.4	91.6
Generation X (aged 32 to 43)	18.1	81.9
Baby Boom (aged 44 to 62)	15.4	84.6
Older Americans (aged 63 or older)	5.8	94.2

Source: Survey Documentation and Analysis, Computer-assisted Survey Methods Program, University of California, Berkeley, General Social Surveys, 1972-2008 Cumulative Data Files, Internet site http://sda.berkeley.edu/cgi-bin32/hsda?harcsda+gss08; calculations by New Strategist

More than One-Third of Gen Xers Are Dissatisfied with Their Finances

Many say that their pay has not kept up with the cost of living.

Few Americans identify with the lower class, but even fewer think they are in the upper class. The 89 percent majority of every generation sees itself as either working class or middle class, but the distribution varies greatly. Whereas Millennials, Xers, and Boomers are more likely to call themselves working class than middle class, the opposite is true for older Americans. The highest share of self-identified lower-class people occurs among Millennials (8 percent). Older Americans are most likely to describe themselves as upper class (5 percent).

A 47 percent plurality of Americans believes their family income is average, while not quite one-third says they make less than average. Baby Boomers are most likely to say they have above average incomes, and they may well be right since they are in their peak earning years.

The share of people who are satisfied with their financial situation stood at 29 percent in 2008, down slightly from the 31 percent of 1998. In parallel, those more or less satisfied with their finances have declined from 44 to 42 percent. Satisfaction with personal finances is greatest among older Americans, only 20 percent of whom are not at all satisfied. The dissatisfied share peaks among Generation Xers at 36 percent, as they juggle college loans, mortgages, and the expenses of growing families.

When asked whether the pay at their current job has kept pace with the cost of living, Boomers are by far most likely to say it has not. The Millennial generation has the largest share of people who say their pay has just about kept pace with inflation. In each generation about one in four say their pay has risen faster than the cost of living.

■ Financial backsliding was common among working Americans even before the current economic disruptions.

Many Boomers and younger adults are dissatisfied with their financial situation

(percent of people aged 18 or older who say they are not at all satisfied with their financial situation, by generation, 2008)

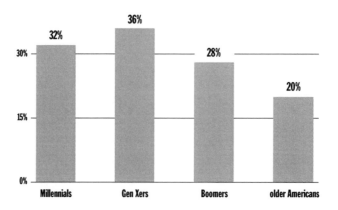

Table 1.8 Social Class Membership, 2008

"If you were asked to use one of four names for your social class, which would you say you belong in: the lower class, the working class, the middle class, or the upper class?"

(percent of people aged 18 or older responding by generation, 2008)

	lower	working	middle	upper
Total people	**7.3%**	**45.7%**	**43.4%**	**3.6%**
Millennial generation (aged 18 to 31)	8.1	49.4	40.1	2.5
Generation X (aged 32 to 43)	6.7	50.5	38.6	4.2
Baby Boom (aged 44 to 62)	7.3	45.5	43.7	3.5
Older Americans (aged 63 or older)	6.6	35.3	53.2	4.8

Source: Survey Documentation and Analysis, Computer-assisted Survey Methods Program, University of California, Berkeley, General Social Surveys, 1972-2008 Cumulative Data Files, Internet site http://sda.berkeley.edu/cgi-bin32/hsda?harcsda+gss08; calculations by New Strategist

Table 1.9 Family Income Relative to Others, 2008

"Compared with American families in general, would you say your family income is far below average, below average, average, above average, or far above average?"

(percent of people aged 18 or older responding by generation, 2008)

	far below average	below average	average	above average	far above average
Total people	**6.3%**	**25.2%**	**46.7%**	**19.8%**	**2.0%**
Millennial generation (aged 18 to 31)	6.6	26.8	49.4	16.5	0.7
Generation X (aged 32 to 43)	7.8	25.5	43.9	20.7	2.2
Baby Boom (aged 44 to 62)	5.6	22.8	46.2	22.4	3.1
Older Americans (aged 63 or older)	5.0	27.8	47.9	17.9	1.4

Source: Survey Documentation and Analysis, Computer-assisted Survey Methods Program, University of California, Berkeley, General Social Surveys, 1972-2008 Cumulative Data Files, Internet site http://sda.berkeley.edu/cgi-bin32/hsda?harcsda+gss08; calculations by New Strategist

Table 1.10 Satisfaction with Financial Situation, 2008

"So far as you and your family are concerned, would you say that you are pretty well satisfied with your present financial situation, more or less satisfied, or not satisfied at all?"

(percent of people aged 18 or older responding by generation, 2008)

	satisfied	more or less satisfied	not at all satisfied
Total people	**28.9%**	**41.7%**	**29.4%**
Millennial generation (aged 18 to 31)	24.8	43.7	31.5
Generation X (aged 32 to 43)	20.5	43.7	35.7
Baby Boom (aged 44 to 62)	27.3	44.2	28.4
Older Americans (aged 63 or older)	48.0	31.6	20.4

Source: Survey Documentation and Analysis, Computer-assisted Survey Methods Program, University of California, Berkeley, General Social Surveys, 1972-2008 Cumulative Data Files, Internet site http://sda.berkeley.edu/cgi-bin32/hsda?harcsda+gss08; calculations by New Strategist

Table 1.11 How Has Pay Changed, 2008

"Thinking about your current employer, how much has your pay changed on your current job since you began? Would you say . . . "

(percent of employed people aged 18 to 62 responding by generation, 2008)

	my pay has gone up more than the cost of living	my pay has stayed about the same as the cost of living	my pay has not kept up with the cost of living
Total people	**23.5%**	**35.6%**	**40.9%**
Millennial generation (aged 18 to 31)	22.7	41.9	35.3
Generation X (aged 32 to 43)	24.9	37.7	37.4
Baby Boom (aged 44 to 62)	22.9	32.3	44.8

Source: Survey Documentation and Analysis, Computer-assisted Survey Methods Program, University of California, Berkeley, General Social Surveys, 1972-2008 Cumulative Data Files, Internet site http://sda.berkeley.edu/cgi-bin32/hsda?harcsda+gss08; calculations by New Strategist

The American Standard of Living May Be Falling

Fewer Americans believe they are better off than their parents.

When comparing their own standard of living now with that of their parents when they were the same age, 63 percent of respondents say they are better off. The figure was 66 percent 10 years earlier. Older Americans are by far most likely to think they are much better off than their parents were at the same age (45 percent). Generation Xers are least likely to agree (24 percent).

When asked whether they think they have a good chance to improve their standard of living, 59 percent of Americans agree. This is down sharply from the 74 percent of a decade earlier. Not surprisingly, younger people—with most of their life ahead of them—are more hopeful than older Americans. Seventy-two percent of Millennials, but only 47 percent of older Americans, believe that their standard of living will improve.

Sixty percent of respondents believe their children will have a better standard of living when they reach the respondent's present age. The share is 67 percent among Millennials, 61 percent among Xers, 57 percent among Boomers, and 53 percent among older Americans. One in four Boomers and older Americans predict their children will be worse off, but fewer Xers (16 percent) and Millennials (13 percent) agree.

■ The Americans who now have the least are most likely to believe things will be better in the future.

Most still believe children will be better off

(percent of people aged 18 or older with children who think their children's standard of living will be somewhat or much better than theirs is now, by generation, 2008)

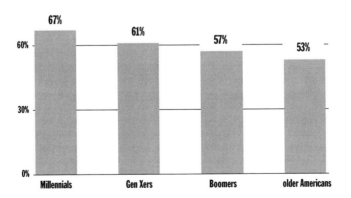

Table 1.12 Parents' Standard of Living, 2008

"Compared to your parents when they were the age you are now, do you think your own standard of living now is much better, somewhat better, about the same, somewhat worse, or much worse than theirs was?"

(percent of people aged 18 or older responding by generation, 2008)

	much better	somewhat better	about the same	somewhat worse	much worse
Total people	**31.6%**	**31.1%**	**21.1%**	**11.5%**	**4.6%**
Millennial generation (aged 18 to 31)	32.9	32.6	20.3	10.5	3.7
Generation X (aged 32 to 43)	24.1	31.6	22.0	16.3	6.1
Baby Boom (aged 44 to 62)	28.9	31.4	22.3	12.4	5.1
Older Americans (aged 63 or older)	45.1	27.9	19.1	5.2	2.7

Source: Survey Documentation and Analysis, Computer-assisted Survey Methods Program, University of California, Berkeley, General Social Surveys, 1972-2008 Cumulative Data Files, Internet site http://sda.berkeley.edu/cgi-bin32/hsda?harcsda+gss08; calculations by New Strategist

Table 1.13 Standard of Living Will Improve, 2008

"The way things are in America, people like me and my family have a good chance of improving our standard of living. Do you agree or disagree?"

(percent of people aged 18 or older responding by generation, 2008)

	strongly agree	agree	neither	disagree	strongly disagree
Total people	**14.7%**	**44.7%**	**13.9%**	**22.9%**	**3.8%**
Millennial generation (aged 18 to 31)	19.6	52.2	11.3	14.0	2.9
Generation X (aged 32 to 43)	15.2	44.7	13.7	21.7	4.6
Baby Boom (aged 44 to 62)	12.0	44.9	11.8	27.9	3.4
Older Americans (aged 63 or older)	13.2	33.6	22.3	26.0	4.9

Source: Survey Documentation and Analysis, Computer-assisted Survey Methods Program, University of California, Berkeley, General Social Surveys, 1972-2008 Cumulative Data Files, Internet site http://sda.berkeley.edu/cgi-bin32/hsda?harcsda+gss08; calculations by New Strategist

Table 1.14 Children's Standard of Living, 2008

"When your children are at the age you are now, do you think their
standard of living will be much better, somewhat better,
about the same, somewhat worse, or much worse than yours is now?"

(percent of people aged 18 or older with children responding by generation, 2008)

	much better	somewhat better	about the same	somewhat worse	much worse
Total people with children	**30.7%**	**29.2%**	**20.0%**	**14.3%**	**5.8%**
Millennial generation (aged 18 to 31)	40.1	27.0	19.3	8.0	5.5
Generation X (aged 32 to 43)	25.5	36.0	22.9	12.4	3.6
Baby Boom (aged 44 to 62)	27.7	29.5	18.4	17.7	6.5
Older Americans (aged 63 or older)	30.3	23.2	21.3	17.5	7.6

Source: Survey Documentation and Analysis, Computer-assisted Survey Methods Program, University of California, Berkeley, General Social Surveys, 1972-2008 Cumulative Data Files, Internet site http://sda.berkeley.edu/cgi-bin32/hsda?harcsda+gss08; calculations by New Strategist

Two Children Are Most Popular

Many Millennials think three children is the ideal number, however.

Across generations a plurality of Americans thinks that two is the ideal number of children. Boomers, who are finished with their childbearing, are most enthusiastic about two—55 percent say two children is ideal and only 29 percent think three or more is best. In contrast, only 41 percent of Millennials think two is ideal and a larger 44 percent say three or more is best. Millennials are more likely than the oldest Americans—who gave birth to the Baby Boom generation—to think three or more children is ideal.

Regardless of their number, most children are subject to a good, hard spanking when they misbehave. Seventy-one percent of Americans believe children sometimes must be spanked, with little difference by generation.

The 52 percent majority of older Americans believes it is better for everyone involved if the man is the achiever outside the home and the woman takes care of the home and family. Only about one-third of the younger generations agree. A similar gap exists with regard to working mothers. Among Boomers and younger generations, about three out of four think a working mother can have just as warm and secure a relationship with her children as a mother who does not work. Only 62 percent of older Americans agree.

Support for the view that government should help people who are sick and in need is strongest among Millennials and declines with age. Twenty-one percent of older Americans—the only age group that is covered by government-provided health insurance—believe people should help themselves. Only 12 percent of Millennials agree.

■ The generation gap in attitudes between Boomers and their parents is greater than the gap between Boomers and their children.

Few among the younger generations think traditional sex roles are best

(percent of people aged 18 or older who think traditional sex roles are best, by generation, 2008)

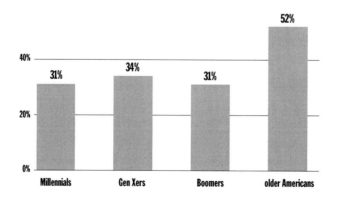

Table 1.15 Ideal Number of Children, 2008

"What do you think is the ideal number of children for a family to have?"

(percent of people aged 18 or older responding by generation, 2008)

	none	one	two	three	four or more	as many as want
Total people	**1.0%**	**2.5%**	**47.7%**	**26.6%**	**10.1%**	**12.1%**
Millennial generation (aged 18 to 31)	0.7	3.9	40.6	34.3	10.1	10.4
Generation X (aged 32 to 43)	0.0	2.5	44.4	29.3	12.0	11.9
Baby Boom (aged 44 to 62)	1.5	1.6	55.2	19.2	9.4	13.2
Older Americans (aged 63 or older)	1.4	2.5	45.5	28.3	9.6	12.6

Source: Survey Documentation and Analysis, Computer-assisted Survey Methods Program, University of California, Berkeley, General Social Surveys, 1972-2008 Cumulative Data Files, Internet site http://sda.berkeley.edu/cgi-bin32/hsda?harcsda+gss08; calculations by New Strategist

Table 1.16 Spanking Children, 2008

"Do you strongly agree, agree, disagree, or strongly disagree that it is sometimes necessary to discipline a child with a good, hard, spanking?"

(percent of people aged 18 or older responding by generation, 2008)

	strongly agree	agree	disagree	strongly disagree
Total people	**24.7%**	**46.2%**	**23.1%**	**6.0%**
Millennial generation (aged 18 to 31)	29.8	41.0	23.0	6.2
Generation X (aged 32 to 43)	19.9	52.3	22.6	5.2
Baby Boom (aged 44 to 62)	24.7	46.1	22.7	6.5
Older Americans (aged 63 or older)	22.9	46.1	25.2	5.7

Source: Survey Documentation and Analysis, Computer-assisted Survey Methods Program, University of California, Berkeley, General Social Surveys, 1972-2008 Cumulative Data Files, Internet site http://sda.berkeley.edu/cgi-bin32/hsda?harcsda+gss08; calculations by New Strategist

Table 1.17 Better for Man to Work, Woman to Tend Home, 2008

"It is much better for everyone involved if the man is the achiever outside
the home and the woman takes care of the home and family."

(percent of people aged 18 or older responding by generation, 2008)

	strongly agree	agree	disagree	strongly disagree
Total people	**8.2%**	**27.0%**	**47.2%**	**17.5%**
Millennial generation (aged 18 to 31)	7.3	24.0	44.5	24.2
Generation X (aged 32 to 43)	8.4	25.2	47.8	18.6
Baby Boom (aged 44 to 62)	7.5	24.0	50.7	17.8
Older Americans (aged 63 or older)	11.3	40.5	42.6	5.5

Source: Survey Documentation and Analysis, Computer-assisted Survey Methods Program, University of California, Berkeley, General Social Surveys, 1972-2008 Cumulative Data Files, Internet site http://sda.berkeley.edu/cgi-bin32/hsda?harcsda+gss08; calculations by New Strategist

Table 1.18 Working Mother's Relationship with Children, 2008

"Do you strongly agree, agree, disagree, or strongly disagree with
the statement: A working mother can establish just as warm and secure
a relationship with her children as a mother who does not work."

(percent of people aged 18 or older responding by generation, 2008)

	strongly agree	agree	disagree	strongly disagree
Total people	**26.3%**	**46.0%**	**22.2%**	**5.4%**
Millennial generation (aged 18 to 31)	26.0	46.1	22.5	5.4
Generation X (aged 32 to 43)	31.4	44.5	20.9	3.2
Baby Boom (aged 44 to 62)	26.3	49.0	19.0	5.6
Older Americans (aged 63 or older)	20.7	41.4	29.9	7.9

Source: Survey Documentation and Analysis, Computer-assisted Survey Methods Program, University of California, Berkeley, General Social Surveys, 1972-2008 Cumulative Data Files, Internet site http://sda.berkeley.edu/cgi-bin32/hsda?harcsda+gss08; calculations by New Strategist

Table 1.19 Should Government Help the Sick, 2008

"Some people think that it is the responsibility of the government in Washington to see to it that people have help in paying for doctors and hospital bills; they are at point 1. Others think that these matters are not the responsibility of the federal government and that people should take care of these things themselves; they are at point 5. Where would you place yourself on this scale?"

(percent of people aged 18 or older responding by generation, 2008)

	1 government should help	2	3 agree with both	4	5 people should help themselves
Total people	**34.9%**	**18.7%**	**30.0%**	**9.3%**	**7.1%**
Millennial generation (aged 18 to 31)	39.0	23.1	25.9	5.2	6.8
Generation X (aged 32 to 43)	35.0	19.8	30.7	9.4	5.1
Baby Boom (aged 44 to 62)	35.2	18.5	28.0	11.4	7.0
Older Americans (aged 63 or older)	28.7	11.2	39.1	10.0	11.0

Source: Survey Documentation and Analysis, Computer-assisted Survey Methods Program, University of California, Berkeley, General Social Surveys, 1972-2008 Cumulative Data Files, Internet site http://sda.berkeley.edu/cgi-bin32/hsda?harcsda+gss08; calculations by New Strategist

Religious Diversity Is on the Rise

Share of Protestants dwindles with each successive generation.

Asked whether science makes our way of life change too fast, the 52 percent majority of Americans disagrees with the statement. Each successive generation is a little surer than the previous one. While 51 percent of older Americans think things change too fast, only 45 percent of Millennials hold that opinion.

Americans are almost equally divided between those who believe in evolution (51 percent) and those who do not (49 percent), but there are large differences by generation. While only 40 percent of older Americans believe in evolution, the share climbs to 48 percent among Boomers, to 52 percent among Gen Xers, and to 62 percent among Millennials.

Among older Americans, 60 percent are Protestants. Among Baby Boomers, the figure is 58 percent. Yet only 39 percent of Generation Xers and Millennials call themselves Protestant. Conversely, the share of people with no religious preference climbs from a mere 7 percent among older Americans to a substantial 27 percent among Millennials. Older Americans are twice as likely as members of younger generations to describe themselves as very religious and they are more likely to see the Bible as the word of God.

The majority of Americans disapproves of the Supreme Court decision barring local governments from requiring religious readings in public schools. While the slight majority of Millennials and nearly half the Generation Xers support the decision, only 36 percent of Baby Boomers and just 31 percent of older Americans back the Supreme Court's decision.

■ Along with the growing racial and ethnic diversity of the American, religious preferences are also growing more diverse.

Younger generations are less Protestant

(percent of people aged 18 or older whose religious preference is Protestant, by generation, 2008)

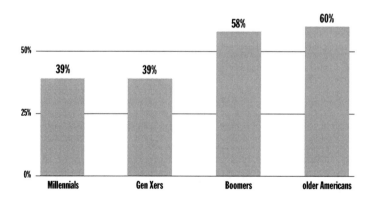

Table 1.20 Attitude toward Science, 2008

"Do you strongly agree, agree, disagree, or strongly disagree with the statement:
Science makes our way of life change too fast."

(percent of people aged 18 or older responding by generation, 2008)

	strongly agree	agree	disagree	strongly disagree
Total people	**9.0%**	**38.8%**	**43.9%**	**8.3%**
Millennial generation (aged 18 to 31)	8.3	36.3	46.1	9.3
Generation X (aged 32 to 43)	8.4	39.4	44.9	7.3
Baby Boom (aged 44 to 62)	10.3	38.0	42.2	9.4
Older Americans (aged 63 or older)	7.6	43.4	43.4	5.7

Source: Survey Documentation and Analysis, Computer-assisted Survey Methods Program, University of California, Berkeley, General Social Surveys, 1972-2008 Cumulative Data Files, Internet site http://sda.berkeley.edu/cgi-bin32/hsda?harcsda+gss08; calculations by New Strategist

Table 1.21 Attitude toward Evolution, 2008

"True or false: Human beings, as we know them today,
developed from earlier species of animals."

(percent of people aged 18 or older responding by generation, 2008)

	true	false
Total people	**50.9%**	**49.1%**
Millennial generation (aged 18 to 31)	62.1	37.9
Generation X (aged 32 to 43)	51.8	48.2
Baby Boom (aged 44 to 62)	47.8	52.2
Older Americans (aged 63 or older)	39.8	60.2

Source: Survey Documentation and Analysis, Computer-assisted Survey Methods Program, University of California, Berkeley, General Social Surveys, 1972-2008 Cumulative Data Files, Internet site http://sda.berkeley.edu/cgi-bin32/hsda?harcsda+gss08; calculations by New Strategist

Table 1.22 Religious Preference, 2008

"What is your religious preference?"

(percent of people aged 18 or older responding by generation, 2008)

	Protestant	Catholic	Jewish	none
Total people	**49.8%**	**25.1%**	**1.7%**	**16.8%**
Millennial generation (aged 18 to 31)	39.0	26.3	1.2	27.1
Generation X (aged 32 to 43)	39.1	28.1	2.9	18.9
Baby Boom (aged 44 to 62)	58.4	21.1	0.9	13.6
Older Americans (aged 63 or older)	60.1	27.3	2.6	7.2

Note: Figures will not sum to 100 percent because "other religion" is not shown.
Source: Survey Documentation and Analysis, Computer-assisted Survey Methods Program, University of California, Berkeley,
General Social Surveys, 1972-2008 Cumulative Data Files, Internet site http://sda.berkeley.edu/cgi-bin32/hsda?harcsda+gss08;
calculations by New Strategist

Table 1.23 Degree of Religiosity, 2008

"To what extent do you consider yourself a religious person?"

(percent of people aged 18 or older responding by generation, 2008)

	very religious	moderately relgious	slightly religious	not religious
Total people	**18.2%**	**42.2%**	**23.4%**	**16.2%**
Millennial generation (aged 18 to 31)	12.1	33.1	28.1	26.7
Generation X (aged 32 to 43)	13.8	40.6	25.7	19.9
Baby Boom (aged 44 to 62)	20.1	45.9	22.1	11.9
Older Americans (aged 63 or older)	27.7	48.6	17.4	6.3

Source: Survey Documentation and Analysis, Computer-assisted Survey Methods Program, University of California, Berkeley,
General Social Surveys, 1972-2008 Cumulative Data Files, Internet site http://sda.berkeley.edu/cgi-bin32/hsda?harcsda+gss08;
calculations by New Strategist

Table 1.24 Belief in the Bible, 2008

"Which of these statements comes closest to describing your feelings about the Bible? 1) The Bible is the actual word of God and is to be taken literally, word for word; 2) The Bible is the inspired word of God but not everything in it should be taken literally, word for word; 3) The Bible is an ancient book of fables, legends, history, and moral precepts recorded by men."

(percent of people aged 18 or older responding by generation, 2008)

	word of God	inspired word	book of fables	other
Total people	**32.0%**	**47.0%**	**19.6%**	**1.4%**
Millennial generation (aged 18 to 31)	27.5	50.3	21.0	1.3
Generation X (aged 32 to 43)	30.8	46.3	20.3	2.6
Baby Boom (aged 44 to 62)	33.6	44.9	20.6	1.0
Older Americans (aged 63 or older)	36.0	48.1	15.0	1.0

Source: Survey Documentation and Analysis, Computer-assisted Survey Methods Program, University of California, Berkeley, General Social Surveys, 1972-2008 Cumulative Data Files, Internet site http://sda.berkeley.edu/cgi-bin32/hsda?harcsda+gss08; calculations by New Strategist

Table 1.25 Bible in the Public Schools, 2008

"The United States Supreme Court has ruled that no state or local government may require the reading of the Lord's Prayer or Bible verses in public schools. What are your views on this? Do you approve or disapprove of the court ruling?"

(percent of people aged 18 or older responding by generation, 2008)

	approve	disapprove
Total people	**41.8%**	**58.2%**
Millennial generation (aged 18 to 31)	52.8	47.2
Generation X (aged 32 to 43)	48.0	52.0
Baby Boom (aged 44 to 62)	36.2	63.8
Older Americans (aged 63 or older)	30.7	69.3

Source: Survey Documentation and Analysis, Computer-assisted Survey Methods Program, University of California, Berkeley, General Social Surveys, 1972-2008 Cumulative Data Files, Internet site http://sda.berkeley.edu/cgi-bin32/hsda?harcsda+gss08; calculations by New Strategist

Growing Tolerance of Sexual Behavior

Americans are growing more accepting of premarital sex and homosexuality.

The share of Americans who believe that premarital sex is not wrong at all grew from 43 percent in 1998 to 55 percent in 2008. While the majority of Boomers and younger generations see nothing wrong with premarital sex, the share is just 38 percent among older Americans.

When it comes to sexual relations between adults of the same sex, the trend of growing tolerance is apparent as well. Each successive generation is less likely to condemn homosexuality. The 52 percent majority of Millennials sees nothing wrong with same-sex sexual relations, but support dwindles to 45 percent among Xers, 34 percent among Boomers, and a mere 19 percent among older Americans.

■ Acceptance of gays and lesbians will grow as tolerant Millennials replace older, less tolerant generations in the population.

Most Millennials see nothing wrong with gays and lesbians

(percent of people aged 18 or older who see nothing wrong with sexual relations between two adults of the same sex, by generation, 2008)

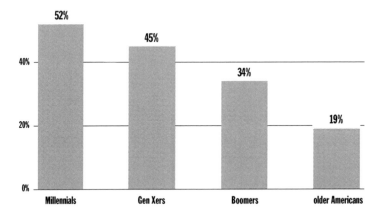

Table 1.26 Premarital Sex, 2008

"If a man and woman have sex relations before marriage, do you think it is always wrong, almost always wrong, wrong only sometimes, or not wrong at all?"

(percent of people aged 18 or older responding by generation, 2008)

	always wrong	almost always wrong	sometimes wrong	not wrong at all
Total people	**22.6%**	**7.2%**	**15.4%**	**54.8%**
Millennial generation (aged 18 to 31)	17.5	6.9	15.8	59.8
Generation X (aged 32 to 43)	21.0	4.9	17.7	56.5
Baby Boom (aged 44 to 62)	23.0	6.5	12.4	58.1
Older Americans (aged 63 or older)	31.0	11.7	18.9	38.4

Source: Survey Documentation and Analysis, Computer-assisted Survey Methods Program, University of California, Berkeley, General Social Surveys, 1972-2008 Cumulative Data Files, Internet site http://sda.berkeley.edu/cgi-bin32/hsda?harcsda+gss08; calculations by New Strategist

Table 1.27 Homosexual Relations, 2008

"What about sexual relations between two adults of the same sex?"

(percent of people aged 18 or older responding by generation, 2008)

	always wrong	almost always wrong	sometimes wrong	not wrong at all
Total people	**52.4%**	**3.1%**	**6.7%**	**37.8%**
Millennial generation (aged 18 to 31)	41.4	1.8	5.3	51.5
Generation X (aged 32 to 43)	47.0	4.3	3.9	44.8
Baby Boom (aged 44 to 62)	53.0	3.3	10.0	33.8
Older Americans (aged 63 or older)	72.6	2.8	5.4	19.2

Source: Survey Documentation and Analysis, Computer-assisted Survey Methods Program, University of California, Berkeley, General Social Surveys, 1972-2008 Cumulative Data Files, Internet site http://sda.berkeley.edu/cgi-bin32/hsda?harcsda+gss08; calculations by New Strategist

Television News Is Most Important

The Internet has jumped into the number two position.

Nearly half of Americans get most of their news from television, 22 percent from the Internet, and 20 percent from the newspaper. Together these three news outlets are the main source of news for 90 percent of the public. But there are big differences by generation. Millennials are far more likely than any other generation to depend on the Internet. Thirty-eight percent of Millennials say the Internet is their most important source of news versus 30 percent of Gen Xers, 15 percent of Boomers and just 5 percent of older Americans. The Millennial attachment to the Internet is so strong that it has boosted the Internet into second place as a news source.

When asked about their political leanings, Americans like to point to the moderate middle (39 percent). A slightly smaller 36 percent say they are conservative, and 26 percent identify themselves as liberal. Millennials are twice as likely as older Americans to hold liberal views. The share of self-described conservatives drops with each successive generation, from 45 percent among older Americans to 28 percent among Millennials. In fact, a larger share of Millennials is liberal than conservative—the only generation in which liberals outnumber conservatives.

■ Millennials depend more on the Internet than on television for the news.

News sources differ dramatically by generation

(percent of people aged 18 or older who turn to each source for the news, by generation, 2008)

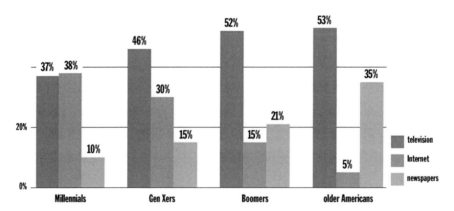

Table 1.28 Main Source of Information about Events in the News, 2008

"We are interested in how people get information about events in the news.
Where do you get most of your information about current news events?"

(percent of people aged 18 or older responding by generation, 2008)

	television	Internet	newspapers	radio	family, friends and colleagues	books, magazines, other
Total people	**47.5%**	**22.0%**	**19.6%**	**6.1%**	**2.8%**	**2.0%**
Millennial generation (aged 18 to 31)	36.8	38.3	9.8	8.4	5.9	0.8
Generation X (aged 32 to 43)	46.3	30.0	15.2	3.1	3.1	2.3
Baby Boom (aged 44 to 62)	52.4	14.8	21.5	7.6	1.5	2.2
Older Americans (aged 63 or older)	53.1	5.0	34.5	3.5	1.0	2.9

Source: Survey Documentation and Analysis, Computer-assisted Survey Methods Program, University of California, Berkeley, General Social Surveys, 1972-2008 Cumulative Data Files, Internet site http://sda.berkeley.edu/cgi-bin32/hsda?harcsda+gss08; calculations by New Strategist

Table 1.29 Political Leanings, 2008

"We hear a lot of talk these days about liberals and conservatives.
On a seven-point scale from extremely liberal (1) to extremely
conservative (7), where would you place yourself?"

(percent of people aged 18 or older responding by generation, 2008)

	1 extremely liberal	2 liberal	3 slightly liberal	4 moderate	5 slightly conservative	6 conservative	7 extremely conservative
Total people	**2.9%**	**12.2%**	**10.6%**	**38.6%**	**15.1%**	**16.7%**	**3.9%**
Millennial generation (aged 18 to 31)	3.0	16.1	15.3	37.6	13.9	12.2	2.0
Generation X (aged 32 to 43)	3.7	12.9	11.1	39.4	15.6	12.3	5.0
Baby Boom (aged 44 to 62)	2.1	11.1	10.2	38.4	15.9	18.1	4.1
Older Americans (aged 63 or older)	3.2	8.8	4.8	38.4	14.8	25.4	4.6

Source: Survey Documentation and Analysis, Computer-assisted Survey Methods Program, University of California, Berkeley, General Social Surveys, 1972-2008 Cumulative Data Files, Internet site http://sda.berkeley.edu/cgi-bin32/hsda?harcsda+gss08; calculations by New Strategist

Millennials and Gen Xers Are at Odds over Death Penalty

Overall opposition to capital punishment is growing.

Opposition to capital punishment is growing. In 1998, 27 percent of the public opposed the death penalty for persons convicted of murder. In 2008, the figure had increased to 32 percent. In a generational pattern rarely seen, support for the death penalty is strongest among Generation X (71 percent) and weakest among Millennials (63 percent).

The vast majority of Americans favors requiring a permit for gun ownership, and there is little variation by generation. Generation Xers are slightly more likely to favor gun permits than the other generations.

Support for legal abortion under certain circumstances is overwhelming. Nine out of 10 Americans approve of abortion if the women's health is in serious danger, and three-quarters if the pregnancy is the result of rape or there is a chance of serious defect in the baby. Economic and lifestyle reasons garner substantially lower approval ratings of 40 to 44 percent. Generally, there are only small differences in opinion by generation, but there are exceptions. Millennials are sharply less likely than the other generations to allow abortion because of a serious defect in the baby, for example. Boomers are much more accepting than other generations of abortion because a woman does not want more children. Older Americans are more likely than younger generations to want to outlaw abortion for economic and lifestyle reasons, but not for health reasons.

The two-thirds majority of Americans favor the right of the terminally ill to die with a doctor's assistance, but support for this measure has fallen slightly over the last decade. Support is strongest among Boomers, who are at an age when they may well see a terminally ill parent suffer, but it is weakest among older Americans themselves.

■ The generation gap between Boomers and older Americans is readily apparent on the issue of abortion for economic or lifestyle reasons.

Most do not favor allowing abortions for any reason

(percent of people aged 18 or older who favor legal abortion for any reason, by generation, 2008)

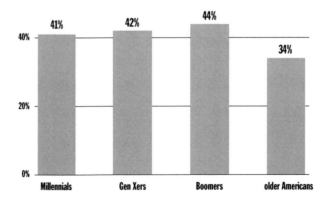

Table 1.30 Favor or Oppose Death Penalty for Murder, 2008

"Do you favor or oppose the death penalty for persons convicted of murder?"

(percent of people aged 18 or older responding by generation, 2008)

	favor	oppose
Total people	**67.6%**	**32.4%**
Millennial generation (aged 18 to 31)	62.8	37.2
Generation X (aged 32 to 43)	71.0	29.0
Baby Boom (aged 44 to 62)	68.0	32.0
Older Americans (aged 63 or older)	69.5	30.5

Source: Survey Documentation and Analysis, Computer-assisted Survey Methods Program, University of California, Berkeley, General Social Surveys, 1972-2008 Cumulative Data Files, Internet site http://sda.berkeley.edu/cgi-bin32/hsda?harcsda+gss08; calculations by New Strategist

Table 1.31 Favor or Oppose Gun Permits, 2008

"Would you favor or oppose a law which would require a person to obtain a police permit before he or she could buy a gun?"

(percent of people aged 18 or older responding by generation, 2008)

	favor	oppose
Total people	**79.1%**	**20.9%**
Millennial generation (aged 18 to 31)	78.3	21.7
Generation X (aged 32 to 43)	81.1	18.8
Baby Boom (aged 44 to 62)	78.4	21.6
Older Americans (aged 63 or older)	78.7	21.3

Source: Survey Documentation and Analysis, Computer-assisted Survey Methods Program, University of California, Berkeley, General Social Surveys, 1972-2008 Cumulative Data Files, Internet site http://sda.berkeley.edu/cgi-bin32/hsda?harcsda+gss08; calculations by New Strategist

Table 1.32 Support for Legal Abortion by Reason, 2008

"Please tell me whether or not you think it should be possible for a pregnant woman to obtain a legal abortion if . . . "

(percent of people aged 18 or older responding yes by generation, 2008)

	her health is seriously endangered	pregnancy is the result of a rape	there is a serious defect in the baby	she cannot afford more children	she does not want more childen	she is single and does not want to marry the man	she wants it for any reason
Total people	**88.6%**	**75.6%**	**73.7%**	**42.3%**	**43.7%**	**40.3%**	**41.2%**
Millennial generation (aged 18 to 31)	85.5	75.8	64.1	43.9	41.5	38.8	41.2
Generation X (aged 32 to 43)	90.6	76.8	75.6	39.4	41.9	40.3	41.8
Baby Boom (aged 44 to 62)	90.4	74.6	78.1	46.2	50.0	43.3	44.5
Older Americans (aged 63 or older)	86.6	75.4	75.2	35.2	35.4	35.1	33.6

Source: Survey Documentation and Analysis, Computer-assisted Survey Methods Program, University of California, Berkeley, General Social Surveys, 1972-2008 Cumulative Data Files, Internet site http://sda.berkeley.edu/cgi-bin32/hsda?harcsda+gss08; calculations by New Strategist

Table 1.33 Doctor-Assisted Suicide, 2008

"When a person has a disease that cannot be cured, do you think doctors should be allowed by law to end the patient's life by some painless means if the patient and his family request it?"

(percent of people aged 18 or older responding by generation, 2008)

	yes	no
Total people	**66.2%**	**33.8%**
Millennial generation (aged 18 to 31)	63.7	36.3
Generation X (aged 32 to 43)	66.1	33.9
Baby Boom (aged 44 to 62)	69.9	30.1
Older Americans (aged 63 or older)	61.1	38.9

Source: Survey Documentation and Analysis, Computer-assisted Survey Methods Program, University of California, Berkeley, General Social Surveys, 1972-2008 Cumulative Data Files, Internet site http://sda.berkeley.edu/cgi-bin32/hsda?harcsda+gss08; calculations by New Strategist

Education

■ The percentage of Americans with a college degree peaks among Generation Xers (aged 32 to 43 in 2008). Just over 33 percent of people aged 35 to 44 have a bachelor's degree or more education, which makes them the best educated among the generations.

■ The women of Generation X are better educated than their male counterparts. They are, in fact, the best-educated people in the nation. Thirty-five percent of women aged 35 to 44 have at least a bachelor's degree. Among men in the age group, 32 percent are college graduates.

■ Among Gen Xers, Asians are by far the best educated. The 58 percent majority of Asian men aged 35 to 44 have a bachelor's degree. In contrast, only 61 percent of Hispanic men in the age group have even graduated from high school.

■ People aged 35 to 44 account for only 6 percent of the nation's undergraduates, but they are 17 percent of graduate students.

■ One-third of people aged 35 to 44 took work-related courses in 2005, and almost one-half participated in an adult learning activity.

Generation X Is the Best Educated

Boomers are in third place among the generations.

The percentage of Americans with a college degree peaks among Generation Xers (aged 32 to 43 in 2008). Just over 33 percent of people aged 35 to 44 have a bachelor's degree or more education, which makes them the best educated among the generations. Millennials are not far behind, at 32 percent. Boomers were once the best-educated generation, but younger adults have surpassed them. Thirty percent of Boomers have at least a bachelor's degree. Among Americans aged 65 or older, only 20 percent are college graduates.

Although Generation X is the best-educated generation overall, the oldest Boomer men are better educated than the men of Generation X. Among Boomer men aged 55 to 64, from 34 to 35 percent have a bachelor's degree—thanks in part to draft deferments offered to college students during the Vietnam War. Among the men of Generation X, only 32 percent have a bachelor's degree.

■ The women of Generation X are better educated than Boomer women, pushing the percentage of Generation Xers with a college degree above that of Boomers.

Generation X is better educated than Boomers

(percent of people aged 25 or older with a bachelor's degree, by age, 2008)

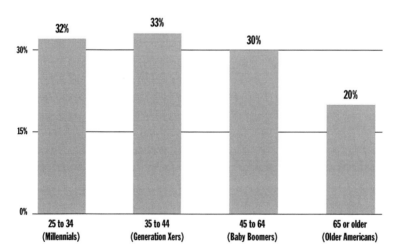

Table 2.1 Educational Attainment by Generation, 2008

(number and percent distribution of people aged 25 or older by highest level of education by generation, 2008; numbers in thousands)

	total 25 or older	Millennials (25 to 34)	Generation X (35 to 44)	Boomers (45 to 64)	older Americans (65 or older)
Total people	**196,305**	**40,146**	**42,132**	**77,237**	**36,790**
Not a high school graduate	26,340	4,768	4,792	8,474	8,306
High school graduate	61,183	11,297	12,040	24,290	13,559
Some college, no degree	33,812	7,396	7,199	13,694	5,523
Associate's degree	17,182	3,717	4,158	7,429	1,877
Bachelor's degree	37,559	9,421	9,204	14,527	4,407
Master's degree	14,765	2,792	3,506	6,337	2,129
Professional degree	2,991	490	693	1,356	453
Doctoral degree	2,472	267	538	1,132	536
High school graduate or more	169,964	35,380	37,338	68,765	28,484
Some college or more	108,781	24,083	25,298	44,475	14,925
Associate's degree or more	74,969	16,687	18,099	30,781	9,402
Bachelor's degree or more	57,787	12,970	13,941	23,352	7,525
Total people	**100.0%**	**100.0%**	**100.0%**	**100.0%**	**100.0%**
Not a high school graduate	13.4	11.9	11.4	11.0	22.6
High school graduate	31.2	28.1	28.6	31.4	36.9
Some college, no degree	17.2	18.4	17.1	17.7	15.0
Associate's degree	8.8	9.3	9.9	9.6	5.1
Bachelor's degree	19.1	23.5	21.8	18.8	12.0
Master's degree	7.5	7.0	8.3	8.2	5.8
Professional degree	1.5	1.2	1.6	1.8	1.2
Doctoral degree	1.3	0.7	1.3	1.5	1.5
High school graduate or more	86.6	88.1	88.6	89.0	77.4
Some college or more	55.4	60.0	60.0	57.6	40.6
Associate's degree or more	38.2	41.6	43.0	39.9	25.6
Bachelor's degree or more	29.4	32.3	33.1	30.2	20.5

Source: Bureau of the Census, Educational Attainment in the United States: 2008, detailed tables, Internet site http://www .census.gov/population/www/socdemo/education/cps2008.html; calculations by New Strategist

Most Gen Xers Have Been to College

One-third are college graduates.

Generation X followed the Baby-Boom generation onto the nation's college campuses. Overall, the 60 percent majority of Gen Xers have been to college—17 percent have college experience but no degree, 10 percent have an associate's degree, 22 percent have a bachelor's degree, and 11 percent have a graduate degree.

Although Generation X is the best-educated generation overall, the oldest Boomer men are better educated than Generation X men. Among Boomer men aged 55 to 64, from 34 to 35 percent have a bachelor's degree—thanks in part to draft deferments offered to college students during the Vietnam War. Among the men of Generation X, only 32 percent have a bachelor's degree. In contrast, Gen X women are better educated than Boomer women. Thirty-five percent of Gen X women have at least a bachelor's degree versus 29 percent of Baby-Boom women.

■ Because most Gen Xers have college experience, they will be eager to see their children go to college as well.

Among Generation Xers, one in nine has a graduate degree

(percent distribution of people aged 35 to 44 by educational attainment, 2008)

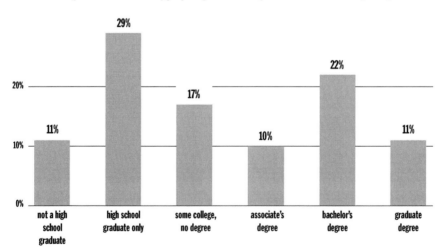

Table 2.2 Educational Attainment of Generation Xers, 2008

(number and percent distribution of people aged 25 or older, aged 35 to 44, and aged 35 to 44 in five-year age groups, by highest level of education, 2008; numbers in thousands)

		aged 35 to 44		
	total 25 or older	total	35 to 39	40 to 44
Total people	**196,305**	**42,132**	**20,733**	**21,399**
Not a high school graduate	26,340	4,792	2,281	2,511
High school graduate	61,183	12,040	5,586	6,454
Some college, no degree	33,812	7,199	3,623	3,576
Associate's degree	17,182	4,158	2,039	2,119
Bachelor's degree	37,559	9,204	4,695	4,509
Master's degree	14,765	3,506	1,865	1,641
Professional degree	2,991	693	375	318
Doctoral degree	2,472	538	268	270
High school graduate or more	169,964	37,338	18,451	18,887
Some college or more	108,781	25,298	12,865	12,433
Associate's degree or more	74,969	18,099	9,242	8,857
Bachelor's degree or more	57,787	13,941	7,203	6,738
Total people	**100.0%**	**100.0%**	**100.0%**	**100.0%**
Not a high school graduate	13.4	11.4	11.0	11.7
High school graduate	31.2	28.6	26.9	30.2
Some college, no degree	17.2	17.1	17.5	16.7
Associate's degree	8.8	9.9	9.8	9.9
Bachelor's degree	19.1	21.8	22.6	21.1
Master's degree	7.5	8.3	9.0	7.7
Professional degree	1.5	1.6	1.8	1.5
Doctoral degree	1.3	1.3	1.3	1.3
High school graduate or more	86.6	88.6	89.0	88.3
Some college or more	55.4	60.0	62.1	58.1
Associate's degree or more	38.2	43.0	44.6	41.4
Bachelor's degree or more	29.4	33.1	34.7	31.5

Source: Bureau of the Census, Educational Attainment in the United States: 2008, detailed tables, Internet site http://www .census.gov/population/www/socdemo/education/cps2008.html; calculations by New Strategist

Nearly 32 Percent of Gen X Men Are College Graduates

Some of those still without a college degree will get one later in life.

The men of Generation X are well educated, although not as highly educated as Baby-Boom men. Eighty-seven percent of men aged 35 to 44 are high school graduates, which leaves a substantial 13 percent who do not have a high school diploma. These men will have a difficult time making ends meet in an economy that rewards the well educated.

Fifty-seven percent of men aged 35 to 44 have attended college. Thirty-two percent have at least a bachelor's degree—meaning many men who start college drop out before getting their degree. Some are likely to return to school as older students to complete their education.

■ Most men are aware of the importance of education for their career. Even if they do not obtain a college degree, attending college for a year or two should boost their earnings significantly.

Most men aged 35 to 44 have at least some college experience

(percent distribution of men aged 35 to 44 by educational attainment, 2008)

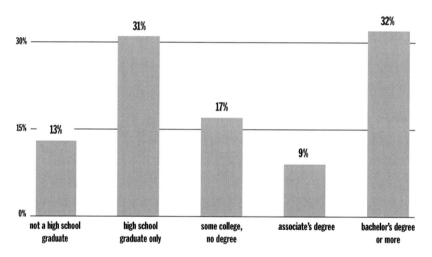

Table 2.3 Educational Attainment of Generation X Men, 2008

(number and percent distribution of men aged 25 or older, aged 35 to 44, and aged 35 to 44 in five-year age groups, by highest level of education, 2008; numbers in thousands)

		aged 35 to 44		
	total 25 or older	total	35 to 39	40 to 44
Total men	**94,470**	**20,880**	**10,291**	**10,589**
Not a high school graduate	13,298	2,648	1,203	1,445
High school graduate	29,491	6,391	3,004	3,387
Some college, no degree	15,810	3,464	1,844	1,620
Associate's degree	7,436	1,794	887	907
Bachelor's degree	18,042	4,252	2,170	2,082
Master's degree	6,886	1,609	819	790
Professional degree	1,877	399	213	186
Doctoral degree	1,628	324	152	172
High school graduate or more	81,170	18,233	9,089	9,144
Some college or more	51,679	11,842	6,085	5,757
Associate's degree or more	35,869	8,378	4,241	4,137
Bachelor's degree or more	28,433	6,584	3,354	3,230
Total men	**100.0%**	**100.0%**	**100.0%**	**100.0%**
Not a high school graduate	14.1	12.7	11.7	13.6
High school graduate	31.2	30.6	29.2	32.0
Some college, no degree	16.7	16.6	17.9	15.3
Associate's degree	7.9	8.6	8.6	8.6
Bachelor's degree	19.1	20.4	21.1	19.7
Master's degree	7.3	7.7	8.0	7.5
Professional degree	2.0	1.9	2.1	1.8
Doctoral degree	1.7	1.6	1.5	1.6
High school graduate or more	85.9	87.3	88.3	86.4
Some college or more	54.7	56.7	59.1	54.4
Associate's degree or more	38.0	40.1	41.2	39.1
Bachelor's degree or more	30.1	31.5	32.6	30.5

Source: Bureau of the Census, Educational Attainment in the United States: 2008, detailed tables, Internet site http://www .census.gov/population/www/socdemo/education/cps2008.html; calculations by New Strategist

Gen X Women Are Better Educated than Gen X Men

They are more likely to have attended and completed college.

As educational opportunities for women broadened over the years, increasing numbers of women took advantage of them. Women aged 35 to 44 are better educated than their male counterparts.

The women of Generation X, in fact, are the best-educated people in the nation. Specifically, 37 percent of women aged 35 to 39 have at least a bachelor's degree, and 65 percent have college experience. Among men aged 35 to 39, a smaller 33 percent have at least a bachelor's degree, while 59 percent have college experience.

The higher educational attainment of Baby-Boom and younger women is the driving factor behind the changing role of women in society. Having been better educated than their forebears, today's women expect to work and are eager to advance in their careers.

■ Among high school graduates, girls have been more likely than boys to go to college. Consequently, among Generation Xers, women are more likely than men to have a college degree.

Most women aged 35 to 44 have at least some college experience

(percent distribution of women aged 35 to 44 by educational attainment, 2008)

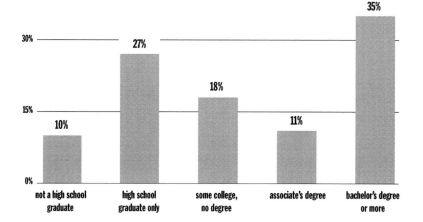

Table 2.4 Educational Attainment of Generation X Women, 2008

(number and percent distribution of women aged 25 or older, aged 35 to 44, and aged 35 to 44 in five-year age groups, by highest level of education, 2008; numbers in thousands)

		aged 35 to 44		
	total 25 or older	total	35 to 39	40 to 44
Total women	**101,835**	**21,252**	**10,442**	**10,810**
Not a high school graduate	13,042	2,143	1,079	1,064
High school graduate	31,692	5,649	2,582	3,067
Some college, no degree	18,002	3,736	1,779	1,957
Associate's degree	9,746	2,365	1,153	1,212
Bachelor's degree	19,517	4,953	2,526	2,427
Master's degree	7,879	1,898	1,046	852
Professional degree	1,114	296	163	133
Doctoral degree	844	215	116	99
High school graduate or more	88,794	19,112	9,365	9,747
Some college or more	57,102	13,463	6,783	6,680
Associate's degree or more	39,100	9,727	5,004	4,723
Bachelor's degree or more	29,354	7,362	3,851	3,511
Total women	**100.0%**	**100.0%**	**100.0%**	**100.0%**
Not a high school graduate	12.8	10.1	10.3	9.8
High school graduate	31.1	26.6	24.7	28.4
Some college, no degree	17.7	17.6	17.0	18.1
Associate's degree	9.6	11.1	11.0	11.2
Bachelor's degree	19.2	23.3	24.2	22.5
Master's degree	7.7	8.9	10.0	7.9
Professional degree	1.1	1.4	1.6	1.2
Doctoral degree	0.8	1.0	1.1	0.9
High school graduate or more	87.2	89.9	89.7	90.2
Some college or more	56.1	63.3	65.0	61.8
Associate's degree or more	38.4	45.8	47.9	43.7
Bachelor's degree or more	28.8	34.6	36.9	32.5

Source: Bureau of the Census, Educational Attainment in the United States: 2008, detailed tables, Internet site http://www .census.gov/population/www/socdemo/education/cps2008.html; calculations by New Strategist

Among Gen Xers, Asian Men Have the Highest Educational Attainment

Hispanics are least likely to have completed high school.

There are substantial socioeconomic differences among Americans by race and Hispanic origin. Differences in educational attainment are the primary reason for the disparity.

Among Gen X men, Asians are by far the best educated. Fully 76 percent of Asian men aged 35 to 44 have college experience and the 58 percent majority have at least a bachelor's degree. Among non-Hispanic white men in the age group, 64 percent have college experience and 36 percent have a bachelor's degree.

Hispanics are the least educated. Only 61 percent of Hispanic men aged 35 to 44 have even graduated from high school. Just 13 percent have a bachelor's degree. Black Gen X men are much better educated than Hispanics. Forty-eight percent have college experience, and 19 percent have a bachelor's degree.

■ The educational attainment of Hispanics is low because many are recent immigrants from countries with little educational opportunity.

Education gaps point to continued socioeconomic differences

(percent of men aged 35 to 44 with a bachelor's degree or more, by race and Hispanic origin, 2008)

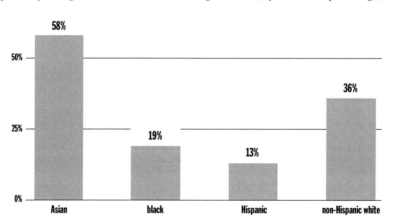

Table 2.5 Educational Attainment of Generation X Men by Race and Hispanic Origin, 2008

(number and percent distribution of men aged 35 to 44 by educational attainment, race, and Hispanic origin, 2008; numbers in thousands)

	total	Asian	black	Hispanic	non-Hispanic white
Total men aged 35 to 44	**20,880**	**1,191**	**2,422**	**3,638**	**13,469**
Not a high school graduate	2,648	87	326	1,424	805
High school graduate only	6,391	195	933	1,105	4,098
Some college, no degree	3,464	129	493	411	2,395
Associate's degree	1,794	85	212	208	1,259
Bachelor's degree	4,252	361	328	316	3,230
Master's degree	1,609	220	101	128	1,149
Professional degree	399	33	19	31	317
Doctoral degree	324	81	13	14	215
High school graduate or more	18,233	1,104	2,099	2,213	12,663
Some college or more	11,842	909	1,166	1,108	8,565
Associate's degree or more	8,378	780	673	697	6,170
Bachelor's degree or more	6,584	695	461	489	4,911
Total men aged 35 to 44	**100.0%**	**100.0%**	**100.0%**	**100.0%**	**100.0%**
Not a high school graduate	12.7	7.3	13.5	39.1	6.0
High school graduate only	30.6	16.4	38.5	30.4	30.4
Some college, no degree	16.6	10.8	20.4	11.3	17.8
Associate's degree	8.6	7.1	8.8	5.7	9.3
Bachelor's degree	20.4	30.3	13.5	8.7	24.0
Master's degree	7.7	18.5	4.2	3.5	8.5
Professional degree	1.9	2.8	0.8	0.9	2.4
Doctoral degree	1.6	6.8	0.5	0.4	1.6
High school graduate or more	87.3	92.7	86.7	60.8	94.0
Some college or more	56.7	76.3	48.1	30.5	63.6
Associate's degree or more	40.1	65.5	27.8	19.2	45.8
Bachelor's degree or more	31.5	58.4	19.0	13.4	36.5

Note: Asians and blacks are those who identify themselves as being of the race alone and those who identify themselves as being of the race in combination with other races. Non-Hispanic whites are those who identify themselves as being white alone and not Hispanic. Numbers do not add to total because not all races are shown and Hispanics may be of any race.
Source: Bureau of the Census, Educational Attainment in the United States: 2008, detailed tables, Internet site http://www .census.gov/population/www/socdemo/education/cps2008.html; calculations by New Strategist

Hispanic Women Are Least Likely to Be High School Graduates

Asians are most likely to be college graduates.

Although the educational attainment of women has been rising for decades, substantial gaps persist among Gen Xers by race and Hispanic origin. From 90 to 95 percent of Asian, black, and non-Hispanic white women aged 35 to 44 have graduated from high school versus only 66 percent of Hispanic women in the age group. The majority of Asian, black, and non-Hispanic white women have college experience compared with only 37 percent of their Hispanic counterparts.

Gen X women of Asian descent are the best educated. Fully 58 percent have at least a bachelor's degree. Among non-Hispanic white women in the age group, the proportion is 39 percent. Twenty-five percent of black women aged 35 to 44 have a bachelor's degree, while the figure is just 16 percent for Hispanics.

■ The educational attainment of Hispanics will remain low as long as immigrants are a large share of the Hispanic population.

Among Gen X women, Asians have the highest educational attainment

(percent of women aged 35 to 44 with a bachelor's degree or more, by race and Hispanic origin, 2008)

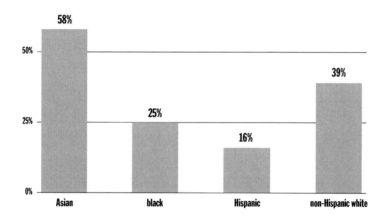

Table 2.6 Educational Attainment of Generation X Women by Race and Hispanic Origin, 2008

(number and percent distribution of women aged 35 to 44 by educational attainment, race, and Hispanic origin, 2008; numbers in thousands)

	total	Asian	black	Hispanic	non-Hispanic white
Total women aged 35 to 44	**21,252**	**1,276**	**2,993**	**3,266**	**13,577**
Not a high school graduate	2,143	115	293	1,110	611
High school graduate only	5,649	205	926	943	3,531
Some college, no degree	3,736	136	648	452	2,474
Associate's degree	2,365	74	383	255	1,631
Bachelor's degree	4,953	442	503	374	3,605
Master's degree	1,898	217	193	111	1,372
Professional degree	296	42	26	14	211
Doctoral degree	215	43	22	8	141
High school graduate or more	19,112	1,159	2,701	2,157	12,965
Some college or more	13,463	954	1,775	1,214	9,434
Associate's degree or more	9,727	818	1,127	762	6,960
Bachelor's degree or more	7,362	744	744	507	5,329
Total women aged 35 to 44	**100.0%**	**100.0%**	**100.0%**	**100.0%**	**100.0%**
Not a high school graduate	10.1	9.0	9.8	34.0	4.5
High school graduate only	26.6	16.1	30.9	28.9	26.0
Some college, no degree	17.6	10.7	21.7	13.8	18.2
Associate's degree	11.1	5.8	12.8	7.8	12.0
Bachelor's degree	23.3	34.6	16.8	11.5	26.6
Master's degree	8.9	17.0	6.4	3.4	10.1
Professional degree	1.4	3.3	0.9	0.4	1.6
Doctoral degree	1.0	3.4	0.7	0.2	1.0
High school graduate or more	89.9	90.8	90.2	66.0	95.5
Some college or more	63.3	74.8	59.3	37.2	69.5
Associate's degree or more	45.8	64.1	37.7	23.3	51.3
Bachelor's degree or more	34.6	58.3	24.9	15.5	39.3

Note: Asians and blacks are those who identify themselves as being of the race alone and those who identify themselves as being of the race in combination with other races. Non-Hispanic whites are those who identify themselves as being white alone and not Hispanic. Numbers do not add to total because not all races are shown and Hispanics may be of any race.
Source: Bureau of the Census, Educational Attainment in the United States: 2008, detailed tables, Internet site http://www .census.gov/population/www/socdemo/education/cps2008.html; calculations by New Strategist

Some Gen Xers Are Still in School

More than 1 million people aged 35 to 44 are students.

School is a major part of life for many people in their twenties and early thirties. But taking classes becomes much less common in the 35-to-44 age group. In 2007, just 4 percent of 35-to-44-year-olds were in school (Gen Xers were aged 31 to 42 in that year).

Because women are more likely to go to college than men, a larger proportion of women than men are enrolled in school. Five percent of women aged 35 to 44 are students compared with 3 percent of men.

■ Among students aged 35 to 44, women outnumber men by more than 380,000.

Among 35-to-44-year-olds, women outnumber men in school

(number of people aged 35 to 44 enrolled in school, by sex, 2007)

men: 618,000
women: 999,000

Table 2.7 School Enrollment by Sex and Age, 2007

(total number of people aged 3 or older, and number and percent enrolled in school by sex and age, 2007; numbers in thousands)

	total	enrolled	
		number	percent
Total people	**285,410**	**75,967**	**26.6%**
Under age 30	110,925	71,591	64.5
Aged 30 to 34	19,179	1,379	7.2
Aged 35 to 44	42,276	1,617	3.8
Aged 35 to 39	20,740	940	4.5
Aged 40 to 44	21,536	677	3.1
Aged 45 or older	113,029	1,380	1.2
Total females	**145,806**	**38,398**	**26.3**
Under age 30	54,583	35,705	65.4
Aged 30 to 34	9,632	765	7.9
Aged 35 to 44	21,420	999	4.7
Aged 35 to 39	10,489	587	5.6
Aged 40 to 44	10,931	412	3.8
Aged 45 or older	60,171	929	1.5
Total males	**139,603**	**37,569**	**26.9**
Under age 30	56,343	35,886	63.7
Aged 30 to 34	9,546	614	6.4
Aged 35 to 44	20,856	618	3.0
Aged 35 to 39	10,251	352	3.4
Aged 40 to 44	10,605	266	2.5
Aged 45 or older	52,858	452	0.9

Source: Bureau of the Census, School Enrollment—Social and Economic Characteristics of Students: October 2007, Internet site http://www.census.gov/population/www/socdemo/school/cps2007.html

Gen Xers Account for Few College Students

They are a significant share of graduate students, however.

Although the college enrollment of older people has grown over the years, young adults still dominate the nation's college campuses. In 2007, nearly 85 percent of college students were under age 35. People aged 35 to 44 (Gen Xers were aged 31 to 42 in that year) accounted for 8 percent of college students, while another 7 percent were people aged 45 or older.

Students aged 35 to 44 account for 6 percent of all undergraduates. The age group accounts for a larger 17 percent of graduate students.

■ Generation Xers are disappearing from college campuses, but many are still in graduate school.

More than half a million graduate students are aged 35 to 44

(number of graduate students by age, 2007)

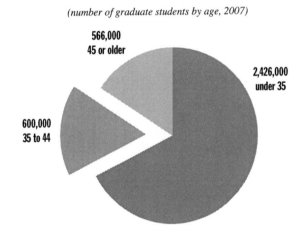

566,000
45 or older

2,426,000
under 35

600,000
35 to 44

Table 2.8 College Students by Age and Enrollment Level, 2007

(number and percent distribution of people aged 15 or older enrolled in institutions of higher education by age and level of enrollment, 2007; numbers in thousands)

	total	undergraduate	graduate school
Total enrolled	**17,956**	**14,365**	**3,591**
Under age 30	13,846	11,972	1,874
Aged 30 to 34	1,341	789	552
Aged 35 to 44	1,519	919	600
Aged 35 to 39	892	519	373
Aged 40 o 44	627	400	227
Aged 45 or older	1,249	683	566

PERCENT DISTRIBUTION BY LEVEL OF ENROLLMENT

Total enrolled	**100.0%**	**80.0%**	**20.0%**
Under age 30	100.0	86.5	13.5
Aged 30 to 34	100.0	58.8	41.2
Aged 35 to 44	100.0	60.5	39.5
Aged 35 to 39	100.0	58.2	41.8
Aged 40 o 44	100.0	63.8	36.2
Aged 45 or older	100.0	54.7	45.3

PERCENT DISTRIBUTION BY AGE

Total enrolled	**100.0%**	**100.0%**	**100.0%**
Under age 30	77.1	83.3	52.2
Aged 30 to 34	7.5	5.5	15.4
Aged 35 to 44	8.5	6.4	16.7
Aged 35 to 39	5.0	3.6	10.4
Aged 40 o 44	3.5	2.8	6.3
Aged 45 or older	7.0	4.8	15.8

Source: Bureau of the Census, School Enrollment—Social and Economic Characteristics of Students: October 2007, Internet site http://www.census.gov/population/www/socdemo/school/cps2007.html; calculations by New Strategist

Many Adults Participate in Education for Job-Related Reasons

Life-long learning is becoming a necessity for job security.

As job security dwindles, many workers are turning to the educational system to try to stay on track. Overall, 27 percent of Americans aged 16 or older participated in work-related adult education in 2005 (the latest available data), while another 21 percent took personal interest courses and 5 percent were enrolled in part-time degree or diploma programs.

The share of Americans involved in work-related adult education rises from less than one-third among 25-to-34-year-olds to its peaks of over 36 percent among 45-to-54-year-olds. Participation in personal interest courses declines slightly with age, as does participation in part-time degree or diploma programs.

■ Many Americans who participate in work-related education are retraining themselves to compete in the increasingly global economy.

Work-related training peaks in the 45-to-54 age group

(percent of workers who participated in work-related adult education activities, by age, 2005)

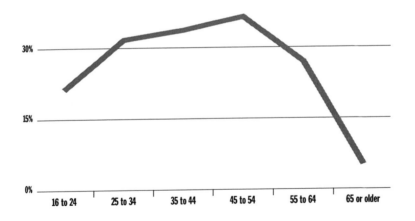

Table 2.9 Participation in Adult Education by Age, 2005

(percent of people aged 16 or older participating in formal adult education activities, by age and type of adult education activity, 2005)

	total	percent participating in any activity	work-related courses	personal interest courses	part-time degree or diploma programs
Total people	**100.0%**	**44.4%**	**26.9%**	**21.4%**	**5.0%**
Aged 16 to 24	100.0	52.9	21.2	26.6	11.4
Aged 25 to 34	100.0	52.2	31.7	22.1	8.7
Aged 35 to 44	100.0	48.7	33.7	22.1	5.3
Aged 45 to 54	100.0	47.9	36.5	19.7	3.8
Aged 55 to 64	100.0	40.3	27.0	20.7	1.5
Aged 65 or older	100.0	22.9	5.2	18.8	0.3

Source: National Center for Education Statistics, The Condition of Education, Participation in Adult Education, Indicator 10 (2007), Internet site http://nces.ed.gov/programs/coe/2007/section1/indicator10.asp; calculations by New Strategist

3

Health

■ The 55 percent majority of Americans aged 18 or older say their health is "excellent" or "very good." Among 35-to-44-year-olds the figure is 61 percent.

■ Americans have a weight problem, and Gen Xers are no exception. The average Gen X man weighs nearly 200 pounds. The average Gen X woman weighs more than 160 pounds.

■ Men aged 15 to 44 have had a median of 5.6 opposite-sex partners in their lifetime. Women in the age group have had a median of 3.3 partners.

■ Women spanning the ages from 30 to 44 accounted for only 36 percent of the nation's births in 2007 (Generation X was aged 31 to 42 in that year).

■ Many Gen Xers do not have health insurance. In 2007, 18 percent of people aged 35 to 44 were without health insurance coverage.

■ Twenty-two percent of Americans aged 18 to 44 have experienced lower back pain for at least one full day in the past three months, making it the most common health condition in the age group.

■ Thirty-eight percent of people aged 25 to 44 have taken at least one prescription drug in the past month, and 10 percent have taken three or more.

■ Among Gen Xers, 40 percent have used alternative medicine in the past year.

Most 35-to-44-Year-Olds Say Their Health Is Excellent or Very Good

The proportion who say they are in very good or excellent health declines with age.

Overall, the 55 percent majority of Americans aged 18 or older say their health is "excellent" or "very good." The figure peaks at 63 percent in the 25-to-34 age group. Among people aged 35 to 44 in 2008 (Gen Xers were aged 32 to 43 in that year), 61 percent say they are in very good or excellent. The figure falls with increasing age as chronic conditions become common.

Fewer than half of people aged 65 or older report that their health is excellent or very good. Nevertheless, the proportion saying they are in poor health remains below 8 percent, regardless of age. Among people aged 65 or older, the proportion saying their health is excellent or very good (38 percent) surpasses the proportion saying their health is only "fair" or "poor" (25 percent).

■ Medical advances that allow people to manage chronic conditions should boost the proportions of people reporting excellent or very good health in the years ahead.

More than 60 percent of 35-to-44-year-olds say their health is excellent or very good

(percent of people aged 18 or older who say their health is excellent or very good, by age, 2008)

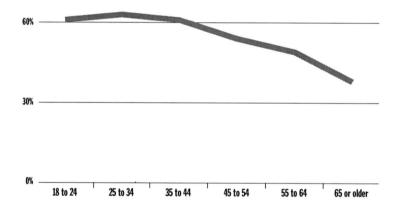

Table 3.1 Health Status by Age, 2008

(percent distribution of people aged 18 or older by self-reported health status, by age, 2008)

	total	excellent	very good	good	fair	poor
Total people	**100.0%**	**20.1%**	**34.9%**	**30.0%**	**10.6%**	**3.8%**
Aged 18 to 24	100.0	25.1	35.7	29.7	6.6	1.0
Aged 25 to 34	100.0	24.8	38.1	28.9	7.3	1.4
Aged 35 to 44	100.0	23.7	37.2	28.3	8.0	2.1
Aged 45 to 54	100.0	19.6	34.5	29.1	10.3	4.2
Aged 55 to 64	100.0	17.3	31.5	30.3	13.8	5.6
Aged 65 or older	100.0	11.4	26.7	34.1	18.0	7.4

Source: Centers for Disease Control and Prevention, Behavioral Risk Factor Surveillance System Prevalence Data, 2008, Internet site http://apps.nccd.cdc.gov/brfss/

Weight Problems Are the Norm for Gen Xers

Most men and women are overweight.

Americans have a weight problem, and Gen Xers are no exception. The average Gen X man weighs nearly 200 pounds. The average Gen X woman weighs more than 160 pounds. Three out of four Gen X men and 61 percent of Gen X women are overweight, and more than one-third are obese.

Although many people say they exercise, only 31 percent of adults participate in regular leisure-time physical activity, according to government data. The figure ranges from a high of 38 percent among 18-to-24-year-olds to a low of 17 percent among people aged 75 or older. Among 25-to-44-year-olds, only 33 percent participate in regular leisure-time physical activity.

■ Most Gen Xers lack the willpower to eat less or exercise more—fueling a diet and weight loss industry that never lacks for customers.

Most Gen Xers weigh more than they should

(percent distribution of people aged 35 to 44 by weight status, by sex, 2003–06)

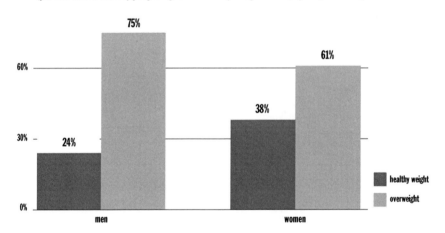

Table 3.2 Average Measured Weight by Age and Sex, 2003–06

(average weight in pounds of people aged 20 or older by age and sex, 2003–06)

	men	women
Total aged 20 or older	**194.7**	**164.7**
Aged 20 to 29	188.3	155.9
Aged 30 to 39	194.1	164.7
Aged 40 to 49	202.3	171.3
Aged 50 to 59	198.8	172.1
Aged 60 to 69	198.3	170.5
Aged 70 to 79	187.4	155.6
Aged 80 or older	168.1	142.2

Note: Data are based on measured weight of a sample of the civilian noninstitutionalized population.
Source: National Center for Health Statistics, Anthropometric Reference Data for Children and Adults: United States, 2003–2006, National Health Statistics Reports, Number 10, 2008, Internet site http://www.cdc.gov/nchs/products/pubs/pubd/nhsr/nhsr.htm; calculations by New Strategist

Table 3.3 Weight Status by Sex and Age, 2003–06

(percent distribution of people aged 20 or older by weight status, sex, and age, 2003–06)

	total	healthy weight	overweight total	obese
TOTAL PEOPLE	**100.0%**	**31.4%**	**66.9%**	**34.1%**
Total men	**100.0**	**26.1**	**72.6**	**33.1**
Aged 20 to 34	100.0	35.9	61.6	26.2
Aged 35 to 44	100.0	24.1	75.2	37.0
Aged 45 to 54	100.0	20.8	78.5	34.6
Aged 55 to 64	100.0	19.3	79.7	39.3
Aged 65 to 74	100.0	21.2	78.0	33.0
Aged 75 or older	100.0	33.1	65.8	24.0
Total women	**100.0**	**36.6**	**61.2**	**35.2**
Aged 20 to 34	100.0	45.1	50.9	28.4
Aged 35 to 44	100.0	37.6	60.7	36.1
Aged 45 to 54	100.0	31.1	67.3	40.0
Aged 55 to 64	100.0	29.5	69.6	41.0
Aged 65 to 74	100.0	28.5	70.5	36.4
Aged 75 or older	100.0	35.4	62.6	24.2

Note: Data are based on measured height and weight of a sample of the civilian noninstitutionalized population. Overweight is defined as a body mass index of 25 or higher. Obesity is defined as a body mass index of 30 or higher. Body mass index is calculated by dividing weight in kilograms by height in meters squared.
Source: National Center for Health Statistics, Health, United States, 2008, Internet site http://www.cdc.gov/nchs/hus.htm

Table 3.4 Leisure-Time Physical Activity Level by Sex and Age, 2006

(percent distribution of people aged 18 or older by leisure-time physical activity level, by sex and age, 2006)

	total	physically inactive	at least some physical activity	regular physical activity
TOTAL PEOPLE	**100.0%**	**39.5%**	**29.6%**	**30.9%**
Aged 18 to 24	100.0	34.8	27.1	38.1
Aged 25 to 44	100.0	35.0	31.6	33.4
Aged 45 to 54	100.0	38.2	30.7	31.1
Aged 55 to 64	100.0	41.9	30.9	27.2
Aged 65 to 74	100.0	48.0	25.8	26.2
Aged 75 or older	100.0	59.6	23.1	17.3
Total men	**100.0**	**38.5**	**27.4**	**33.1**
Aged 18 to 44	100.0	34.2	28.8	36.9
Aged 45 to 54	100.0	39.0	28.4	32.7
Aged 55 to 64	100.0	41.1	30.6	28.2
Aged 65 to 74	100.0	46.9	25.0	28.2
Aged 75 or older	100.0	52.1	26.6	21.4
Total women	**100.0**	**40.3**	**30.7**	**29.0**
Aged 18 to 44	100.0	35.6	32.0	32.4
Aged 45 to 54	100.0	37.5	33.0	29.5
Aged 55 to 64	100.0	42.6	31.1	26.3
Aged 65 to 74	100.0	49.0	26.5	24.5
Aged 75 or older	100.0	64.4	20.8	14.7

Note: "Physically inactive" are those with no sessions of light-to-moderate or vigorous leisure-time physical activity of at least 10 minutes duration during past week. "At least some physical activity" includes those with at least one light-to-moderate or vigorous leisure-time physical activity of at least 10 minutes duration during past week, but who did not meet the definition for regular leisure-time activity. "Regular physical activity" includes those who did three or more sessions per week of vigorous activity lasting at least 20 minutes or five or more sessions per week of light-to-moderate activity lasting at least 30 minutes.
Source: National Center for Health Statistics, Health, United States, 2008, Internet site http://www.cdc.gov/nchs/hus.htm

Americans Report on Their Sexual Behavior

For most, sexual activity is limited to one partner.

Every few years the federal government fields the National Survey of Family Growth, which examines the sexual behavior, contraceptive use, and childbearing patterns of Americans aged 15 to 44. Results from the latest survey, taken in 2002, have been released by the National Center for Health Statistics.

Overall 90 percent of men and 91 percent of women aged 15 to 44 have had at least one opposite-sex partner in their lifetime. Even among 15-to-19-year-olds, 57 percent of men and 62 percent of women are sexually experienced. Men aged 15 to 44 have had a median of 5.6 opposite-sex partners in their lifetime, with the figure peaking at 8.2 among men aged 40 to 44. Women have had a median of 3.3 partners in their lifetime, with a peak of 3.8 to 3.9 partners among women aged 30 or older. Among those with an opposite-sex partner in the past year, most had only one.

Ninety percent of men and women aged 15 to 44 identify themselves as heterosexual. Only 2 percent of men and 1 percent of women say they are homosexual. But 6 percent of men and 11 percent of women say they have had sexual activity with a same-sex partner in their lifetime (the 2002 survey questions regarding same-sex activity were worded differently for men and women, a factor that may explain the different percentages reporting same-sex activity).

■ Twenty-three percent of men and 9 percent of women report having had 15 or more opposite-sex partners in their lifetime.

Most Americans aged 18 or older are sexually active

(percent of people aged 15 to 44 who have had at least one opposite-sex partner during the past 12 months, by sex and age, 2002)

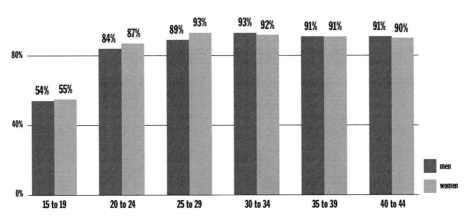

Table 3.5 Lifetime Sexual Activity of 15-to-44-Year-Olds by Sex, 2002

(number of people aged 15 to 44 and percent distribution by sexual experience with opposite-sex partners during lifetime, by sex and age, 2002; numbers in thousands)

	total		number of opposite-sex partners in lifetime							
	number	percent	none	1 or more	1	2	3 to 6	7 to 14	15 or more	median
Total men aged 15 to 44	**61,147**	**100.0**	**9.6**	**90.4**	**12.5**	**8.0**	**27.2**	**19.5**	**23.2**	**5.6**
Aged 15 to 19	10,208	100.0	43.5	56.6	23.4	9.0	17.0	4.9	2.3	1.6
Aged 20 to 24	9,883	100.0	9.9	90.1	15.7	11.6	33.1	13.9	15.8	3.8
Aged 25 to 29	9,226	100.0	5.0	94.9	10.0	8.7	29.3	23.1	23.8	5.9
Aged 30 to 34	10,138	100.0	3.0	97.0	10.7	6.9	28.4	21.9	29.1	6.4
Aged 35 to 39	10,557	100.0	2.1	97.9	8.9	7.0	27.9	25.4	28.7	6.9
Aged 40 to 44	11,135	100.0	1.9	98.2	8.8	5.4	25.6	24.2	34.2	8.2
Total women aged 15 to 44	**61,561**	**100.0**	**8.6**	**91.4**	**22.5**	**10.8**	**32.6**	**16.3**	**9.2**	**3.3**
Aged 15 to 19	9,834	100.0	37.8	62.2	27.2	9.0	19.1	5.0	1.9	1.4
Aged 20 to 24	9,840	100.0	8.9	91.1	24.6	13.0	32.2	14.4	6.9	2.8
Aged 25 to 29	9,249	100.0	2.5	97.5	22.5	11.7	31.3	20.1	11.9	3.5
Aged 30 to 34	10,272	100.0	1.9	98.0	20.5	9.4	38.8	18.0	11.3	3.8
Aged 35 to 39	10,853	100.0	1.1	98.9	20.2	11.2	35.8	20.5	11.2	3.9
Aged 40 to 44	11,512	100.0	1.4	98.6	20.4	10.5	37.4	19.1	11.2	3.8

Source: National Center for Health Statistics, Sexual Behavior and Selected Health Measures: Men and Women 15–44 Years of Age, United States, 2002, Advance Data, No. 362, 2005, Internet site http://www.cdc.gov/nchs/nsfg.htm

Table 3.6 Past Year Sexual Activity of 15-to-44-Year-Olds by Sex, 2002

(percent distribution of people aged 15 to 44 by sexual experience with opposite-sex partners during the past 12 months, and percent distribution by number of opposite partners in past 12 months, by sex and age, 2002; numbers in thousands)

	total	no opposite-sex partners in past year	one or more opposite-sex partners in past year
Sexual activity in past year			
Total men	**100.0%**	**16.4%**	**83.6%**
Aged 15 to 19	100.0	46.2	53.8
Aged 20 to 24	100.0	15.6	84.4
Aged 25 to 29	100.0	11.4	88.6
Aged 30 to 34	100.0	7.4	92.7
Aged 35 to 39	100.0	9.3	90.8
Aged 40 to 44	100.0	9.0	91.1
Total women	**100.0**	**15.3**	**84.7**
Aged 15 to 19	100.0	44.8	55.3
Aged 20 to 24	100.0	13.4	86.7
Aged 25 to 29	100.0	6.9	93.0
Aged 30 to 34	100.0	7.9	92.1
Aged 35 to 39	100.0	9.2	90.8
Aged 40 to 44	100.0	10.5	89.5

	total with one or more	one	two	three or more	not reported
Number of sex partners in past year					
Total men	**100.0%**	**75.0%**	**9.6%**	**12.4%**	**3.0%**
Aged 15 to 19	100.0	56.3	21.9	19.9	1.9
Aged 20 to 24	100.0	58.4	15.0	22.9	3.7
Aged 25 to 29	100.0	75.7	7.4	14.1	2.7
Aged 30 to 34	100.0	80.7	7.3	9.4	2.6
Aged 35 to 39	100.0	84.6	5.5	7.5	2.4
Aged 40 to 44	100.0	83.9	6.0	5.8	4.3
Total women	**100.0**	**80.5**	**9.0**	**8.0**	**2.5**
Aged 15 to 19	100.0	58.2	17.5	20.4	3.8
Aged 20 to 24	100.0	70.2	14.5	13.3	2.0
Aged 25 to 29	100.0	81.6	10.1	6.1	2.2
Aged 30 to 34	100.0	86.5	6.1	5.4	2.0
Aged 35 to 39	100.0	86.2	6.7	4.8	2.2
Aged 40 to 44	100.0	88.7	3.8	4.1	3.4

Source: National Center for Health Statistics, Sexual Behavior and Selected Health Measures: Men and Women 15–44 Years of Age, United States, 2002, Advance Data, No. 362, 2005, Internet site http://www.cdc.gov/nchs/nsfg.htm; calculations by New Strategist

Table 3.7 Sexual Orientation of 18-to-44-Year-Olds, 2002

(number of people aged 18 to 44 and percent distribution by sexual orientation, by sex and age, 2002; numbers in thousands)

| | total | | sexual orientation | | | | |
	number	percent	heterosexual	homosexual	bisexual	something else	did not report
Total men 18 to 44	**55,399**	**100.0%**	**90.2%**	**2.3%**	**1.8%**	**3.9%**	**1.8%**
Aged 18 to 19	4,460	100.0	91.3	1.7	1.4	3.5	2.1
Aged 20 to 24	9,883	100.0	91.0	2.3	2.0	3.5	1.3
Aged 25 to 29	9,226	100.0	87.3	2.8	0.9	5.7	3.3
Aged 30 to 34	10,138	100.0	91.1	2.0	1.7	4.0	1.2
Aged 35 to 44	21,692	100.0	90.3	2.4	2.2	3.5	1.6
Total women 18 to 44	**55,742**	**100.0**	**90.3**	**1.3**	**2.8**	**3.8**	**1.8**
Aged 18 to 19	4,015	100.0	84.2	0.9	7.4	5.7	1.9
Aged 20 to 24	9,840	100.0	90.0	0.8	3.5	4.4	1.3
Aged 25 to 29	9,249	100.0	89.9	1.5	2.8	2.8	3.1
Aged 30 to 34	10,272	100.0	91.2	1.3	2.1	3.8	1.6
Aged 35 to 44	22,365	100.0	91.4	1.5	2.0	3.5	1.6

Source: National Center for Health Statistics, Sexual Behavior and Selected Health Measures: Men and Women 15–44 Years of Age, United States, 2002, Advance Data, No. 362, 2005, Internet site http://www.cdc.gov/nchs/nsfg.htm

Table 3.8 Lifetime Same-Sex Sexual Activity of 15-to-44-Year-Olds, 2002

(percent of people aged 15 to 44 reporting any sexual activity with same-sex partners in their lifetime, by age and sex, 2002)

	men	women
Total aged 15 to 44	**6.0%**	**11.2%**
Aged 15 to 19	4.5	10.6
Aged 20 to 24	5.5	14.2
Aged 25 to 29	5.7	14.1
Aged 30 to 34	6.2	9.1
Aged 35 to 39	8.0	12.3
Aged 40 to 44	6.0	7.8

Note: The question about same-sex sexual contact was worded differently for men and women. Women were asked whether they had ever had a sexual experience of any kind with another female. Men were asked whether they had performed any of four specific sexual acts with another male. The question asked of women may have elicited more yes answers than the questions asked of men.
Source: National Center for Health Statistics, Sexual Behavior and Selected Health Measures: Men and Women 15–44 Years of Age, United States, 2002, Advance Data, No. 362, 2005, Internet site http://www.cdc.gov/nchs/nsfg.htm

Birth Rate Has Increased among Women Aged 30 or Older

Rate has fallen among women under age 30.

Between 1990 and 2006, the birth rate fell for women under age 30. The biggest decline occurred among teenagers, the number of births per 1,000 women aged 15 to 19 falling by 20 percent. The birth rate among 20-to-29-year-olds fell 6 percent during those years. Interestingly, the birth rate among 25-to-29-year old women bottomed out in 1997 and has been rising since then.

The birth rate has climbed substantially among women aged 30 or older since 1990. Behind the increase is catch-up childbearing by women who had postponed starting a family while they went to college and embarked on a career.

■ One reason for the recent rise in the birth rate among women aged 25 to 29 is the growing Hispanic population.

Birth rate peaks in the 25-to-29 age group

(births per 1,000 women in age group, 2006)

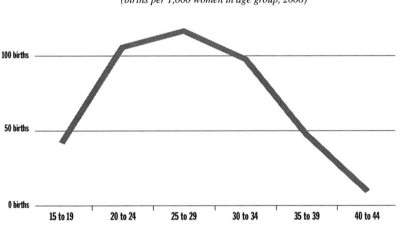

Table 3.9 Birth Rate by Age, 1990 to 2006

(number of live births per 1,000 women in age group, 1990 to 2006; percent change in rate, 1990–2000 and 2000–06)

	total	15 to 19	20 to 24	25 to 29	30 to 34	35 to 39	40 to 44	45 to 49
2006	68.5	41.9	105.9	116.7	97.7	47.3	9.4	0.6
2005	66.7	40.5	102.2	115.5	95.8	46.3	9.1	0.6
2004	66.3	41.1	101.7	115.5	95.3	45.4	8.9	0.5
2003	66.1	41.6	102.6	115.6	95.1	43.8	8.7	0.5
2002	64.8	43.0	103.6	113.6	91.5	41.4	8.3	0.5
2001	65.3	45.3	106.2	113.4	91.9	40.6	8.1	0.5
2000	65.9	47.7	109.7	113.5	91.2	39.7	8.0	0.5
1999	64.4	48.8	107.9	111.2	87.1	37.8	7.4	0.4
1998	64.3	50.3	108.4	110.2	85.2	36.9	7.4	0.4
1997	63.6	51.3	107.3	108.3	83.0	35.7	7.1	0.4
1996	64.1	53.5	107.8	108.6	82.1	34.9	6.8	0.3
1995	64.6	56.0	107.5	108.8	81.1	34.0	6.6	0.3
1994	65.9	58.2	109.2	111.0	80.4	33.4	6.4	0.3
1993	67.0	59.0	111.3	113.2	79.9	32.7	6.1	0.3
1992	68.4	60.3	113.7	115.7	79.6	32.3	5.9	0.3
1991	69.3	61.8	115.3	117.2	79.2	31.9	5.5	0.2
1990	70.9	59.9	116.5	120.2	80.8	31.7	5.5	0.2
Percent change								
2000 to 2006	3.9%	−12.2%	−3.5%	2.8%	7.1%	19.1%	17.5%	20.0%
1990 to 2000	−7.1	−20.4	−5.8	−5.6	12.9	25.2	45.5	150.0

Source: National Center for Health Statistics, Births: Final Data for 2006, National Vital Statistics Reports, Vol. 57, No. 7, 2009, Internet site http://www.cdc.gov/nchs/births.htm; calculations by New Strategist

Most Women Are Mothers by Age 30

Among women aged 15 to 44, the largest share has had two children.

The proportion of women who have never had a child falls from 93 percent among 15-to-19-year-olds to a much smaller (but still substantial) 19 percent among women aged 35 to 39. Overall, 55 percent of women aged 15 to 44 have had at least one child. The largest share (22 percent) have had two.

Six percent of women aged 15 to 44 had a baby in the past year, according to a 2006 survey. Women aged 25 to 29 are most likely to have had a baby in the past year, with 10 percent giving birth. By race and Hispanic origin, Hispanics are most likely to have had a baby in the past year, at 8 percent. Six percent of native-born women aged 15 to 44 had a child in the past year. Among foreign-born women, the figure is a larger 8 percent.

■ The two-child family has been the norm in the United States for several decades.

Most women aged 25 or older have had at least one child

(percent of women aged 15 to 44 who have had one or more children, by age, 2006)

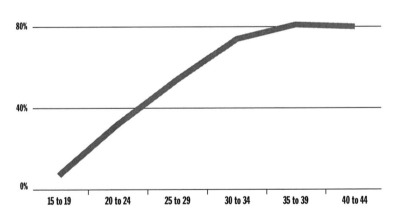

Table 3.10 Number of Children Born to Women Aged 15 to 44, 2006

(total number of women aged 15 to 44, and percent distribution by number of children ever borne, by age, 2006; numbers in thousands)

| | total | | number of children | | | | | | | |
	number	percent	none	one or more	one	two	three	four	five or six	seven or more
Total aged 15 to 44	**61,683**	**100.0%**	**45.1%**	**54.9%**	**17.0%**	**21.7%**	**10.8%**	**3.7%**	**1.4%**	**0.3%**
Aged 15 to 19	10,269	100.0	93.3	6.7	4.5	1.5	0.5	0.2	0.0	0.0
Aged 20 to 24	10,079	100.0	68.6	31.6	18.8	9.3	2.7	0.6	0.1	0.1
Aged 25 to 29	10,004	100.0	45.6	54.4	22.9	19.4	8.5	2.8	0.7	0.1
Aged 30 to 34	9,647	100.0	26.2	73.9	21.8	29.3	15.3	5.3	1.9	0.3
Aged 35 to 39	10,450	100.0	18.9	81.0	17.6	35.4	18.5	6.5	2.5	0.5
Aged 40 to 44	11,235	100.0	20.4	79.7	16.9	34.4	18.5	6.4	3.0	0.5

Source: Bureau of the Census, Fertility of American Women, Current Population Survey—June 2006, Detailed Tables, Internet site http://www.census.gov/population/www/socdemo/fertility/cps2006.html; calculations by New Strategist

Table 3.11 Women Giving Birth in the Past Year, 2006

(total number of women aged 15 to 44, number and percent who gave birth in the past year, and number and percent who had a first birth in past year, by age, 2006; numbers in thousands)

	total	gave birth in past year		first birth in past year	
		number	percent	number	percent
TOTAL AGED 15 TO 44	**61,683**	**3,974**	**6.4%**	**1,551**	**2.5%**
Age					
Aged 15 to 19	10,269	417	4.1	243	2.4
Aged 20 to 24	10,079	935	9.3	483	4.8
Aged 25 to 29	10,004	1,046	10.5	401	4.0
Aged 30 to 34	9,647	888	9.2	277	2.9
Aged 35 to 39	10,450	579	5.5	121	1.2
Aged 40 to 44	11,235	109	1.0	26	0.2
Race and Hispanic origin					
Asian	3,391	202	6.0	88	2.6
Black	9,272	538	5.8	218	2.4
Hispanic	10,099	830	8.2	309	3.1
Non-Hispanic white	38,532	2,383	6.2	923	2.4
Nativity status					
Native born	52,002	3,203	6.2	1,237	2.4
Foreign born	9,681	771	8.0	314	3.2
Region					
Northeast	11,176	667	6.0	262	2.3
Midwest	13,557	905	6.7	356	2.6
South	22,546	1,406	6.2	560	2.5
West	14,404	996	6.9	373	2.6

Note: Numbers by race and Hispanic origin do not add to total because Asians and blacks include those who identified themselves as being of the race alone and those who identified themselves as being of the race in combination with other races, and because Hispanics may be of any race. Non-Hispanic whites are those who identified themselves as being white alone and not Hispanic.
Source: Bureau of the Census, Fertility of American Women, Current Population Survey—June 2006, Detailed Tables, Internet site http://www.census.gov/population/www/socdemo/fertility/cps2006.html; calculations by New Strategist

Generation X No Longer Dominates Births

Only about one-third of babies are born to women aged 30 or older.

Despite an increase in the number of older mothers during the past few decades, the great majority of women who give birth are under age 30. Women aged 30 or older accounted for only 36 percent of the nation's births in 2007 (Generation X was aged 31 to 42 in that year). A much larger 64 percent of babies were born to women under age 30.

The age at which women give birth varies by race and Hispanic origin. Among blacks and Hispanics, women aged 30 to 44 account for only 26 to 30 percent of births. Among Asians, the women of Generation X account for the 56 percent majority of births. Many Asian women postpone childbearing until their thirties because most spend much of their twenties in college.

Among women aged 30 to 44 who gave birth in 2007, only 26 percent were having their first child. A larger 34 percent were having their second child, and the 40 percent plurality was having a third or subsequent child.

■ The Millennial generation has replaced Generation X as the dominant group entering parenthood.

The women of Generation X account for just over one-third of births

(percent distribution of births by age of mother, 2007)

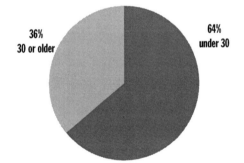

36%
30 or older

64%
under 30

Table 3.12 Births by Age, Race, and Hispanic Origin, 2007

(number and percent distribution of births by age, race, and Hispanic origin of mother, 2007)

	total	American Indian	Asian	non-Hispanic black	Hispanic	non-Hispanic white
Total births	**4,317,119**	**49,284**	**254,734**	**627,230**	**1,061,970**	**2,312,473**
Under age 15	6,218	120	92	2,326	2,407	1,269
Aged 15 to 19	445,045	8,925	8,022	106,224	148,453	173,104
Aged 20 to 24	1,082,837	16,759	32,309	200,273	305,107	526,943
Aged 25 to 29	1,208,504	12,420	71,465	157,173	287,730	676,599
Aged 30 to 44	1,567,166	11,021	142,207	160,374	317,179	930,015
Aged 30 to 34	962,179	7,052	86,949	97,332	201,212	566,197
Aged 35 to 39	499,916	3,265	46,379	50,614	95,694	301,666
Aged 40 to 44	105,071	704	8,879	12,428	20,273	62,152
Aged 45 to 54	7,349	38	639	860	1,095	4,544

PERCENT DISTRIBUTION BY RACE AND HISPANIC ORIGIN

	total	American Indian	Asian	non-Hispanic black	Hispanic	non-Hispanic white
Total births	**100.0%**	**1.1%**	**5.9%**	**14.5%**	**24.6%**	**53.6%**
Under age 15	100.0	1.9	1.5	37.4	38.7	20.4
Aged 15 to 19	100.0	2.0	1.8	23.9	33.4	38.9
Aged 20 to 24	100.0	1.5	3.0	18.5	28.2	48.7
Aged 25 to 29	100.0	1.0	5.9	13.0	23.8	56.0
Aged 30 to 44	100.0	0.7	9.1	10.2	20.2	59.3
Aged 30 to 34	100.0	0.7	9.0	10.1	20.9	58.8
Aged 35 to 39	100.0	0.7	9.3	10.1	19.1	60.3
Aged 40 to 44	100.0	0.7	8.5	11.8	19.3	59.2
Aged 45 to 54	100.0	0.5	8.7	11.7	14.9	61.8

PERCENT DISTRIBUTION BY AGE

	total	American Indian	Asian	non-Hispanic black	Hispanic	non-Hispanic white
Total births	**100.0%**	**100.0%**	**100.0%**	**100.0%**	**100.0%**	**100.0%**
Under age 15	0.1	0.2	0.0	0.4	0.2	0.1
Aged 15 to 19	10.3	18.1	3.1	16.9	14.0	7.5
Aged 20 to 24	25.1	34.0	12.7	31.9	28.7	22.8
Aged 25 to 29	28.0	25.2	28.1	25.1	27.1	29.3
Aged 30 to 44	36.3	22.4	55.8	25.6	29.9	40.2
Aged 30 to 34	22.3	14.3	34.1	15.5	18.9	24.5
Aged 35 to 39	11.6	6.6	18.2	8.1	9.0	13.0
Aged 40 to 44	2.4	1.4	3.5	2.0	1.9	2.7
Aged 45 to 54	0.2	0.1	0.3	0.1	0.1	0.2

Note: Births by race and Hispanic origin do not add to total because Hispanics may be of any race and "not stated" is not shown.
Source: National Center for Health Statistics, Births: Preliminary Data for 2007, National Vital Statistics Reports, Vol. 57, No. 12, 2009, Internet site http://www.cdc.gov/nchs/products/nvsr.htm#57_12; calculations by New Strategist

Table 3.13 Births by Age of Mother and Birth Order, 2007

(number and percent distribution of births by age of mother and birth order, 2007)

	total	first child	second child	third child	fourth or later child
Total births	**4,317,119**	**1,726,523**	**1,364,048**	**722,883**	**483,766**
Under age 15	6,218	6,088	99	2	1
Aged 15 to 19	445,045	357,092	73,891	10,863	1,472
Aged 20 to 24	1,082,837	524,240	359,732	141,942	52,063
Aged 25 to 29	1,208,504	432,011	400,000	230,640	140,490
Aged 30 to 44	1,567,166	405,212	528,529	338,131	287,431
Aged 30 to 34	962,179	270,057	334,881	201,033	151,655
Aged 35 to 39	499,916	112,833	163,927	114,878	105,601
Aged 40 to 44	105,071	22,322	29,721	22,220	30,175
Aged 45 to 54	7,349	1,881	1,797	1,307	2,310
PERCENT DISTRIBUTION BY BIRTH ORDER					
Total births	**100.0%**	**40.0%**	**31.6%**	**16.7%**	**11.2%**
Under age 15	100.0	97.9	1.6	0.0	0.0
Aged 15 to 19	100.0	80.2	16.6	2.4	0.3
Aged 20 to 24	100.0	48.4	33.2	13.1	4.8
Aged 25 to 29	100.0	35.7	33.1	19.1	11.6
Aged 30 to 44	100.0	25.9	33.7	21.6	18.3
Aged 30 to 34	100.0	28.1	34.8	20.9	15.8
Aged 35 to 39	100.0	22.6	32.8	23.0	21.1
Aged 40 to 44	100.0	21.2	28.3	21.1	28.7
Aged 45 to 54	100.0	25.6	24.5	17.8	31.4
PERCENT DISTRIBUTION BY AGE					
Total births	**100.0%**	**100.0%**	**100.0%**	**100.0%**	**100.0%**
Under age 15	0.1	0.4	0.0	0.0	0.0
Aged 15 to 19	10.3	20.7	5.4	1.5	0.3
Aged 20 to 24	25.1	30.4	26.4	19.6	10.8
Aged 25 to 29	28.0	25.0	29.3	31.9	29.0
Aged 30 to 44	36.3	23.5	38.7	46.8	59.4
Aged 30 to 34	22.3	15.6	24.6	27.8	31.3
Aged 35 to 39	11.6	6.5	12.0	15.9	21.8
Aged 40 to 44	2.4	1.3	2.2	3.1	6.2
Aged 45 to 54	0.2	0.1	0.1	0.2	0.5

Note: Numbers do not add to total because "not stated" is not shown.
Source: National Center for Health Statistics, Births: Preliminary Data for 2007, National Vital Statistics Reports, Vol. 57, No. 12, 2009, Internet site http://www.cdc.gov/nchs/products/nvsr.htm#57_12; calculations by New Strategist

Many Generation X Mothers Are Not Married

Out-of-wedlock births fall with age.

Nearly 40 percent of babies born in 2007 had a mother who was not married. There are sharp differences by age in the percentage of new mothers who are not married, however. The younger the woman, the more likely she is to give birth out of wedlock.

Among babies born to women under age 25 in 2007, most were born to single mothers. The figure falls to 32 percent in the 25-to-29 age group. Among babies born to women aged 30 or older, from 17 to 20 percent had a single mother.

■ Out-of-wedlock childbearing has increased enormously over the past few decades and has become common even among older mothers.

About one in five babies born to women aged 30 or older is out of wedlock

(percent of babies born to unmarried women, by age of mother, 2007)

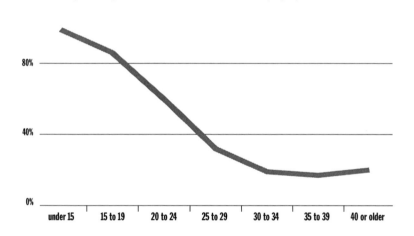

Table 3.14 Births to Unmarried Women by Age, 2007

(total number of births and number and percent to unmarried women, by age of mother, 2007)

	total	unmarried women		
		number	percent distribution	percent of total
Total births	**4,317,119**	**1,714,643**	**100.0%**	**39.7%**
Under age 15	6,218	6,142	0.4	98.8
Aged 15 to 19	445,045	380,560	22.2	85.5
Aged 20 to 24	1,082,837	644,591	37.6	59.5
Aged 25 to 29	1,208,504	389,169	22.7	32.2
Aged 30 to 34	962,179	185,425	10.8	19.3
Aged 35 to 39	499,916	86,343	5.0	17.3
Aged 40 to 54	112,420	22,411	1.3	19.9

Source: National Center for Health Statistics, Births: Preliminary Data for 2007, National Vital Statistics Reports, Vol. 57, No. 12, 2009, Internet site http://www.cdc.gov/nchs/products/nvsr.htm#57_12; calculations by New Strategist

Caesarean Deliveries Are Common among Women of All Ages

The rate is highest among older women, however.

Delayed childbearing can have an unanticipated cost. The older a woman is when she has a child, the greater the likelihood of complications that necessitate Caesarean delivery.

Among babies born in 2006, fully 31 percent were delivered by Caesarean section. The figure ranges from only 22 percent of babies born to women under age 20 to 41 percent of babies born to women aged 35 to 39 and nearly half (47 percent) of those born to women aged 40 or older.

■ As women delay childbearing, the rate of Caesarean delivery increases. With new fertility technologies enabling more women to have children later in life, the rate is likely to rise further.

Younger mothers are least likely to require a Caesarean delivery

(percent of births delivered by Caesarean section, by age of mother, 2006)

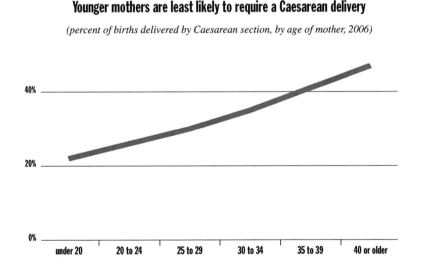

Table 3.15 Births by Age and Method of Delivery, 2006

(number and percent distribution of births by age of mother and method of delivery, 2006)

	total births	vaginal	Caesarean
Total births	**4,265,555**	**2,929,590**	**1,321,054**
Under age 20	441,832	342,977	97,806
Aged 20 to 24	1,080,437	792,028	285,227
Aged 25 to 29	1,181,899	826,822	351,002
Aged 30 to 34	950,258	615,784	330,783
Aged 35 to 39	498,616	293,352	202,987
Aged 40 or older	112,513	58,627	53,249

PERCENT DISTRIBUTION BY METHOD OF DELIVERY

Total births	**100.0%**	**68.7%**	**31.0%**
Under age 20	100.0	77.6	22.1
Aged 20 to 24	100.0	73.3	26.4
Aged 25 to 29	100.0	70.0	29.7
Aged 30 to 34	100.0	64.8	34.8
Aged 35 to 39	100.0	58.8	40.7
Aged 40 or older	100.0	52.1	47.3

PERCENT DISTRIBUTION BY AGE

Total births	**100.0%**	**100.0%**	**100.0%**
Under age 20	10.4	11.7	7.4
Aged 20 to 24	25.3	27.0	21.6
Aged 25 to 29	27.7	28.2	26.6
Aged 30 to 34	22.3	21.0	25.0
Aged 35 to 39	11.7	10.0	15.4
Aged 40 or older	2.6	2.0	4.0

Note: Numbers do not add to total because "not stated" is not shown.
Source: National Center for Health Statistics, Births: Final Data for 2006, National Vital Statistics Reports, Vol. 57, No. 7, 2009, Internet site http://www.cdc.gov/nchs/births.htm; calculations by New Strategist

Twenty Percent of 35-to-44-Year-Olds Smoke Cigarettes

Smoking rate peaks among 25-to-35-year-olds.

The percentage of Americans who smoke cigarettes is sharply lower than what it was a few decades ago. Nevertheless, a substantial 18 percent of people aged 18 or older were current smokers in 2007. Among people aged 35 to 44, one in five smokes cigarettes. Nineteen percent of 35-to-44-year-olds are former smokers.

Drinking is much more popular than smoking. Overall, 54 percent of people aged 18 or older have had an alcoholic beverage in the past month. The proportion peaks at 61 percent in the broad 25-to-44 age group.

Although many Gen Xers have experience with illicit drugs, particularly marijuana, few continue to use them. Only 7 percent of people aged 35 to 44 have used illicit drugs in the past month. But most people between the ages of 19 and 59 have used illicit drugs at some point in their lives. Many 35-to-44-year-olds have used marijuana in the past, although only about 5 percent have used it in the past month.

■ As Gen Xers age and health concerns become increasingly important, proportions of smokers and drinkers will decline.

Many Gen Xers never smoked

(percent distribution of people aged 35 to 44 by cigarette smoking status, 2007)

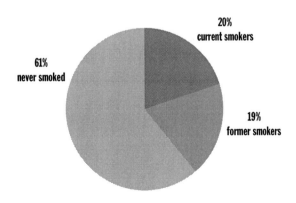

20%
current smokers

61%
never smoked

19%
former smokers

Table 3.16 Cigarette Smoking Status by Age, 2008

(percent distribution of people aged 18 or older by age and cigarette smoking status, 2008)

	total	current smokers			former smoker	never smoked
		total	smoke every day	smoke some days		
Total people	**100.0%**	**18.2%**	**13.4%**	**4.8%**	**25.2%**	**55.3%**
Aged 18 to 24	100.0	23.0	15.8	7.2	7.2	70.0
Aged 25 to 34	100.0	23.5	16.8	6.7	17.6	58.4
Aged 35 to 44	100.0	20.0	14.9	5.1	18.7	60.6
Aged 45 to 54	100.0	20.5	16.0	4.5	25.2	52.4
Aged 55 to 64	100.0	16.4	12.4	4.0	35.0	46.6
Aged 65 or older	100.0	8.0	6.0	2.0	42.9	48.8

Source: Centers for Disease Control and Prevention, Behavioral Risk Factor Surveillance System Prevalence Data, 2008, Internet site http://apps.nccd.cdc.gov/brfss/index.asp; calculations by New Strategist

Table 3.17 Alcohol Use by Age, 2008

(percent distribution of people aged 18 or older by whether they have had at least one drink of alcohol within the past 30 days, by age, 2008)

	total	yes	no
Total people	**100.0%**	**54.4%**	**45.5%**
Aged 18 to 24	100.0	49.9	50.0
Aged 25 to 34	100.0	60.5	39.4
Aged 35 to 44	100.0	60.5	39.4
Aged 45 to 54	100.0	58.4	41.5
Aged 55 to 64	100.0	53.4	46.5
Aged 65 or older	100.0	40.6	59.3

Source: Centers for Disease Control and Prevention, Behavioral Risk Factor Surveillance System Prevalence Data, 2008, Internet site http://apps.nccd.cdc.gov/brfss/index.asp

Table 3.18 Illicit Drug Use by People Aged 12 or Older, 2007

(percent of people aged 12 or older who ever used any illicit drug, who used an illicit drug in the past year, and who used an illicit drug in the past month, by age, 2007)

	ever used	used in past year	used in past month
Total people	**46.1%**	**14.4%**	**8.0%**
Aged 12	9.9	5.4	2.7
Aged 13	16.4	10.2	4.0
Aged 14	21.4	14.7	6.7
Aged 15	29.0	21.4	11.0
Aged 16	37.6	28.6	14.8
Aged 17	41.5	30.8	17.4
Aged 18	46.9	34.8	20.7
Aged 19	53.3	36.6	22.3
Aged 20	57.1	36.6	22.0
Aged 21	60.3	37.6	23.1
Aged 22	59.6	32.8	20.0
Aged 23	62.7	31.6	17.5
Aged 24	62.1	28.7	16.1
Aged 25	60.1	25.4	15.4
Aged 26 to 29	57.8	23.0	12.8
Aged 30 to 34	55.5	16.9	9.4
Aged 35 to 39	56.1	13.9	7.3
Aged 40 to 44	58.6	13.1	7.0
Aged 45 to 49	61.0	11.9	7.2
Aged 50 to 54	58.9	10.6	5.7
Aged 55 to 59	51.6	8.0	4.1
Aged 60 to 64	35.0	4.4	1.9
Aged 65 or older	10.7	1.0	0.7

Note: Illicit drugs include marijuana, hashish, cocaine (including crack), heroin, hallucinogens, inhalants, and any prescription-type psychotherapeutic used nonmedically.
Source: SAMHSA, Office of Applied Studies, National Survey on Drug Use and Health, 2007, Internet site http://www.oas.samhsa.gov/nsduh/2k7nsduh/2k7Results.pdf

Table 3.19 Marijuana Use by People Aged 12 or Older, 2007

(percent of people aged 12 or older who ever used marijuana, who used marijuana in the past year, and who used marijuana in the past month, by age, 2007)

	ever used	used in past year	used in past month
Total people	**40.6%**	**10.1%**	**5.8%**
Aged 12	1.3	1.0	0.6
Aged 13	4.1	2.9	1.3
Aged 14	9.9	7.8	3.7
Aged 15	17.9	14.4	7.6
Aged 16	27.5	21.8	11.4
Aged 17	34.9	25.8	14.9
Aged 18	39.5	28.3	17.1
Aged 19	46.8	31.4	18.9
Aged 20	50.8	31.5	19.2
Aged 21	53.8	31.0	18.9
Aged 22	53.1	27.4	16.7
Aged 23	57.0	25.1	14.6
Aged 24	55.2	23.0	12.7
Aged 25	52.8	20.3	12.5
Aged 26 to 29	52.0	17.4	9.8
Aged 30 to 34	48.8	11.1	6.3
Aged 35 to 39	49.8	8.9	5.4
Aged 40 to 44	53.5	8.0	4.5
Aged 45 to 49	56.9	7.9	4.9
Aged 50 to 54	54.8	6.7	3.8
Aged 55 to 59	46.2	4.4	2.1
Aged 60 to 64	29.6	1.9	0.6
Aged 65 or older	8.4	0.3	0.2

Source: SAMHSA, Office of Applied Studies, National Survey on Drug Use and Health, 2007, Internet site http://oas.samhsa .gov/NSDUH/2k7NSDUH/tabs/Sect1peTabs1to46.htm#Tab1.1A

Eighteen Percent of Generation Xers Lack Health Insurance

The figure is even higher among younger adults.

People aged 18 to 24 are more likely than older adults to be without health insurance. Entering the workforce at the age of 18, or graduating from college at the age of 21, usually means health insurance coverage is no longer available through a parent's plan. This partly explains why a substantial 28 percent of the nation's 18-to-24-year-olds lack health insurance. The figure stood at 18 percent among 35-to-44-year-olds in 2007 (Gen Xers were 31 to 42 in that year).

Most Americans obtain health insurance coverage through their employer. Among 35-to-44-year-olds, 69 percent had employment-based coverage in 2007. But only 49 percent had their own employment-based coverage. Among all 18-to-44-year-olds without health insurance in 2007, the single biggest reason for not having coverage was the high cost (cited by 49 percent), followed by losing employment (23 percent).

■ The economic downturn is likely to increase the percentage of Gen Xers without health insurance.

Many Americans do not have health insurance coverage

(percent of people aged 18 or older without health insurance, by age, 2007)

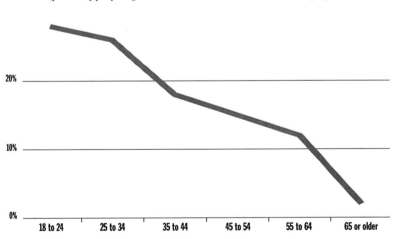

Table 3.20 Health Insurance Coverage by Age, 2007

(number and percent distribution of people by age and health insurance coverage status, 2007; numbers in thousands)

	total	with health insurance total	with health insurance private	with health insurance government	not covered
Total people	**299,106**	**253,449**	**201,991**	**83,031**	**45,657**
Under age 65	262,316	217,345	180,785	48,567	44,971
Under age 18	74,403	66,254	47,750	23,041	8,149
Aged 18 to 24	28,398	20,407	17,074	4,428	7,991
Aged 25 to 34	40,146	29,817	26,430	4,539	10,329
Aged 35 to 44	42,132	34,415	31,067	4,546	7,717
Aged 45 to 54	43,935	37,161	33,350	5,363	6,774
Aged 55 to 64	33,302	29,291	25,114	6,651	4,011
Aged 65 or older	36,790	36,103	21,206	34,464	686
PERCENT DISTRIBUTION BY COVERAGE STATUS					
Total people	**100.0%**	**84.7%**	**67.5%**	**27.8%**	**15.3%**
Under age 65	100.0	82.9	68.9	18.5	17.1
Under age 18	100.0	89.0	64.2	31.0	11.0
Aged 18 to 24	100.0	71.9	60.1	15.6	28.1
Aged 25 to 34	100.0	74.3	65.8	11.3	25.7
Aged 35 to 44	100.0	81.7	73.7	10.8	18.3
Aged 45 to 54	100.0	84.6	75.9	12.2	15.4
Aged 55 to 64	100.0	88.0	75.4	20.0	12.0
Aged 65 or older	100.0	98.1	57.6	93.7	1.9
PERCENT DISTRIBUTION BY AGE					
Total people	**100.0%**	**100.0%**	**100.0%**	**100.0%**	**100.0%**
Under age 65	87.7	85.8	89.5	58.5	98.5
Under age 18	24.9	26.1	23.6	27.7	17.8
Aged 18 to 24	9.5	8.1	8.5	5.3	17.5
Aged 25 to 34	13.4	11.8	13.1	5.5	22.6
Aged 35 to 44	14.1	13.6	15.4	5.5	16.9
Aged 45 to 54	14.7	14.7	16.5	6.5	14.8
Aged 55 to 64	11.1	11.6	12.4	8.0	8.8
Aged 65 or older	12.3	14.2	10.5	41.5	1.5

Note: Numbers may not add to total because some people have more than one type of health insurance coverage.
Source: Bureau of the Census, Health Insurance, Table HI01, Internet site http://pubdb3.census.gov/macro/032008/health/toc .htm; calculations by New Strategist

Table 3.21 Private Health Insurance Coverage by Age, 2007

(number and percent distribution of people by age and private health insurance coverage status, 2007; numbers in thousands)

		with private health insurance			
		total	employment based		
	total	total	total	own	direct purchase
Total people	**299,106**	**201,991**	**177,446**	**93,774**	**26,673**
Under age 65	262,316	180,785	164,888	84,332	17,127
Under age 18	74,403	47,750	44,252	227	3,930
Aged 18 to 24	28,398	17,074	13,747	5,386	1,635
Aged 25 to 34	40,146	26,430	24,505	19,005	2,347
Aged 35 to 44	42,132	31,067	29,009	20,616	2,687
Aged 45 to 54	43,935	33,350	30,805	22,486	3,292
Aged 55 to 64	33,302	25,114	22,569	16,612	3,237
Aged 65 or older	36,790	21,206	12,558	9,442	9,546

PERCENT DISTRIBUTION BY COVERAGE STATUS

Total people	**100.0%**	**67.5%**	**59.3%**	**31.4%**	**8.9%**
Under age 65	100.0	68.9	62.9	32.1	6.5
Under age 18	100.0	64.2	59.5	0.3	5.3
Aged 18 to 24	100.0	60.1	48.4	19.0	5.8
Aged 25 to 34	100.0	65.8	61.0	47.3	5.8
Aged 35 to 44	100.0	73.7	68.9	48.9	6.4
Aged 45 to 54	100.0	75.9	70.1	51.2	7.5
Aged 55 to 64	100.0	75.4	67.8	49.9	9.7
Aged 65 or older	100.0	57.6	34.1	25.7	25.9

PERCENT DISTRIBUTION BY AGE

Total people	**100.0%**	**100.0%**	**100.0%**	**100.0%**	**100.0%**
Under age 65	87.7	89.5	92.9	89.9	64.2
Under age 18	24.9	23.6	24.9	0.2	14.7
Aged 18 to 24	9.5	8.5	7.7	5.7	6.1
Aged 25 to 34	13.4	13.1	13.8	20.3	8.8
Aged 35 to 44	14.1	15.4	16.3	22.0	10.1
Aged 45 to 54	14.7	16.5	17.4	24.0	12.3
Aged 55 to 64	11.1	12.4	12.7	17.7	12.1
Aged 65 or older	12.3	10.5	7.1	10.1	35.8

Note: Numbers may not add to total because some people have more than one type of health insurance coverage.
Source: Bureau of the Census, Health Insurance, Table HI01, Internet site http://pubdb3.census.gov/macro/032008/health/toc
.htm; calculations by New Strategist

Table 3.22 Government Health Insurance Coverage by Age, 2007

(number and percent distribution of people by age and government health insurance coverage status, 2007; numbers in thousands)

	total	with government health insurance			
		total	Medicaid	Medicare	military
Total people	**299,106**	**83,031**	**39,554**	**41,375**	**10,955**
Under age 65	262,316	48,567	36,291	7,097	8,351
Under age 18	74,403	23,041	20,899	518	2,101
Aged 18 to 24	28,398	4,428	3,563	180	823
Aged 25 to 34	40,146	4,539	3,237	501	1,047
Aged 35 to 44	42,132	4,546	3,027	924	1,016
Aged 45 to 54	43,935	5,363	3,103	1,795	1,285
Aged 55 to 64	33,302	6,651	2,462	3,179	2,079
Aged 65 or older	36,790	34,464	3,263	34,278	2,604
PERCENT DISTRIBUTION BY COVERAGE STATUS					
Total people	**100.0%**	**27.8%**	**13.2%**	**13.8%**	**3.7%**
Under age 65	100.0	18.5	13.8	2.7	3.2
Under age 18	100.0	31.0	28.1	0.7	2.8
Aged 18 to 24	100.0	15.6	12.5	0.6	2.9
Aged 25 to 34	100.0	11.3	8.1	1.2	2.6
Aged 35 to 44	100.0	10.8	7.2	2.2	2.4
Aged 45 to 54	100.0	12.2	7.1	4.1	2.9
Aged 55 to 64	100.0	20.0	7.4	9.5	6.2
Aged 65 or older	100.0	93.7	8.9	93.2	7.1
PERCENT DISTRIBUTION BY AGE					
Total people	**100.0%**	**100.0%**	**100.0%**	**100.0%**	**100.0%**
Under age 65	87.7	58.5	91.8	17.2	76.2
Under age 18	24.9	27.7	52.8	1.3	19.2
Aged 18 to 24	9.5	5.3	9.0	0.4	7.5
Aged 25 to 34	13.4	5.5	8.2	1.2	9.6
Aged 35 to 44	14.1	5.5	7.7	2.2	9.3
Aged 45 to 54	14.7	6.5	7.8	4.3	11.7
Aged 55 to 64	11.1	8.0	6.2	7.7	19.0
Aged 65 or older	12.3	41.5	8.2	82.8	23.8

Note: Numbers may not add to total because some people have more than one type of health insurance coverage.
Source: Bureau of the Census, Health Insurance, Table HI01, Internet site http://pubdb3.census.gov/macro/032008/health/toc .htm; calculations by New Strategist

Table 3.23 People Aged 18 to 44 by Health Insurance Coverage Status and Reason for No Coverage, 2007

(number and percent distribution of people aged 18 to 44 by health insurance coverage status and reason for lack of coverage, 2007)

	number	percent
HEALTH INSURANCE STATUS		
Total people aged 18 to 44	**110,890**	**100.0%**
With health insurance	84,711	76.4
Without health insurance	26,179	23.6
REASON FOR LACK OF HEALTH INSURANCE		
People aged 18 to 44 without health insurance	**26,179**	**100.0**
Cost	12,775	48.8
Lost job or change in employment	5,916	22.6
Employer didn't offer insurance/company refused	4,372	16.7
Ineligible due to age/left school	3,272	12.5
Medicaid stopped	2,801	10.7
Change in marital status or death of parent	550	2.1
Other reason	1,545	5.9

Note: Numbers do not sum to total because "unknown" is not shown and people could report more than one reason.
Source: National Center for Health Statistics, Summary Health Statistics for the U.S. Population: National Health Interview Survey, 2007, Vital and Health Statistics, Series 10, No. 238, 2008, Internet site http://www.cdc.gov/nchs/nhis.htm; calculations by New Strategist

Table 3.24 Spending on Health Care by Age, 2006

(percent of people with health care expense, median expense per person, total expenses, and percent distribution of total expenses by source of payment, by age, 2006)

	total (thousands)	percent with expense	median expense per person	total expenses amount (millions)	total expenses percent distribution
Total people	**299,267**	**84.6%**	**$1,185**	**$1,033,056**	**100.0%**
Under age 18	74,106	85.4	462	98,789	9.6
Aged 18 to 29	49,243	73.5	685	79,302	7.7
Aged 30 to 39	39,719	78.5	1,017	94,457	9.1
Aged 40 to 49	44,328	83.8	1,100	129,809	12.6
Aged 50 to 59	39,458	90.0	2,220	207,157	20.1
Aged 60 to 64	14,433	91.8	2,855	90,222	8.7
Aged 65 or older	37,980	96.7	4,215	333,320	32.3

PERCENT DISTRIBUTION BY SOURCE OF PAYMENT

	total	out of pocket	private insurance	Medicare	Medicaid	other
Total people	**100.0%**	**19.0%**	**41.7%**	**23.5%**	**8.7%**	**7.1%**
Under age 18	100.0	20.5	50.7	0.5	23.7	4.6
Aged 18 to 29	100.0	24.8	46.3	0.8	20.0	8.1
Aged 30 to 39	100.0	19.5	62.3	3.0	8.3	6.8
Aged 40 to 49	100.0	20.3	55.3	6.1	10.0	8.3
Aged 50 to 59	100.0	19.6	57.6	8.9	7.0	6.9
Aged 60 to 64	100.0	22.1	52.2	10.7	7.8	7.2
Aged 65 or older	100.0	15.2	14.1	60.9	2.4	7.3

Note: "Other" insurance includes Department of Veterans Affairs (except Tricare), American Indian Health Service, state and local clinics, worker's compensation, homeowner's and automobile insurance, etc.
Source: Agency for Healthcare Research and Quality, Medical Expenditure Panel Survey, 2006, Internet site http://www.meps .ahrq.gov/mepsweb/data_stats/quick_tables_results.jsp?component=1&subcomponent=0&tableSeries=1&year=-1&SearchMet hod=1&Action=Search; calculations by New Strategist

Health Problems Are Few in the 18-to-44 Age Group

Lower back pain is by far the most common health condition in the age group.

Twenty-two percent of Americans aged 18 to 44 have experienced lower back pain for at least one full day in the past three months, making it the most common health condition in the age group. Migraines or severe headaches are second, with 15 percent having the problem. Chronic joint symptoms are third, with 13 percent reporting this problem. The 18-to-44 age group accounts for more than half of those ever experiencing asthma.

As Americans became more aware of the problems associated with high cholesterol over the past few decades, cholesterol levels have dropped in most age groups—although they have increased slightly among 20-to-44-year-olds. The percentage of women aged 35 to 44 with high blood pressure has also increased slightly since the 1988–94 time period.

Nearly 1 million Americans have been diagnosed with AIDS over the decades. The largest share were diagnosed in their thirties—the age group now filled with Generation X.

■ As Generation X ages into its late forties and fifties, the percentage with chronic health problems will rise.

The percentage of people with arthritis rises with age

(percent of people with arthritis, by age, 2007)

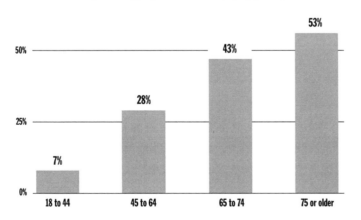

Table 3.25 Number of Adults with Health Conditions by Age, 2007

(number of people aged 18 or older with selected health conditions, by type of condition and age, 2007; numbers in thousands)

	total	18 to 44	45 to 64	aged 65 or older total	65 to 74	75 or older
TOTAL PEOPLE 18 OR OLDER	223,181	110,890	76,136	36,155	19,258	16,897
Selected circulatory diseases						
Heart disease, all types	25,095	4,591	9,266	11,239	5,199	6,040
Coronary	13,674	1,041	5,091	7,542	3,571	3,971
Hypertension	52,920	9,094	24,383	19,442	9,763	9,679
Stroke	5,426	285	2,156	2,985	1,205	1,780
Selected respiratory conditions						
Emphysema	3,736	226	1,765	1,745	861	884
Asthma, ever	24,402	12,996	7,895	3,511	2,030	1,481
Asthma, still	16,177	7,996	5,476	2,704	1,591	1,113
Hay fever	16,882	7,420	7,210	2,252	1,302	950
Sinusitis	25,953	10,261	11,154	4,538	2,589	1,949
Chronic bronchitis	7,604	2,515	3,226	1,863	1,050	813
Selected types of cancer						
Any cancer	16,370	2,085	6,305	7,980	3,757	4,223
Breast cancer	2,630	178	1,028	1,424	626	798
Cervical cancer	1,011	437	417	157	92	65
Prostate cancer	2,037	0	543	1,494	651	843
Other selected diseases and conditions						
Diabetes	17,273	2,432	8,093	6,748	3,840	2,908
Ulcers	14,501	4,616	5,641	4,244	2,119	2,125
Kidney disease	3,343	759	1,226	1,359	593	766
Liver disease	2,649	749	1,374	526	368	158
Arthritis	46,429	7,810	21,428	17,192	8,322	8,870
Chronic joint symptoms	53,945	14,776	24,820	14,350	7,140	7,210
Migraines or severe headaches	27,364	16,427	9,277	1,660	1,075	585
Pain in neck	29,019	11,833	12,073	5,113	2,833	2,280
Pain in lower back	57,070	24,555	21,860	10,655	5,650	5,005
Pain in face or jaw	9,062	4,649	3,455	957	607	350
Selected sensory problems						
Hearing	33,318	6,597	13,400	13,320	5,739	7,581
Vision	22,378	7,596	9,297	5,484	2,472	3,012
Absence of all natural teeth	16,997	2,066	5,606	9,325	4,284	5,041

Note: The conditions shown are those that have ever been diagnosed by a doctor, except as noted. Hay fever, sinusitis, and chronic bronchitis have been diagnosed in the past 12 months. Kidney and liver diseases have been diagnosed in the past 12 months and exclude kidney stones, bladder infections, and incontinence. Chronic joint symptoms are shown if respondent had pain, aching, or stiffness in or around a joint (excluding back and neck) and the condition began more than three months ago. Migraines, and pain in neck, lower back, face, or jaw are shown only if pain lasted a whole day or more.
Source: National Center for Health Statistics, Summary Health Statistics for U.S. Adults: National Health Interview Survey, 2007, Vital and Health Statistics, Series 10, No. 240, 2008, Internet site http://www.cdc.gov/nchs/nhis.htm

Table 3.26 Distribution of Health Conditions among Adults by Age, 2007

(percent distribution of people aged 18 or older with selected health conditions, by type of condition and age, 2007)

	total	18 to 44	45 to 64	aged 65 or older total	65 to 74	75 or older
TOTAL PEOPLE 18 OR OLDER	100.0%	49.7%	34.1%	16.2%	8.6%	7.6%
Selected circulatory diseases						
Heart disease, all types	100.0	18.3	36.9	44.8	20.7	24.1
Coronary	100.0	7.6	37.2	55.2	26.1	29.0
Hypertension	100.0	17.2	46.1	36.7	18.4	18.3
Stroke	100.0	5.3	39.7	55.0	22.2	32.8
Selected respiratory conditions						
Emphysema	100.0	6.0	47.2	46.7	23.0	23.7
Asthma, ever	100.0	53.3	32.4	14.4	8.3	6.1
Asthma, still	100.0	49.4	33.9	16.7	9.8	6.9
Hay fever	100.0	44.0	42.7	13.3	7.7	5.6
Sinusitis	100.0	39.5	43.0	17.5	10.0	7.5
Chronic bronchitis	100.0	33.1	42.4	24.5	13.8	10.7
Selected types of cancer						
Any cancer	100.0	12.7	38.5	48.7	23.0	25.8
Breast cancer	100.0	6.8	39.1	54.1	23.8	30.3
Cervical cancer	100.0	43.2	41.2	15.5	9.1	6.4
Prostate cancer	100.0	0	26.7	73.3	32.0	41.4
Other selected diseases and conditions						
Diabetes	100.0	14.1	46.9	39.1	22.2	16.8
Ulcers	100.0	31.8	38.9	29.3	14.6	14.7
Kidney disease	100.0	22.7	36.7	40.7	17.7	22.9
Liver disease	100.0	28.3	51.9	19.9	13.9	6.0
Arthritis	100.0	16.8	46.2	37.0	17.9	19.1
Chronic joint symptoms	100.0	27.4	46.0	26.6	13.2	13.4
Migraines or severe headaches	100.0	60.0	33.9	6.1	3.9	2.1
Pain in neck	100.0	40.8	41.6	17.6	9.8	7.9
Pain in lower back	100.0	43.0	38.3	18.7	9.9	8.8
Pain in face or jaw	100.0	51.3	38.1	10.6	6.7	3.9
Selected sensory problems						
Hearing	100.0	19.8	40.2	40.0	17.2	22.8
Vision	100.0	33.9	41.5	24.5	11.0	13.5
Absence of all natural teeth	100.0	12.2	33.0	54.9	25.2	29.7

Note: The conditions shown are those that have ever been diagnosed by a doctor, except as noted. Hay fever, sinusitis, and chronic bronchitis have been diagnosed in the past 12 months. Kidney and liver diseases have been diagnosed in the past 12 months and exclude kidney stones, bladder infections, and incontinence. Chronic joint symptoms are shown if respondent had pain, aching, or stiffness in or around a joint (excluding back and neck) and the condition began more than three months ago. Migraines, and pain in neck, lower back, face, or jaw are shown only if pain lasted a whole day or more.
Source: National Center for Health Statistics, Summary Health Statistics for U.S. Adults: National Health Interview Survey, 2007, Vital and Health Statistics, Series 10, No. 240, 2008, Internet site http://www.cdc.gov/nchs/nhis.htm; calculations by New Strategist

Table 3.27 Percent of Adults with Health Conditions by Age, 2007

(percent of people aged 18 or older with selected health conditions, by type of condition and age, 2007)

	total	18 to 44	45 to 64	65 to 74	75 or older
TOTAL PEOPLE 18 OR OLDER	100.0%	100.0%	100.0%	100.0%	100.0%
Selected circulatory diseases					
Heart disease, all types	11.3	4.1	12.2	27.1	35.8
Coronary	6.1	0.9	6.7	18.6	23.6
Hypertension	23.7	8.2	32.1	50.9	57.4
Stroke	2.4	0.3	2.8	6.3	10.6
Selected respiratory conditions					
Emphysema	1.7	0.2	2.3	4.5	5.2
Asthma, ever	10.9	11.7	10.4	10.6	8.8
Asthma, still	7.3	7.2	7.2	8.3	6.6
Hay fever	7.6	6.7	9.5	6.8	5.6
Sinusitis	11.6	9.3	14.7	13.5	11.6
Chronic bronchitis	3.4	2.3	4.2	5.5	4.8
Selected types of cancer					
Any cancer	7.3	1.9	8.3	19.6	25.0
Breast cancer	1.2	0.2	1.4	3.3	4.7
Cervical cancer	0.9	0.8	1.1	0.9	0.6
Prostate cancer	1.9	0	1.5	7.4	12.8
Other selected diseases and conditions					
Diabetes	7.8	2.2	10.7	20.3	17.6
Ulcers	6.5	4.2	7.4	11.0	12.6
Kidney disease	1.5	0.7	1.6	3.1	4.5
Liver disease	1.2	0.7	1.8	1.9	0.9
Arthritis	20.8	7.1	28.2	43.4	52.7
Chronic joint symptoms	24.2	13.3	32.6	37.2	42.9
Migraines or severe headaches	12.3	14.8	12.2	5.6	3.5
Pain in neck	13.0	10.7	15.9	14.7	13.5
Pain in lower back	25.6	22.2	28.7	29.4	29.7
Pain in face or jaw	4.1	4.2	4.5	3.2	2.1
Selected sensory problems					
Hearing	14.9	6.0	17.6	29.8	45.0
Vision	10.0	6.9	12.2	12.9	17.9
Absence of all natural teeth	7.6	1.9	7.4	22.4	30.1

Note: The conditions shown are those that have ever been diagnosed by a doctor, except as noted. Hay fever, sinusitis, and chronic bronchitis have been diagnosed in the past 12 months. Kidney and liver diseases have been diagnosed in the past 12 months and exclude kidney stones, bladder infections, and incontinence. Chronic joint symptoms are shown if respondent had pain, aching, or stiffness in or around a joint (excluding back and neck) and the condition began more than three months ago. Migraines, and pain in neck, lower back, face, or jaw are shown only if pain lasted a whole day or more.
Source: National Center for Health Statistics, Summary Health Statistics for U.S. Adults: National Health Interview Survey, 2007, Vital and Health Statistics, Series 10, No. 240, 2008, Internet site http://www.cdc.gov/nchs/nhis.htm; calculations by New Strategist

Table 3.28 Hypertension by Sex and Age, 1988–94 and 2003–06

(percent of people aged 20 or older who have hypertension or take antihypertensive medication, by sex and age, 1988–94 and 2003–06; percentage point change, 1988–94 to 2003–06)

	2003–06	1988–94	percentage point change
TOTAL PEOPLE	**32.1%**	**24.1%**	**8.0**
Total men	**31.3**	**23.8**	**7.5**
Aged 20 to 34	9.2	7.1	2.1
Aged 35 to 44	21.1	17.1	0.0
Aged 45 to 54	36.2	29.2	7.0
Aged 55 to 64	50.2	40.6	9.6
Aged 65 to 74	64.1	54.4	9.7
Aged 75 or older	65.0	60.4	4.6
Total women	**32.9**	**24.4**	**8.5**
Aged 20 to 34	2.2	2.9	–0.7
Aged 35 to 44	12.6	11.2	1.4
Aged 45 to 54	36.2	23.9	12.3
Aged 55 to 64	54.4	42.6	11.8
Aged 65 to 74	70.8	56.2	14.6
Aged 75 or older	80.2	73.6	6.6

Note: A person is defined as having hypertension if he or she has a systolic pressure of at least 140 mmHg, diastolic pressure of at least 90 mmHg, or takes antihypertensive medication.
Source: National Center for Health Statistics, Health, United States, 2008, Internet site http://www.cdc.gov/nchs/hus.htm; calculations by New Strategist

Table 3.29 High Cholesterol by Sex and Age, 1988–94 and 2003–06

(percent of people aged 20 or older who have high serum cholesterol, by sex and age, 1988–94 and 2003–06; percentage point change, 1988–94 to 2003–06)

	2003–06	1988–94	percentage point change
TOTAL PEOPLE	**16.4%**	**19.6%**	**–3.2**
Total men	**15.2**	**17.7**	**–2.5**
Aged 20 to 34	9.5	8.2	1.3
Aged 35 to 44	20.5	19.4	1.1
Aged 45 to 54	20.8	26.6	–5.8
Aged 55 to 64	16.0	28.0	–12.0
Aged 65 to 74	10.9	21.9	–11.0
Aged 75 or older	9.6	20.4	–10.8
Total women	**17.5**	**21.3**	**–3.8**
Aged 20 to 34	10.3	7.3	3.0
Aged 35 to 44	12.7	12.3	0.4
Aged 45 to 54	19.7	26.7	–7.0
Aged 55 to 64	30.5	40.9	–10.4
Aged 65 to 74	24.2	41.3	–17.1
Aged 75 or older	18.6	38.2	–19.6

Note: High cholesterol is defined as 240 mg/dL or more.
Source: National Center for Health Statistics, Health, United States, 2008, Internet site http://www.cdc.gov/nchs/hus.htm; calculations by New Strategist

Table 3.30 Cumulative Number of AIDS Cases by Sex and Age, through 2006

(cumulative number and percent distribution of AIDS cases by sex and age at diagnosis, through 2006)

	number	percent distribution
TOTAL CASES	**982,498**	**100.0%**
Sex		
Males aged 13 or older	783,786	79.8
Females aged 13 or older	189,566	19.3
Age		
Under age 13	9,156	0.9
Aged 13 to 14	1,078	0.1
Aged 15 to 19	5,626	0.6
Aged 20 to 24	36,225	3.7
Aged 25 to 29	117,099	11.9
Aged 30 to 34	197,530	20.1
Aged 35 to 39	213,573	21.7
Aged 40 to 44	170,531	17.4
Aged 45 to 49	107,207	10.9
Aged 50 to 54	59,907	6.1
Aged 55 to 59	32,190	3.3
Aged 60 to 64	17,303	1.8
Aged 65 or older	15,074	1.5

Source: Centers for Disease Control and Prevention, Cases of HIV/AIDS and AIDS, Internet site http://www.cdc.gov/hiv/topics/ surveillance/resources/reports/2006report/table3.htm

Prescription Drug Use Is Increasing

More Americans use a growing number of prescriptions.

The use of prescription drugs to treat a variety of illnesses, particularly chronic conditions, increased substantially between 1988–94 and 2001–04. The percentage of people who take at least one drug in the past month rose from 38 to 47 percent during those years. The percentage who use three or more prescription drugs in the past month climbed from 11 to 20 percent. In the broad 18-to-44 age group, 38 percent took at least one prescription drug in the past month and 10 percent took three or more.

Regardless of age, most people have incurred a prescription drug expense during the past year, the proportion rising from a low of 50 percent among 18-to-29-year-olds to a high of 92 percent among people aged 65 or older, according to the federal government's Medical Expenditure Panel Survey. Expenses for prescription drugs rise with age, to more than $1,300 per year for people aged 65 or older.

■ Behind the increase in the use of prescriptions is the introduction and marketing of new drugs to treat chronic health problems.

Most have prescription drug expenses

(percent of people with prescription drug expenses, by age, 2006)

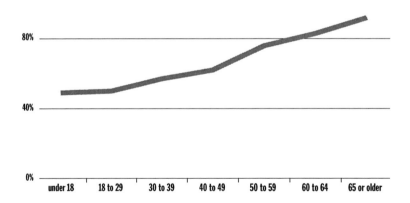

Table 3.31 Prescription Drug Use by Sex and Age, 1988–94 and 2001–04

(percent of people aged 18 or older who take at least one or three or more prescription drugs in the past month, by sex and age, 1988–94 and 2001–04; percentage point change, 1988–94 to 2001–04)

	at least one			three or more		
	2001–04	1988–94	percentage point change	2001–04	1988–94	percentage point change
TOTAL PEOPLE	**46.5%**	**37.8%**	**8.7**	**19.9%**	**11.0%**	**8.9**
Under age 18	23.9	20.5	3.4	4.0	2.4	1.6
Aged 18 to 44	37.6	31.3	6.3	10.2	5.7	4.5
Aged 45 to 64	66.2	54.8	11.4	34.2	20.0	14.2
Aged 65 or older	87.3	73.6	13.7	59.6	35.3	24.3
Total females	**52.2**	**44.6**	**7.6**	**23.3**	**13.6**	**9.7**
Under age 18	22.4	20.6	1.8	3.9	2.3	1.6
Aged 18 to 44	45.9	40.7	5.2	12.3	7.6	4.7
Aged 45 to 64	73.4	62.0	11.4	39.8	24.7	15.1
Aged 65 or older	90.1	78.3	11.8	63.8	38.2	25.6
Total males	**40.5**	**30.6**	**9.9**	**16.3**	**8.3**	**8.0**
Under age 18	25.3	20.4	4.9	4.1	2.6	1.5
Aged 18 to 44	29.2	21.5	7.7	8.0	3.6	4.4
Aged 45 to 64	58.7	47.2	11.5	28.3	15.1	13.2
Aged 65 or older	83.6	67.2	16.4	53.9	31.3	22.6

Source: National Center for Health Statistics, Health, United States, 2008, Internet site http://www.cdc.gov/nchs/hus.htm

Table 3.32 Spending on Prescription Medications by Age, 2006

(percent of people with prescription medication expense, median expense per person, total expenses, and percent distribution of total expenses by source of payment, by age, 2006)

	total (thousands)	percent with expense	median expense per person	total expenses amount (millions)	total expenses percent distribution
Total people	**299,267**	**62.6%**	**$364**	**$223,330**	**100.0%**
Under age 18	74,106	48.9	77	15,180	6.8
Aged 18 to 29	49,243	49.9	133	12,285	5.5
Aged 30 to 39	39,719	57.1	210	15,978	7.2
Aged 40 to 49	44,328	61.8	330	28,273	12.7
Aged 50 to 59	39,458	75.6	776	57,071	25.6
Aged 60 to 64	14,433	83.1	994	20,122	9.0
Aged 65 or older	37,980	91.7	1,367	73,422	32.9

PERCENT DISTRIBUTION BY SOURCE OF PAYMENT	total	out of pocket	private insurance	Medicare	Medicaid	other
Total people	**100.0%**	**34.9%**	**34.0%**	**19.9%**	**7.0%**	**4.3%**
Under age 18	100.0	26.1	47.4	0.7	24.8	0.9
Aged 18 to 29	100.0	52.5	34.2	1.5	9.5	2.3
Aged 30 to 39	100.0	37.7	44.7	4.9	10.1	2.6
Aged 40 to 49	100.0	34.1	42.5	8.6	11.2	3.6
Aged 50 to 59	100.0	32.3	48.0	9.2	7.0	3.5
Aged 60 to 64	100.0	35.6	44.0	8.4	7.2	4.8
Aged 65 or older	100.0	35.3	11.7	46.0	0.5	6.5

Note: "Other" insurance includes Department of Veterans Affairs (except Tricare), American Indian Health Service, state and local clinics, worker's compensation, homeowner's and automobile insurance, etc.
Source: Agency for Healthcare Research and Quality, Medical Expenditure Panel Survey, 2006, Internet site http://www.meps. ahrq.gov/mepsweb/data_stats/quick_tables_results.jsp?component=1&subcomponent=0&tableSeries=1&year=-1&SearchMet hod=1&Action=Search; calculations by New Strategist

Adults Aged 25 to 44 Account for More than One in Five Physician Visits

Among 25-to-44-year-olds, 66 percent of physician visits are made by women.

In 2006, Americans visited physicians a total of 902 million times. Twenty-one percent of visits were made by people aged 25 to 44. Women account for two-thirds of physician visits by those in the age group because of pregnancy and childbirth.

People aged 25 to 44 account for 25 percent of visits to hospital outpatient departments. Among outpatient visitors in the 25-to-44 age group, the largest share (37 percent) are there because of an acute problem.

People aged 25 to 44 account for the largest single share of visits to hospital emergency departments (29 percent) among age groups. This makes sense since many people in the age group lack health insurance, and people without health insurance often end up in emergency rooms.

When people visiting a doctor or health care clinic are asked to rate the care they receive, fewer than half give it the highest rating (a 9 or 10 on a scale of 0 to 10). The proportion rating their experience a 9 or 10 rises with age to a peak of 62 percent among Medicare recipients. A much smaller 43 to 44 percent of people under age 50 give the health care they received the highest rating.

■ Without better health insurance coverage, more patients will be seen in emergency rooms rather than doctor's offices or health clinics.

People aged 25 to 44 see a doctor between two and three times a year

(average number of physician visits per person per year, by age, 2006)

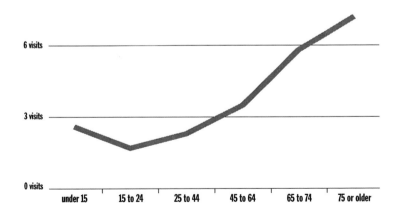

Table 3.33 Physician Office Visits by Sex and Age, 2006

(total number, percent distribution, and number of physician office visits per person per year, by sex and age, 2006; numbers in thousands)

	total	percent distribution	average visits per year
TOTAL VISITS	**901,954**	**100.0%**	**3.1**
Under age 15	157,906	17.5	2.6
Aged 15 to 24	72,411	8.0	1.7
Aged 25 to 44	185,305	20.5	2.3
Aged 45 to 64	256,494	28.4	3.5
Aged 65 to 74	108,063	12.0	5.8
Aged 75 or older	121,774	13.5	7.2
Visits by females	**533,292**	**59.1**	**3.6**
Under age 15	76,300	8.5	2.6
Aged 15 to 24	49,641	5.5	2.4
Aged 25 to 44	122,261	13.6	3.0
Aged 45 to 64	149,778	16.6	3.9
Aged 65 to 74	60,699	6.7	6.0
Aged 75 or older	74,613	8.3	7.3
Visits by males	**368,662**	**40.9**	**2.6**
Under age 15	81,607	9.0	2.6
Aged 15 to 24	22,770	2.5	1.1
Aged 25 to 44	63,044	7.0	1.6
Aged 45 to 64	106,716	11.8	3.0
Aged 65 to 74	47,364	5.3	5.5
Aged 75 or older	47,161	5.2	7.1

Source: National Center for Health Statistics, National Ambulatory Medical Care Survey: 2006 Summary, National Health Statistics Report, No. 3, 2008, Internet site http://www.cdc.gov/nchs/about/major/ahcd/adata.htm

Table 3.34 Hospital Outpatient Department Visits by Age and Reason, 2006

(number and percent distribution of visits to hospital outpatient departments by age and major reason for visit, 2006; numbers in thousands)

	total		major reason for visit						
	number	percent distribution	total	acute problem	chronic problem, routine	chronic problem, flare-up	pre- or post-surgery	preventive care	unknown
Total visits	**102,208**	**100.0%**	**100.0%**	**36.7%**	**31.1%**	**6.8%**	**4.3%**	**19.4%**	**1.7%**
Under age 15	19,864	19.4	100.0	48.9	17.6	3.7	2.0	24.8	2.8
Aged 15 to 24	12,012	11.8	100.0	38.9	16.0	4.7	3.5	34.8	2.1
Aged 25 to 44	25,104	24.6	100.0	37.3	27.2	7.0	4.3	22.6	1.5
Aged 45 to 64	28,707	28.1	100.0	32.2	41.4	8.4	5.4	11.5	1.1
Aged 65 or older	16,522	16.2	100.0	27.4	46.2	8.8	5.9	10.3	1.4

Source: National Center for Health Statistics, National Hospital Ambulatory Medical Care Survey: 2006 Outpatient Department Summary, National Health Statistics Reports, No. 4, 2008, Internet site http://www.cdc.gov/nchs/about/major/ahcd/adata .htm; calculations by New Strategist

Table 3.35 Emergency Department Visits by Age and Urgency of Problem, 2006

(number of visits to emergency rooms and percent distribution by urgency of problem, by age, 2006; numbers in thousands)

	total		percent distribution by urgency of problem						
	number	percent distribution	total	immediate	emergent	urgent	semiurgent	nonurgent	unknown
Total visits	**119,191**	**100.0%**	**100.0%**	**5.1%**	**10.8%**	**36.6%**	**22.0%**	**12.1%**	**13.4%**
Under age 15	21,876	18.4	100.0	3.1	7.8	35.0	25.6	14.6	13.9
Aged 15 to 24	19,525	16.4	100.0	4.1	8.4	34.3	24.7	14.3	14.1
Aged 25 to 44	35,034	29.4	100.0	4.3	10.1	36.4	22.7	12.9	13.6
Aged 45 to 64	25,466	21.4	100.0	5.9	12.8	37.1	20.0	11.1	13.2
Aged 65 or older	17,290	14.5	100.0	9.2	15.4	41.3	15.5	6.7	11.9

Note: "Immediate" is a visit in which the patient should be seen immediately. "Emergent" is a visit in which the patient should be seen within 1 to 14 minutes; "urgent" is a visit in which the patient should be seen within 15 to 60 minutes; "semiurgent" is a visit in which the patient should be seen within 61 to 120 minutes; "nonurgent" is a visit in which the patient should be seen within 121 minutes to 24 hours; "unknown" is a visit with no mention of immediacy or triage or the patient was dead on arrival.
Source: National Center for Health Statistics, National Hospital Ambulatory Medical Care Survey: 2006 Emergency Department Summary, National Health Statistics Reports, No. 7, 2008, Internet site http://www.cdc.gov/nchs/about/major/ahcd/adata .htm

Table 3.36 Rating of Health Care Received from Doctor's Office or Clinic, 2006

(number of people aged 18 or older visiting a doctor or health care clinic in past 12 months, and percent distribution by rating for health care received on a scale from 0 (worst) to 10 (best), by age, 2006; people in thousands)

	with health care visit		rating		
	number	percent	9 to 10	7 to 8	0 to 6
Total people	**140,898**	**100.0%**	**49.3%**	**35.8%**	**13.9%**
Aged 18 to 29	24,274	100.0	42.6	40.2	16.5
Aged 30 to 39	23,007	100.0	43.8	41.3	14.0
Aged 40 to 49	26,565	100.0	45.6	37.6	16.2
Aged 50 to 59	27,436	100.0	48.1	37.0	14.0
Aged 60 to 64	10,666	100.0	54.8	32.6	12.1
Aged 65 or older	28,951	100.0	61.9	26.1	10.2

Source: Agency for Healthcare Research and Quality, Medical Expenditure Panel Survey, 2006, Internet site http://www.meps .ahrq.gov/mepsweb/data_stats/quick_tables_results.jsp?component=1&subcomponent=0&tableSeries=3&year=-1&SearchMet hod=1&Action=Search; calculations by New Strategist

Many Americans Turn to Alternative Medicine

People in their fifties are most likely to seek alternative therapies.

Alternative medicine is big business. In 2007, fully 38 percent of Americans aged 18 or older used a complementary or alternative medicine or therapy, according to a study by the National Center for Health Statistics. Alternative treatments range from popular regimens such as the South Beach diet to chiropractic care, yoga, and acupuncture.

Middle-aged adults are most likely to use alternative medicine. Forty-four percent of people aged 50 to 59 used alternative medicine in 2007. Among Gen Xers (people in their thirties and forties) 40 percent used alternative medicine in the past year—20 percent used biologically based therapies (which include special diets) and 20 percent used mind-body therapy (which includes meditation and yoga).

■ The use of alternative medicine falls steeply with age as health problems become more severe.

The use of alternative medicine peaks in middle age

(percent of people aged 18 or older who have used alternative medicine in the past 12 months, by age, 2007)

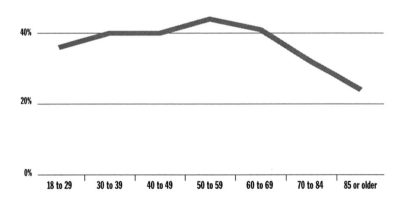

Table 3.37 Adults Who Use Complementary and Alternative Medicine by Age, 2007

(percent of people aged 18 or older who used complementary or alternative medicine in the past 12 months, by age, 2007)

	any use	biologically based therapies	mind-body therapies	alternative medical systems	manipulative and body-based therapies
Total adults	**38.3%**	**19.9%**	**19.2%**	**3.4%**	**15.2%**
Aged 18 to 29	36.3	15.9	21.3	3.2	15.1
Aged 30 to 39	39.6	19.8	19.9	3.6	17.2
Aged 40 to 49	40.1	20.4	19.7	4.6	17.4
Aged 50 to 59	44.1	24.2	22.9	4.9	17.3
Aged 60 to 69	41.0	25.4	17.3	2.8	13.8
Aged 70 to 84	32.1	19.3	11.9	1.8	9.9
Aged 85 or older	24.2	13.7	9.8	1.9	7.0

Definitions: Biologically based therapies include chelation therapy, nonvitamin, nonmineral, natural products, and diet-based therapies. Mind-body therapies include biofeedback; meditation; guided imagery; progressive relaxation; deep breathing exercises; hypnosis; yoga; tai chi; and qi gong. Alternative medical systems include acupuncture; ayurveda; homeopathic treatment; naturopathy; and traditional healers. Manipulative body-based therapies include chiropractic or osteopathic manipulation; massage; and movement therapies.
Source: National Center for Health Statistics, Complementary and Alternative Medicine Use Among Adults and Children: United States, 2007, National Health Statistics Report, No. 12, 2008, Internet site http://nccam.nih.gov/news/camstats/2007/index.htm

Most Deaths of Younger Adults Are Preventable

Accidents are the leading killers of 25-to-44-year-olds.

When adults under age 45 die, it is often preventable. Accidents are the most important cause of death among 25-to-44-year-olds, accounting for 35 percent of deaths among 25-to-34-year-olds and 21 percent of deaths among 35-to-44-year-olds. Suicide ranks second among 25-to-34-year-olds, and homicide is third. Among 35-to-44-year-olds, cancer is the second most important cause of death followed by heart disease. HIV infection ranks sixth as a cause of death among 25-to-34-year-olds and a higher fifth among 35-to-44-year-olds.

Although more could be done to reduce deaths among young adults, some progress has been made. The life expectancy of Americans continues to rise. At age 35, life expectancy is another 44 years. At age 40, another 40 years of life should remain—marking the true age of middle age.

■ As Gen Xers age, heart disease and cancer will become increasingly important causes of death.

Cancer and heart disease are important causes of death among 35-to-44-year-olds

(percent of deaths among 35-to-44-year-olds by top three causes of death, 2006)

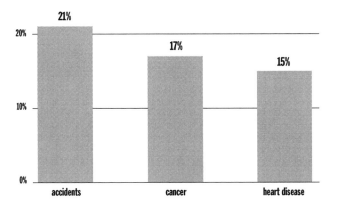

Table 3.38 Leading Causes of Death for People Aged 25 to 34, 2006

(number and percent distribution of deaths accounted for by the 10 leading causes of death for people aged 25 to 34, 2006)

		number	percent distribution
All causes		**42,952**	**100.0%**
1.	Accidents (unintentional injuries) (5)	14,954	34.8
2.	Suicide (11)	4,985	11.6
3.	Homicide (15)	4,725	11.0
4.	Malignant neoplasms (cancer) (2)	3,656	8.5
5.	Diseases of the heart (1)	3,307	7.7
6.	Human immunodeficiency virus infection	1,182	2.8
7.	Diabetes mellitus (6)	673	1.6
8.	Cerebrovascular diseases (3)	527	1.2
9.	Congenital malformations, deformations	437	1.0
10.	Influenza and pneumonia (8)	335	0.8
	All other causes	8,171	19.0

Note: Number in parentheses shows rank for all Americans if the cause of death is among top 15.
Source: National Center for Health Statistics, Deaths: Final Data for 2006, National Vital Statistics Reports, Vol. 57, No. 14, 2009, Internet site http://www.cdc.gov/nchs/products/nvsr.htm#vol57; calculations by New Strategist

Table 3.39 Leading Causes of Death for People Aged 35 to 44, 2006

(number and percent distribution of deaths accounted for by the 10 leading causes of death for people aged 35 to 44, 2006)

		number	percent distribution
All causes		**83,043**	**100.0%**
1.	Accidents (unintentional injuries) (5)	17,534	21.1
2.	Malignant neoplasms (cancer) (2)	13,917	16.8
3.	Diseases of the heart (1)	12,339	14.9
4.	Suicide (11)	6,591	7.9
5.	Human immunodeficiency virus infection	4,010	4.8
6.	Homicide (15)	3,020	3.6
7.	Chronic liver disease and cirrhosis (12)	2,551	3.1
8.	Cerebrovascular diseases (3)	2,221	2.7
9.	Diabetes mellitus (6)	2,094	2.5
10.	Septicemia (10)	870	1.0
	All other causes	17,896	21.6

Note: Number in parentheses shows rank for all Americans if the cause of death is among top 15.
Source: National Center for Health Statistics, Deaths: Final Data for 2006, National Vital Statistics Reports, Vol. 57, No. 14, 2009, Internet site http://www.cdc.gov/nchs/products/nvsr.htm#vol57; calculations by New Strategist

Table 3.40 Life Expectancy by Age and Sex, 2006

(expected years of life remaining at selected ages, by sex, 2006)

	total	females	males
At birth	77.7	80.2	75.1
Aged 1	77.2	79.7	74.7
Aged 5	73.3	75.8	70.8
Aged 10	68.4	70.8	65.8
Aged 15	63.4	65.9	60.9
Aged 20	58.6	61.0	56.1
Aged 25	53.9	56.1	51.5
Aged 30	49.2	51.3	46.9
Aged 35	44.4	46.4	42.2
Aged 40	39.7	41.7	37.6
Aged 45	35.2	37.0	33.1
Aged 50	30.7	32.5	28.8
Aged 55	26.5	28.0	24.7
Aged 60	22.4	23.8	20.7
Aged 65	18.5	19.7	17.0
Aged 70	14.9	15.9	13.6
Aged 75	11.6	12.3	10.5
Aged 80	8.7	9.3	7.8
Aged 85	6.4	6.8	5.7
Aged 90	4.6	4.8	4.1
Aged 95	3.2	3.3	2.9
Aged 100	2.3	2.3	2.0

Source: National Center for Health Statistics, Deaths: Final Data for 2006, National Vital Statistics Reports, Vol. 57, No. 14, 2009tsite http://www.cdc.gov/nchs/products/nvsr.htm#vol57; calculations by New Strategist

4

Housing

■ **The homeownership rate has declined.** Between 2004 and 2008, the homeownership rate fell the most among householders aged 30 to 34 (Gen Xers were aged 32 to 43 in 2008)—a 3.9 percentage point decline.

■ **Most of Generation X has made the transition from renting to home owning.** The 53 percent majority of householders aged 30 to 34 were homeowners in 2008, as were 65 percent of householders aged 35 to 39 and 69 percent of those aged 40 to 44.

■ **Married couples are most likely to own a home.** Among Gen X couples, the homeownership rate ranges from 70.3 percent in the 30-to-34 age group to 83.7 percent among couples aged 40 to 44.

■ **Most (64 percent) householders aged 30 to 44 live in a single-family, detached house.** But a substantial 25 percent live in an apartment building.

■ **The median value of homes owned by married couples aged 35 to 44 stood at $244,492 in 2007**—28 percent greater than the $191,471 median value of all owned homes in that year. Many of those homes have lost value since 2007 because of the collapse of the housing market.

■ **Fifteen percent of people aged 30 to 44 moved between March 2007 and March 2008.** Within the age group, the mobility rate falls to just 10 percent among 40-to-44-year-olds.

Homeownership Rate Has Declined

Since 2004, the rate has fallen the most among 30-to-34-year-olds.

The homeownership rate in the United States reached a peak of 69.0 percent in 2004. Since then, the rate has fallen by 1.2 percentage points, to 67.8 percent in 2008, as the housing market collapsed. Householders aged 30 to 34 experienced the greatest decline in homeownership, their rate falling by nearly 4 percentage points between 2004 and 2008.

In 2008, the overall homeownership rate was 0.4 percentage points greater than in 2000. But for householders aged 30 to 44 (Gen Xers were aged 32 to 43 in 2008), homeownership was lower in 2008 than in 2000. Many Gen Xers purchased homes when housing prices were at their peak, and they have lost their homes in the economic downturn.

■ If the housing market stabilizes, the homeownership rate should increase among Gen Xers as they get older.

After peaking in 2004, homeownership rate among 30-to-44-year-olds has fallen

(homeownership rate for householders aged 30 to 44, by age, 2004 and 2008)

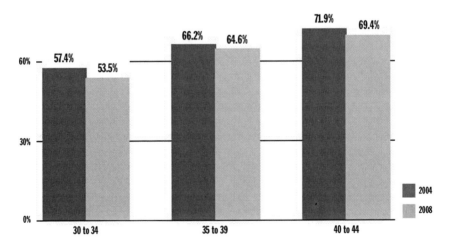

Table 4.1 Homeownership by Age of Householder, 2000 to 2008

(percentage of householders who own their home by age of householder, 2000 to 2008; percentage point change, 2004–08, and 2000–08)

				percentage point change	
	2008	**2004**	**2000**	**2004–08**	**2000–08**
Total households	**67.8%**	**69.0%**	**67.4%**	**−1.2**	**0.4**
Under age 25	23.6	25.2	21.7	−1.6	1.9
Aged 25 to 29	40.0	40.2	38.1	−0.2	1.9
Aged 30 to 34	53.5	57.4	54.6	−3.9	−1.1
Aged 35 to 39	64.6	66.2	65.0	−1.6	−0.4
Aged 40 to 44	69.4	71.9	70.6	−2.5	−1.2
Aged 45 to 54	75.0	77.2	76.5	−2.2	−1.5
Aged 55 to 64	80.1	81.7	80.3	−1.6	−0.2
Aged 65 or older	80.1	81.1	80.4	−1.0	−0.3

Source: Bureau of the Census, Housing Vacancies and Homeownership Survey, Internet site http://www.census.gov/hhes/www/ housing/hvs/annual08/ann08ind.html; calculations by New Strategist

Homeownership Rises with Age

Most householders aged 30 to 44 own their home.

Most of Generation X has made the transition from renting to home owning, although some are losing their homes in the economic downturn. The 53 percent majority of householders aged 30 to 34 were homeowners in 2008. (Gen Xers were aged 32 to 43 in that year.) Among householders aged 35 to 39, the proportion who own their home rises to 65 percent. Among those aged 40 to 44, fully 69 percent are homeowners.

Overall, 63 percent of householders aged 30 to 44 are homeowners and 37 percent are renters. The 30-to-44 age group accounts for 26 percent of the nation's homeowners and 32 percent of its renters.

■ Now that the large Millennial generation is replacing the smaller Generation X in the young-adult age group, the rental market is getting a boost.

Homeownership becomes the norm in the 30-to-34 age group

(percent distribution of householders aged 30 to 44 by homeownership status, 2008)

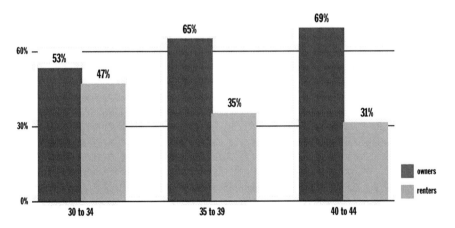

Table 4.2 Owners and Renters by Age of Householder, 2008

(number and percent distribution of householders by homeownership status, and owner and renter share of total, by age of householder, 2008; numbers in thousands)

	total	owners			renters		
		number	percent distribution	share of total	number	percent distribution	share of total
Total households	**111,409**	**75,566**	**100.0%**	**67.8%**	**35,843**	**100.0%**	**32.2%**
Under age 25	6,272	1,482	2.0	23.6	4,790	13.4	76.4
Aged 25 to 29	9,094	3,641	4.8	40.0	5,453	15.2	60.0
Aged 30 to 44	30,867	19,423	25.7	62.9	11,444	31.9	37.1
Aged 30 to 34	9,343	4,998	6.6	53.5	4,346	12.1	46.5
Aged 35 to 39	10,550	6,811	9.0	64.6	3,739	10.4	35.4
Aged 40 to 44	10,974	7,614	10.1	69.4	3,359	9.4	30.6
Aged 45 to 54	23,382	17,537	23.2	75.0	5,845	16.3	25.0
Aged 55 to 64	18,818	15,069	19.9	80.1	3,748	10.5	19.9
Aged 65 or older	22,976	18,414	24.4	80.1	4,562	12.7	19.9

Source: Bureau of the Census, Housing Vacancies and Homeownership Survey, Internet site http://www.census.gov/hhes/www/housing/hvs/historic/index.html; calculations by New Strategist

Married Couples Are Most Likely to Be Homeowners

Two incomes make homes more affordable.

The homeownership rate among all married couples stood at 83.4 percent in 2008, much higher than the 67.8 percent rate for all households. Among Gen X couples (Gen Xers were aged 32 to 43 in 2008), the homeownership rate ranges from 70.3 percent in the 30-to-34 age group to 83.7 percent among couples aged 40 to 44.

Homeownership is much lower for other types of households and lowest for female-headed families, at 49.5 percent in 2008. Regardless of household type, however, most householders aged 45 or older are homeowners.

■ The lax lending standards of the housing bubble did not eliminate differences in homeownership rates by household type.

More than 70 percent of couples aged 30 to 44 own their home

(percent of married-couple householders who own their home, by age, 2008)

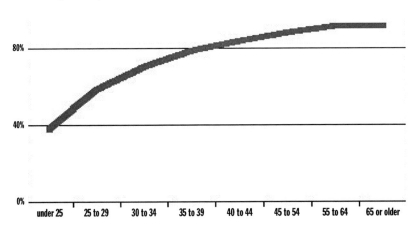

Table 4.3 Homeownership Rate by Age of Householder and Type of Household, 2008

(percent of households that own their home, by age of householder and type of household, 2008)

	total	family households			people living alone	
		married couples	female householder, no spouse present	male householder, no spouse present	females	males
Total households	**67.8%**	**83.4%**	**49.5%**	**57.6%**	**58.6%**	**50.6%**
Under age 25	23.6	37.3	23.4	41.7	11.2	16.7
Aged 25 to 29	40.0	58.7	24.0	40.2	24.1	30.0
Aged 30 to 34	53.5	70.3	30.7	44.9	34.0	36.1
Aged 35 to 39	64.6	78.7	41.3	55.1	45.2	44.2
Aged 40 to 44	69.4	83.7	48.9	58.0	49.5	46.9
Aged 45 to 54	75.0	88.2	60.1	69.4	55.0	53.9
Aged 55 to 64	80.1	91.4	66.7	76.1	66.0	60.2
Aged 65 or older	80.1	91.7	81.2	81.2	69.4	68.2

Source: Bureau of the Census, Housing Vacancies and Homeownership Survey, Internet site http://www.census.gov/hhes/www/housing/hvs/annual08/ann08ind.html

Most Black Gen Xers Are Not Yet Homeowners

Among Hispanics aged 35 to 44, the majority owns a home.

The homeownership rate of blacks and Hispanics is well below average. The overall homeownership rate stood at 68.3 percent for all households in 2007 (the latest data available by race, Hispanic origin, and age). Among blacks, the rate was a smaller 46.7 percent. The Hispanic rate was slightly greater at 50.5 percent.

Homeownership is below 50 percent among black householders until the 45-to-54 age group. Among Hispanics, the rate surpasses 50 percent in the 35-to-44 age group. Homeownership peaks in the 65-or-older age group for both blacks and Hispanics.

■ Blacks are less likely than Hispanics to be homeowners because married couples head a smaller share of black households.

Forty-five percent of black householders aged 35 to 44 own their home

(homeownership rate of total householders and householders aged 30 to 44, by race and Hispanic origin, 2007)

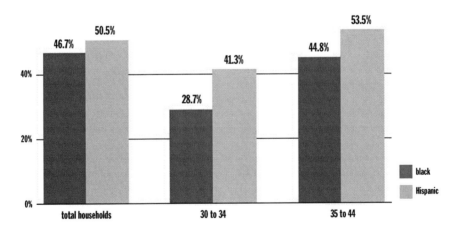

Table 4.4 Black and Hispanic Homeownership Rate by Age, 2007

(percent of total, black, and Hispanic households that own their home, by age of householder, 2007)

	total	black	Hispanic
Total households	**68.3%**	**46.7%**	**50.5%**
Under age 30	34.0	17.3	25.8
Aged 30 to 34	54.7	28.7	41.3
Aged 35 to 44	67.9	44.8	53.5
Aged 45 to 54	75.6	55.1	61.1
Aged 55 to 64	80.7	60.6	64.2
Aged 65 to 74	82.2	64.2	67.4
Aged 75 or older	77.5	66.4	63.7

Note: Blacks include only those who identify themselves as being black alone. Hispanics may be of any race.
Source: Bureau of the Census, American Housing Survey for the United States: 2007, Internet site http://www.census.gov/hhes/ www/housing/ahs/ahs07/ahs07.html; calculations by New Strategist

Most Americans Live in a Single-Family Home

Many Gen Xers live in apartment buildings, however.

The 65 percent majority of American households live in detached, single-family homes. People aged 30 to 44 are about as likely as the average householder to live in this type of home, with 64 percent in a single-family detached house.

A substantial 25 percent of householders aged 30 to 44 live in an apartment building, 6 percent in a duplex, and 6 percent in a mobile home. The median age of householders in detached, single-family homes is 51 years. The median age of householders in apartment buildings is a full 10 years less.

■ The demand for apartments has been growing as the large Millennial generation replaces the small Generation X in the young-adult population.

Generation Xers are likely to live in a detached, single-family home

(percent of households living in detached, single-family homes, by age of householder, 2007)

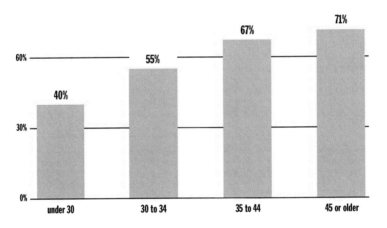

Table 4.5 Number of Units in Structure by Age of Householder, 2007

(number and percent distribution of households by age of householder and type of structure, 2007; numbers in thousands)

	total	one, detached	one, attached	multi-unit dwellings total	2 to 4	5 to 9	10 to 19	20 to 49	50 or more	mobile homes
Total households	**110,692**	**71,435**	**6,083**	**26,256**	**8,790**	**5,258**	**4,697**	**3,645**	**3,866**	**6,919**
Under age 30	15,082	6,011	951	7,285	2,319	1,712	1,613	1,048	592	834
Aged 30 to 44	31,327	19,907	1,789	7,763	2,765	1,663	1,458	1,143	732	1,869
Aged 30 to 34	9,571	5,263	643	3,058	1,058	677	601	459	262	607
Aged 35 to 44	21,756	14,644	1,146	4,705	1,707	986	857	684	470	1,262
Aged 45 to 54	23,208	16,683	1,153	3,906	1,440	760	724	484	497	1,467
Aged 55 to 64	18,211	13,125	1,033	2,832	1,020	499	440	351	521	1,222
Aged 65 or older	22,865	15,710	1,157	4,470	1,246	622	461	617	1,524	1,528
Median age	49	51	48	41	41	37	37	40	57	50

PERCENT DISTRIBUTION BY AGE OF HOUSEHOLDER

	total	one, detached	one, attached	multi-unit dwellings total	2 to 4	5 to 9	10 to 19	20 to 49	50 or more	mobile homes
Total households	**100.0%**	**100.0%**	**100.0%**	**100.0%**	**100.0%**	**100.0%**	**100.0%**	**100.0%**	**100.0%**	**100.0%**
Under age 30	13.6	8.4	15.6	27.7	26.4	32.6	34.3	28.8	15.3	12.1
Aged 30 to 44	28.3	27.9	29.4	29.6	31.5	31.6	31.0	31.4	18.9	27.0
Aged 30 to 34	8.6	7.4	10.6	11.6	12.0	12.9	12.8	12.6	6.8	8.8
Aged 35 to 44	19.7	20.5	18.8	17.9	19.4	18.8	18.2	18.8	12.2	18.2
Aged 45 to 54	21.0	23.4	19.0	14.9	16.4	14.5	15.4	13.3	12.9	21.2
Aged 55 to 64	16.5	18.4	17.0	10.8	11.6	9.5	9.4	9.6	13.5	17.7
Aged 65 or older	20.7	22.0	19.0	17.0	14.2	11.8	9.8	16.9	39.4	22.1

PERCENT DISTRIBUTION BY UNITS IN STRUCTURE

	total	one, detached	one, attached	multi-unit dwellings total	2 to 4	5 to 9	10 to 19	20 to 49	50 or more	mobile homes
Total households	**100.0%**	**64.5%**	**5.5%**	**23.7%**	**7.9%**	**4.8%**	**4.2%**	**3.3%**	**3.5%**	**6.3%**
Under age 30	100.0	39.9	6.3	48.3	15.4	11.4	10.7	6.9	3.9	5.5
Aged 30 to 44	100.0	63.5	5.7	24.8	8.8	5.3	4.7	3.6	2.3	6.0
Aged 30 to 34	100.0	55.0	6.7	32.0	11.1	7.1	6.3	4.8	2.7	6.3
Aged 35 to 44	100.0	67.3	5.3	21.6	7.8	4.5	3.9	3.1	2.2	5.8
Aged 45 to 54	100.0	71.9	5.0	16.8	6.2	3.3	3.1	2.1	2.1	6.3
Aged 55 to 64	100.0	72.1	5.7	15.6	5.6	2.7	2.4	1.9	2.9	6.7
Aged 65 or older	100.0	68.7	5.1	19.5	5.4	2.7	2.0	2.7	6.7	6.7

Source: Bureau of the Census, American Housing Survey for the United States: 2007, Internet site http://www.census.gov/hhes/ www/housing/ahs/ahs07/ahs07.html; calculations by New Strategist

Many Generation Xers Live in New Homes

Older homeowners are least likely to live in recently built homes.

New homes are the province of the young. Overall, only 6 percent of homeowners live in a new home—one built in the past four years. The share is much greater among Gen Xers, however. Among 30-to-34-year-old homeowners, 13 percent live in a new home. The figure is 9 percent among those aged 35 to 44. Among homeowners aged 45 or older, only 3 to 5 percent live in a new home. Householders aged 30 to 44 account for a substantial 42 percent of homeowners who live in a newly built home.

Overall, 3.0 percent of the nation's renters live in newly built housing units. The figure among householders aged 30 to 34 is only slightly higher than average, at 3.3 percent.

■ Many Gen Xers who bought new homes now owe more on the mortgage than the home is worth.

Generation Xers account for a large share of the owners of new homes

(percent distribution of homeowners who live in homes built in the past four years, by age of householder, 2007)

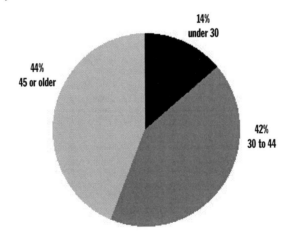

14%
under 30

44%
45 or older

42%
30 to 44

Table 4.6 Owners and Renters of New Homes by Age of Householder, 2007

(number of total occupied housing units, number and percent built in the past four years, and percent distribution of new units by housing tenure and age of householder, 2007; numbers in thousands)

		new homes		
	total	number	percent of total	percent distribution
Total households	**110,692**	**5,747**	**5.2%**	**100.0%**
Under age 30	15,082	1,025	6.8	17.8
Aged 30 to 44	31,327	2,371	7.6	41.3
Aged 30 to 34	9,571	835	8.7	14.5
Aged 35 to 44	21,756	1,536	7.1	26.7
Aged 45 to 54	23,208	1,056	4.6	18.4
Aged 55 to 64	18,211	683	3.8	11.9
Aged 65 or older	22,865	611	2.7	10.6
Total owner households	**75,647**	**4,710**	**6.2**	**100.0**
Under age 30	5,126	679	13.2	14.4
Aged 30 to 44	20,016	1,993	10.0	42.3
Aged 30 to 34	5,235	675	12.9	14.3
Aged 35 to 44	14,781	1,318	8.9	28.0
Aged 45 to 54	17,539	935	5.3	19.9
Aged 55 to 64	14,695	616	4.2	13.1
Aged 65 or older	18,271	487	2.7	10.3
Total renter households	**35,045**	**1,036**	**3.0**	**100.0**
Under age 30	9,955	347	3.5	33.5
Aged 30 to 44	11,311	377	3.3	36.4
Aged 30 to 34	4,336	160	3.7	15.4
Aged 35 to 44	6,975	217	3.1	20.9
Aged 45 to 54	5,669	121	2.1	11.7
Aged 55 to 64	3,516	67	1.9	6.5
Aged 65 or older	4,593	124	2.7	12.0

Source: Bureau of the Census, American Housing Survey for the United States: 2007, Internet site http://www.census.gov/hhes/ www/housing/ahs/ahs07/ahs07.html; calculations by New Strategist

Housing Costs Are Highest for Homeowner Couples Aged 35 to 44

Costs are lowest for homeowners aged 65 or older.

Monthly housing costs for the average household in 2007 stood at $843, including utilities. For homeowners, median monthly housing cost was $927 including mortgages, and for renters the figure was a smaller $755.

Housing costs are highest for married-couple homeowners aged 35 to 44, not only because their homes are larger than average to make room for children but also because many are recent buyers who bought homes during the housing bubble. The median monthly housing cost for married-couple homeowners aged 35 to 44 was $1,466 in 2007—or 74 percent higher than average.

Housing costs are lowest for homeowners aged 65 or older regardless of household type. For older renters, housing costs do not decline much with age. Among married householders aged 65 or older, homeowners paid a median of $514 for housing, while renters paid a median of $814.

■ The financial advantages of homeownership grow as householders age and pay off their mortgages.

Housing costs fall after age 45

(median monthly housing costs for married-couple homeowners, by age of householder, 2007)

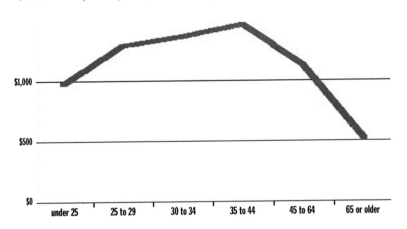

Table 4.7 Median Monthly Housing Costs by Household Type and Age of Householder, 2007

(median monthly housing costs and indexed costs by type of household, age of householder, and housing tenure, 2007)

	median monthly cost			indexed cost		
	total	owners	renters	total	owners	renters
Total households	$843	$927	$755	100	110	90
TWO-OR-MORE-PERSON HOUSEHOLDS						
Married couples	1,026	1,088	878	122	129	104
Under age 25	810	979	716	96	116	85
Aged 25 to 29	1,100	1,286	871	130	153	103
Aged 30 to 34	1,200	1,366	897	142	162	106
Aged 35 to 44	1,349	1,466	937	160	174	111
Aged 45 to 64	1,078	1,113	895	128	132	106
Aged 65 or older	536	514	814	64	61	97
Other male householder	870	960	817	103	114	97
Under age 45	903	1,131	832	107	134	99
Aged 45 to 64	877	951	782	104	113	93
Aged 65 or older	550	505	739	65	60	88
Other female householder	801	867	773	95	103	92
Under age 45	830	1,029	775	98	122	92
Aged 45 to 64	849	935	769	101	111	91
Aged 65 or older	559	496	750	66	59	89
SINGLE-PERSON HOUSEHOLDS						
Male householder	665	681	658	79	81	78
Under age 45	757	996	694	90	118	82
Aged 45 to 64	654	691	631	78	82	75
Aged 65 or older	463	426	524	55	51	62
Female householder	585	523	640	69	62	76
Under age 45	774	991	708	92	118	84
Aged 45 to 64	666	717	616	79	85	73
Aged 65 or older	425	390	528	50	46	63

Note: Housing costs include utilities, mortgages, real estate taxes, property insurance, and regime fees. The index is calculated by dividing median monthly housing costs for each household type by the median cost for total households and multiplying by 100.
Source: Bureau of the Census, American Housing Survey for the United States: 2007, Internet site http://www.census.gov/hhes/ www/housing/ahs/ahs07/ahs07.html; calculations by New Strategist

Married Couples Aged 35 to 44 Own the Most Expensive Homes

The value of their homes has probably declined, however.

The median value of homes owned by married couples aged 35 to 44 stood at $244,492 in 2007—28 percent greater than the $191,471 median value of all owned homes in that year. More than one in four married couples ranging in age from 35 to 64 owned a home with a value of $400,000 or more in 2007. Many of those homes are worth far less today, however, because of the bursting of the housing bubble.

Among homeowning families headed by men and women without a spouse, those aged 45 to 64 have the most valuable homes—although the properties are not as highly valued as the homes of married couples aged 35 to 44. Among men and women who live alone, younger homeowners have the most valuable homes, and female householders under age 65 own homes of greater value than their male counterparts.

■ Home values have been falling and are now significantly lower than the 2007 figures shown below.

Home values were close to their peak in 2007

(median value of homes owned by married couples, by age of householder, 2007)

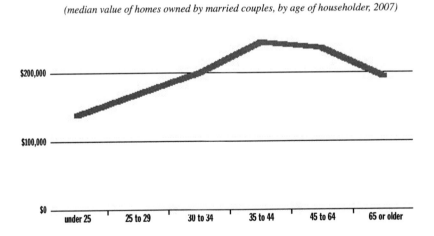

Table 4.8 Value of Owner-Occupied Homes by Type of Household and Age of Householder, 2007

(number of homeowners by value of home, median value of home, and indexed median value, by type of household and age of householder, 2007)

	number (in 000s)	under $100,000	$100,000– $149,999	$150,000– $199,999	$200,000– $299,999	$300,000– $399,999	$400,000– $499,999	$500,000– $749,999	$750,000 or more	median value of home ($)	indexed median value
Total homeowners	75,647	18,779	11,048	9,643	13,132	8,060	4,740	6,234	4,013	191,471	100
TWO-OR-MORE-PERSON HOUSEHOLDS											
Married couples	46,570	9227	6,282	5,992	8,660	5,664	3,348	4,443	2,955	220,607	115
Under age 25	540	176	122	55	66	55	17	37	11	138,617	72
Aged 25 to 29	2,133	494	438	359	415	257	72	89	10	168,736	88
Aged 30 to 34	3,456	709	500	525	739	357	234	264	128	199,431	104
Aged 35 to 44	10,245	1560	1,331	1,334	2,020	1,375	852	1,073	701	244,492	128
Aged 45 to 64	21,119	4048	2,655	2,502	3,795	2,714	1,568	2,274	1,564	235,723	123
Aged 65 or older	9,078	2242	1,237	1,216	1,625	906	605	706	541	193,584	101
Other male householder	4,408	1256	642	597	723	422	205	366	196	175,616	92
Under age 45	2,050	558	349	298	363	174	94	146	67	169,745	89
Aged 45 to 64	1,792	495	245	241	269	174	95	173	102	182,457	95
Aged 65 or older	565	204	48	57	91	75	16	48	27	177,446	93
Other female householder	7,984	2644	1,323	925	1,196	643	427	523	305	151,366	79
Under age 45	3,076	1036	609	406	403	229	138	176	78	141,246	74
Aged 45 to 64	3,349	1037	484	345	543	300	210	250	180	172,275	90
Aged 65 or older	1,558	571	230	173	250	113	79	96	46	145,242	76
SINGLE-PERSON HOUSEHOLDS											
Men living alone	6,930	2321	1,147	935	1,007	563	318	403	235	149,840	78
Under age 45	2,235	663	413	335	392	166	99	122	45	156,298	82
Aged 45 to 64	2,813	991	436	371	385	232	123	161	113	147,605	77
Aged 65 or older	1,882	667	299	229	229	165	96	120	77	145,811	76
Women living alone	9,756	3330	1,653	1,195	1,547	768	442	499	322	146,812	77
Under age 45	1,408	416	225	192	270	138	77	65	25	166,550	87
Aged 45 to 64	3,161	1035	500	453	546	246	157	146	78	155,029	81
Aged 65 or older	5,187	1880	928	550	731	384	208	288	219	138,439	72

Source: Bureau of the Census, American Housing Survey for the United States: 2007, Internet site http://www.census.gov/hhes/ www/housing/ahs/ahs07/ahs07.html; calculations by New Strategist

Mobility Rate Falls Steeply in the 30-to-44 Age Group

Most move for housing-related reasons.

Twelve percent of Americans aged 1 or older moved between March 2007 and March 2008, but the proportion was a larger 15 percent among people aged 30 to 44. Within the age group, the mobility rate falls from 17 percent among 30-to-34-year-olds to 10 percent among 40-to-44-year-olds. The majority of all movers stay within the same county. Only 13 percent of people who moved between 2007 and 2008 went to a different state.

Regardless of age, housing is the primary motivation for moving. The 42 percent plurality of movers aged 30 to 44 say housing was the main reason for the move. Family reasons ranked second as a motivation for moving, and employment ranked a close third. Among those who moved between 2007 and 2008 because of a change in marital status, a substantial 29 percent were aged 30 to 44.

■ Americans are moving less than they once did. Several factors are behind the decline in mobility including the collapse of the housing market, the aging of the population, and the growing number of dual-income couples.

Seventeen percent of 30-to-34-year-olds moved between 2007 and 2008

(percent of people who moved between March 2007 and March 2008, by age)

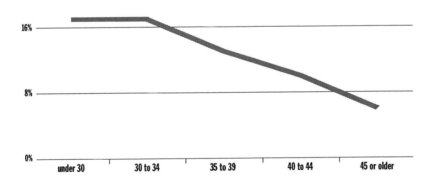

Table 4.9 Geographic Mobility by Age and Type of Move, 2007–08

(total number of people aged 1 or older, and number and percent who moved between March 2007 and March 2008, by age and type of move; numbers in thousands)

	total	total movers	same county	different county, same state	different state total	different state same region	different state different region	movers from abroad
Total, aged 1 or older	**294,851**	**35,166**	**23,013**	**6,282**	**4,727**	**2,248**	**2,479**	**1,145**
Under age 30	119,604	20,898	13,973	3,578	2,648	1,280	1,368	694
Total aged 30 to 44	61,221	9,185	5,171	1,411	1,155	540	615	287
Aged 30 to 34	19,089	3,321	2,066	597	504	229	275	154
Aged 35 to 39	20,733	2,620	1,718	438	381	179	202	83
Aged 40 to 44	21,399	2,083	1,387	376	270	132	138	50
Aged 45 or older	114,026	6,873	3,870	1,290	924	430	494	162

PERCENT DISTRIBUTION BY MOBILITY STATUS

	total	total movers	same county	different county, same state	different state total	different state same region	different state different region	movers from abroad
Total, aged 1 or older	**100.0%**	**11.9%**	**7.8%**	**2.1%**	**1.6%**	**0.8%**	**0.8%**	**0.4%**
Under age 30	100.0	17.5	11.7	3.0	2.2	1.1	1.1	0.6
Total aged 30 to 44	100.0	15.0	8.4	2.3	1.9	0.9	1.0	0.5
Aged 30 to 34	100.0	17.4	10.8	3.1	2.6	1.2	1.4	0.8
Aged 35 to 39	100.0	12.6	8.3	2.1	1.8	0.9	1.0	0.4
Aged 40 to 44	100.0	9.7	6.5	1.8	1.3	0.6	0.6	0.2
Aged 45 or older	100.0	6.0	3.4	1.1	0.8	0.4	0.4	0.1

PERCENT DISTRIBUTION OF MOVERS BY TYPE OF MOVE

	total	total movers	same county	different county, same state	different state total	different state same region	different state different region	movers from abroad
Total, aged 1 or older	**–**	**100.0%**	**65.4%**	**17.9%**	**13.4%**	**6.4%**	**7.0%**	**3.3%**
Under age 30	–	100.0	66.9	17.1	12.7	6.1	6.5	3.3
Total aged 30 to 44	–	100.0	56.3	15.4	12.6	5.9	6.7	3.1
Aged 30 to 34	–	100.0	62.2	18.0	15.2	6.9	8.3	4.6
Aged 35 to 39	–	100.0	65.6	16.7	14.5	6.8	7.7	3.2
Aged 40 to 44	–	100.0	66.6	18.1	13.0	6.3	6.6	2.4
Aged 45 or older	–	100.0	56.3	18.8	13.4	6.3	7.2	2.4

Note: "–" means not applicable.
Source: Bureau of the Census, Geographic Mobility: 2007 to 2008, Detailed Tables, Internet site http://www.census.gov/population/www/socdemo/migrate/cps2008.html; calculations by New Strategist

Table 4.10 Reason for Moving among People Aged 30 to 44, 2007–08

(number and percent distribution of movers aged 30 to 44 by primary reason for move and share of total movers between March 2007 and March 2008; numbers in thousands)

	total movers	movers aged 30 to 44		
		number	percent distribution	share of total
TOTAL MOVERS	35,167	8,023	100.0%	22.8%
Family reasons	**10,738**	**2,265**	**28.2**	**21.1**
Change in marital status	1,987	570	7.1	28.7
To establish own household	3,682	679	8.5	18.4
Other family reasons	5,069	1,016	12.7	20.0
Employment reasons	**7,352**	**1,916**	**23.9**	**26.1**
New job or job transfer	2,940	823	10.3	28.0
To look for work or lost job	794	244	3.0	30.7
To be closer to work/easier commute	2,183	549	6.8	25.1
Retired	140	1	0.0	0.7
Other job-related reason	1,295	299	3.7	23.1
Housing reasons	**14,098**	**3,331**	**41.5**	**23.6**
Wanted own home, not rent	2,033	543	6.8	26.7
Wanted better home/apartment	4,866	1,153	14.4	23.7
Wanted better neighborhood	1,778	448	5.6	25.2
Wanted cheaper housing	2,872	655	8.2	22.8
Other housing reasons	2,549	532	6.6	20.9
Other reasons	**2,978**	**512**	**6.4**	**17.2**
To attend or leave college	872	118	1.5	13.5
Change of climate	212	47	0.6	22.2
Health reasons	460	82	1.0	17.8
Natural disaster	61	12	0.1	19.7
Other reasons	1,373	253	3.2	18.4

Source: Bureau of the Census, Geographic Mobility: 2007 to 2008, Detailed Tables, Internet site http://www.census.gov/population/www/socdemo/migrate/cps2008.html; calculations by New Strategist

5

Income

■ Between 2000 and 2007, the median income of households headed by people aged 35 to 44 (Gen Xers were aged 31 to 42 in 2007) fell 4 percent, after adjusting for inflation. Despite the decline, their median household income was 5 percent higher in 2007 than in 1990.

■ Among householders aged 30 to 44, the incomes of Asians are far higher than those of other racial or ethnic groups.

■ Among Gen Xers, married couples have the highest incomes by far. In 2007 married couples headed by people aged 30 to 44 had a median income of $79,275.

■ The incomes of men aged 35 to 44 fell between 2000 and 2007—a decline that does not reflect the economic downturn of 2008. In fact, the decline in men's incomes began long before 2000.

■ Generation Xers are less likely to be poor than the average American. Overall, 12 percent of Americans lived in poverty in 2007. Among people aged 31 to 42, however, a smaller 10 percent were poor.

Household Incomes of Gen Xers Have Declined

But incomes are higher than they were in 1990.

Between 2000 and 2007, the median income of households headed by people aged 35 to 44 fell 4 percent, after adjusting for inflation. (Generation Xers were aged 31 to 42 in 2007.) Behind the decline was the lackluster recovery following the recession of 2001. Not yet appearing in these statistics is the effect of the economic downturn of 2008, which is certain to have reduced median household even more.

Despite the decline between 2000 and 2007, the median income of householders aged 35 to 44 was 5 percent higher in 2007 than in 1990. At $62,124 in 2007, the median income of householders aged 35 to 44 was 24 percent greater than the national median of $50,233.

■ The median income of householders aged 35 to 44 is probably even lower today because of the economic downturn.

Household incomes have fallen since 2000

(median income of households headed by people aged 35 to 44, 2000–07; in 2007 dollars)

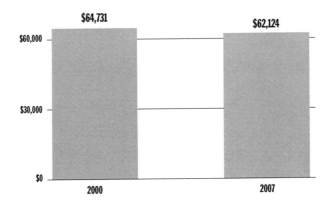

Table 5.1 Median Income of Households Headed by People Aged 35 to 44, 1990 to 2007

(median income of total households and households headed by people aged 35 to 44, and index of age group to total, 1990 to 2007; percent change for selected years; in 2007 dollars)

	total households	35 to 44	index, 35–44 to total
2007	$50,233	$62,124	124
2006	49,568	62,119	125
2005	49,202	61,690	125
2004	48,665	62,219	128
2003	48,835	62,054	127
2002	48,878	61,685	126
2001	49,455	62,446	126
2000	50,557	64,731	128
1999	50,641	63,226	125
1998	49,397	61,549	125
1997	47,665	59,714	125
1996	46,704	58,452	125
1995	46,034	58,718	128
1994	44,636	57,645	129
1993	44,143	57,738	131
1992	44,359	57,704	130
1991	44,726	58,419	131
1990	46,049	59,302	129
Percent change			
2000 to 2007	–0.6%	–3.9%	–
1990 to 2007	9.1	4.9	–

Note: The index is calculated by dividing the median income of the age group by the national median and multiplying by 100. "–" means not applicable.
Source: Bureau of the Census, Current Population Survey Annual Social and Economic Supplements, Internet site http://www .census.gov/hhes//www/income/histinc/inchhtoc.html; calculations by New Strategist

Household Income Rises with Age

Household income begins to exceed the average in the 30-to-34 age group.

The median income of householders aged 25 to 29, at $47,358 in 2007, was below the national median of $50,233. But householders aged 30 to 34 had a median income 10 percent above the national average, at $55,077. Behind the substantially higher incomes of the 30-to-34 age group is their lifestyle. At this age, most men and women are married and most couples have two incomes.

In the nation as a whole, nearly 24 million households had incomes of $100,000 or more in 2007. One-third of those householders were aged 30 to 44 (Gen Xers were aged 31 to 42 in 2007). Among all households, 20 percent have incomes of $100,000 or more. For householders aged 30 to 44, the figure is a higher 24 percent.

■ Gen Xers may see little income growth in the years ahead as Boomers postpone retirement and clog up the promotion pipeline.

Householders aged 30 to 44 have above-average incomes

(median income of total households and households headed by people aged 30 to 44, 2007)

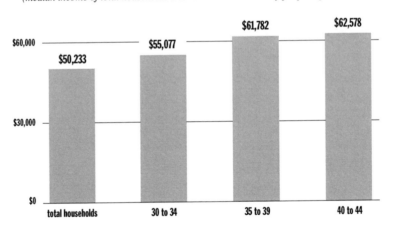

Table 5.2 Income of Households Headed by People Aged 30 to 44, 2007: Total Households

(number and percent distribution of total households and households headed by people aged 30 to 44, by income, 2007; households in thousands as of 2008)

	total	aged 30 to 44			
		total	30 to 34	35 to 39	40 to 44
Total households	**116,783**	**32,273**	**9,825**	**10,900**	**11,548**
Under $10,000	8,455	1,591	512	485	594
$10,000 to $19,999	13,778	2,440	835	784	821
$20,000 to $29,999	13,115	2,872	1,016	947	909
$30,000 to $39,999	12,006	3,147	1,089	989	1,069
$40,000 to $49,999	10,733	2,972	954	981	1,037
$50,000 to $59,999	9,565	2,960	920	1,003	1,037
$60,000 to $69,999	8,009	2,585	794	950	841
$70,000 to $79,999	7,006	2,376	732	810	834
$80,000 to $89,999	5,788	1,950	570	651	729
$90,000 to $99,999	4,741	1,570	446	544	580
$100,000 or more	23,586	7,809	1,955	2,756	3,098
Median income	$50,233	$60,026	$55,077	$61,782	$62,578
Total households	**100.0%**	**100.0%**	**100.0%**	**100.0%**	**100.0%**
Under $10,000	7.2	4.9	5.2	4.4	5.1
$10,000 to $19,999	11.8	7.6	8.5	7.2	7.1
$20,000 to $29,999	11.2	8.9	10.3	8.7	7.9
$30,000 to $39,999	10.3	9.8	11.1	9.1	9.3
$40,000 to $49,999	9.2	9.2	9.7	9.0	9.0
$50,000 to $59,999	8.2	9.2	9.4	9.2	9.0
$60,000 to $69,999	6.9	8.0	8.1	8.7	7.3
$70,000 to $79,999	6.0	7.4	7.5	7.4	7.2
$80,000 to $89,999	5.0	6.0	5.8	6.0	6.3
$90,000 to $99,999	4.1	4.9	4.5	5.0	5.0
$100,000 or more	20.2	24.2	19.9	25.3	26.8

Source: Bureau of the Census, 2008 Current Population Survey Annual Social and Economic Supplement, Internet site http://www.census.gov/hhes/www/macro/032008/hhinc/new02_001.htm; calculations by New Strategist

Incomes Are Highest for Asian Households

Among householders aged 30 to 44, the incomes of Asians are far higher than those of other racial or ethnic groups.

The median income of households headed by Asians aged 3 to 44 stood at $78,674 in 2007. (Gen Xers were aged 31 to 42 in that year.) Among Asian householders aged 40 to 44, median income was an even higher $86,808. The median income of non-Hispanic whites aged 3 to 44, at $69,089, was lower than that of Asians. The median incomes of Hispanic and black householders aged 30 to 44 were much lower—$42,158 and $41,328, respectively.

One factor behind the income differences by race and Hispanic origin is the number of earners per household. Because Asian and non-Hispanic white households are more likely than black or Hispanic households to be two-earner married couples, their incomes are considerably higher. Education also accounts for some of the gap. Asians are the best-educated Americans, followed by non-Hispanic whites. Hispanics are the least educated.

■ Black and Hispanic householders will not close the income gap until dual-earner couples make up a larger share of their households and college graduation rates approach those of Asians and non-Hispanic whites.

The incomes of middle-aged householders vary by race and Hispanic origin

(median income of households headed by people aged 30 to 44 by race and Hispanic origin, 2007)

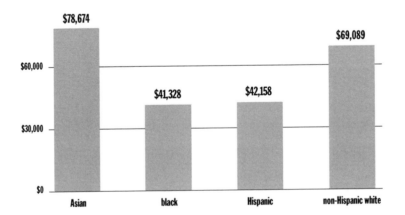

Table 5.3 Income of Households Headed by People Aged 30 to 44, 2007: Asian Households

(number and percent distribution of total Asian households and Asian households headed by people aged 30 to 44, by income, 2007; households in thousands as of 2008)

	total	aged 30 to 44			
		total	30 to 34	35 to 39	40 to 44
Total Asian households	**4,715**	**1768**	**620**	**628**	**520**
Under $10,000	311	70	23	31	16
$10,000 to $19,999	365	102	44	29	29
$20,000 to $29,999	388	99	35	44	20
$30,000 to $39,999	357	113	37	50	26
$40,000 to $49,999	372	128	50	46	32
$50,000 to $59,999	336	122	46	37	39
$60,000 to $69,999	327	128	47	46	35
$70,000 to $79,999	307	138	45	51	42
$80,000 to $89,999	243	97	27	35	35
$90,000 to $99,999	240	101	49	30	22
$100,000 or more	1,468	671	217	230	224
Median income	$65,876	$78,674	$76,532	$74,053	$86,808
Total Asian households	**100.0%**	**100.0%**	**100.0%**	**100.0%**	**100.0%**
Under $10,000	6.6	4.0	3.7	4.9	3.1
$10,000 to $19,999	7.7	5.8	7.1	4.6	5.6
$20,000 to $29,999	8.2	5.6	5.6	7.0	3.8
$30,000 to $39,999	7.6	6.4	6.0	8.0	5.0
$40,000 to $49,999	7.9	7.2	8.1	7.3	6.2
$50,000 to $59,999	7.1	6.9	7.4	5.9	7.5
$60,000 to $69,999	6.9	7.2	7.6	7.3	6.7
$70,000 to $79,999	6.5	7.8	7.3	8.1	8.1
$80,000 to $89,999	5.2	5.5	4.4	5.6	6.7
$90,000 to $99,999	5.1	5.7	7.9	4.8	4.2
$100,000 or more	31.1	38.0	35.0	36.6	43.1

Note: Asians include those who identify themselves as being of the race alone and those who identify themselves as being of the race in combination with other races.
Source: Bureau of the Census, 2008 Current Population Survey Annual Social and Economic Supplement, Internet site http://www.census.gov/hhes/www/macro/032008/hhinc/new02_001.htm; calculations by New Strategist

Table 5.4 Income of Households Headed by People Aged 30 to 44, 2007: Black Households

(number and percent distribution of total black households and black households headed by people aged 30 to 44, by income, 2007; households in thousands as of 2008)

	total	aged 30 to 44 total	30 to 34	35 to 39	40 to 44
Total black households	**14,976**	**4,623**	**1,421**	**1,621**	**1,581**
Under $10,000	2,256	489	194	133	162
$10,000 to $19,999	2,444	610	220	205	185
$20,000 to $29,999	1,988	567	191	215	161
$30,000 to $39,999	1,746	584	204	188	192
$40,000 to $49,999	1,379	472	119	187	166
$50,000 to $59,999	1,161	397	111	135	151
$60,000 to $69,999	867	309	96	111	102
$70,000 to $79,999	683	253	65	95	93
$80,000 to $89,999	549	215	49	69	97
$90,000 to $99,999	403	167	41	67	59
$100,000 or more	1,500	559	133	215	211
Median income	$34,091	$41,328	$35,216	$43,312	$44,786
Total black households	**100.0%**	**100.0%**	**100.0%**	**100.0%**	**100.0%**
Under $10,000	15.1	10.6	13.7	8.2	10.2
$10,000 to $19,999	16.3	13.2	15.5	12.6	11.7
$20,000 to $29,999	13.3	12.3	13.4	13.3	10.2
$30,000 to $39,999	11.7	12.6	14.4	11.6	12.1
$40,000 to $49,999	9.2	10.2	8.4	11.5	10.5
$50,000 to $59,999	7.8	8.6	7.8	8.3	9.6
$60,000 to $69,999	5.8	6.7	6.8	6.8	6.5
$70,000 to $79,999	4.6	5.5	4.6	5.9	5.9
$80,000 to $89,999	3.7	4.7	3.4	4.3	6.1
$90,000 to $99,999	2.7	3.6	2.9	4.1	3.7
$100,000 or more	10.0	12.1	9.4	13.3	13.3

Note: Blacks include those who identify themselves as being of the race alone and those who identify themselves as being of the race in combination with other races.
Source: Bureau of the Census, 2008 Current Population Survey Annual Social and Economic Supplement, Internet site http:// www.census.gov/hhes/www/macro/032008/hhinc/new02_001.htm; calculations by New Strategist

Table 5.5 Income of Households Headed by People Aged 30 to 44, 2007: Hispanic Households

(number and percent distribution of total Hispanic households and Hispanic households headed by people aged 30 to 44, by income, 2007; households in thousands as of 2008)

	total	aged 30 to 44			
		total	30 to 34	35 to 39	40 to 44
Total Hispanic households	**13,339**	**5,185**	**1,800**	**1,789**	**1,596**
Under $10,000	1,184	305	106	103	96
$10,000 to $19,999	1,901	649	255	192	202
$20,000 to $29,999	1,961	782	310	261	211
$30,000 to $39,999	1,787	709	237	252	220
$40,000 to $49,999	1,387	580	193	208	179
$50,000 to $59,999	1,119	469	159	144	166
$60,000 to $69,999	921	399	149	139	111
$70,000 to $79,999	758	315	101	125	89
$80,000 to $89,999	534	239	74	92	73
$90,000 to $99,999	401	144	49	51	44
$100,000 or more	1,385	592	168	221	203
Median income	$38,679	$42,158	$39,584	$43,337	$43,741
Total Hispanic households	**100.0%**	**100.0%**	**100.0%**	**100.0%**	**100.0%**
Under $10,000	8.9	5.9	5.9	5.8	6.0
$10,000 to $19,999	14.3	12.5	14.2	10.7	12.7
$20,000 to $29,999	14.7	15.1	17.2	14.6	13.2
$30,000 to $39,999	13.4	13.7	13.2	14.1	13.8
$40,000 to $49,999	10.4	11.2	10.7	11.6	11.2
$50,000 to $59,999	8.4	9.0	8.8	8.0	10.4
$60,000 to $69,999	6.9	7.7	8.3	7.8	7.0
$70,000 to $79,999	5.7	6.1	5.6	7.0	5.6
$80,000 to $89,999	4.0	4.6	4.1	5.1	4.6
$90,000 to $99,999	3.0	2.8	2.7	2.9	2.8
$100,000 or more	10.4	11.4	9.3	12.4	12.7

Source: Bureau of the Census, 2008 Current Population Survey Annual Social and Economic Supplement, Internet site http:// www.census.gov/hhes/www/macro/032008/hhinc/new02_001.htm; calculations by New Strategist

Table 5.6 Income of Households Headed by People Aged 30 to 44, 2007: Non-Hispanic White Households

(number and percent distribution of total non-Hispanic white households and non-Hispanic white households headed by people aged 30 to 44, by income, 2007; households in thousands as of 2008)

| | | aged 30 to 44 | | | |
	total	total	30 to 34	35 to 39	40 to 44
Total non-Hispanic white households	**82,765**	**20,466**	**5,937**	**6,786**	**7,743**
Under $10,000	4,607	707	199	203	305
$10,000 to $19,999	8,971	1,077	327	356	394
$20,000 to $29,999	8,639	1,394	463	431	500
$30,000 to $39,999	8,017	1,717	594	500	623
$40,000 to $49,999	7,479	1,767	586	537	644
$50,000 to $59,999	6,854	1,941	593	670	678
$60,000 to $69,999	5,836	1,734	503	651	580
$70,000 to $79,999	5,213	1,658	521	533	604
$80,000 to $89,999	4,419	1,392	414	451	527
$90,000 to $99,999	3,664	1,138	304	385	449
$100,000 or more	19,062	5,941	1,434	2,071	2,436
Median income	$54,920	$69,089	$63,502	$70,588	$72,059
Total non-Hispanic white households	**100.0%**	**100.0%**	**100.0%**	**100.0%**	**100.0%**
Under $10,000	5.6	3.5	3.4	3.0	3.9
$10,000 to $19,999	10.8	5.3	5.5	5.2	5.1
$20,000 to $29,999	10.4	6.8	7.8	6.4	6.5
$30,000 to $39,999	9.7	8.4	10.0	7.4	8.0
$40,000 to $49,999	9.0	8.6	9.9	7.9	8.3
$50,000 to $59,999	8.3	9.5	10.0	9.9	8.8
$60,000 to $69,999	7.1	8.5	8.5	9.6	7.5
$70,000 to $79,999	6.3	8.1	8.8	7.9	7.8
$80,000 to $89,999	5.3	6.8	7.0	6.6	6.8
$90,000 to $99,999	4.4	5.6	5.1	5.7	5.8
$100,000 or more	23.0	29.0	24.2	30.5	31.5

Note: Non-Hispanic whites are those who identify themselves as being white alone and not Hispanic.
Source: Bureau of the Census, 2008 Current Population Survey Annual Social and Economic Supplement, Internet site http://www.census.gov/hhes/www/macro/032008/hhinc/new02_001.htm; calculations by New Strategist

Couples Have the Highest Incomes

Female family heads have the lowest incomes.

The incomes of households headed by people aged 30 to 44 vary sharply by household type. Married couples have the highest incomes by far. Among households headed by people aged 30 to 44 (Gen Xers were aged 31 to 42 in 2007), married couples had a median income of $79,275 in 2007. In the 40-to-44 age group, the median income of married couples was a lofty $85,686. Behind the higher incomes is the fact that most couples are dual earners.

Female-headed families in the 30-to-44 age group had a median income of only $31,103 in 2007. Most are single parents. The median income of male-headed families, at $51,358, was much higher than that of female-headed families. The median income of women aged 30 to 44 who live alone was almost as high as that of their male counterparts, $36,407 versus $39,351.

■ Female-headed families have the lowest incomes because their households usually include only one earner and the presence of children diminishes flexibility in job choices.

Incomes of Gen X couples are above average

(median income of householders aged 30 to 44 by household type, 2007)

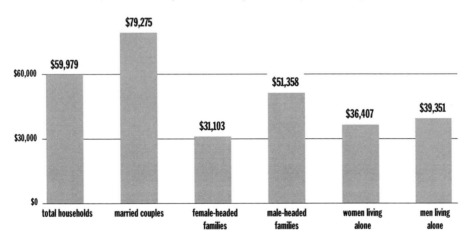

Table 5.7 Income of Households by Household Type, 2007: Aged 30 to 44

(number and percent distribution of households headed by people aged 30 to 44, by income and household type, 2007; households in thousands as of 2008)

| | | family households | | | nonfamily households | | | |
| | | | | | female householder | | male householder | |
	total	married couples	female hh, no spouse present	male hh, no spouse present	total	living alone	total	living alone
Total households headed by 30-to-44-year-olds	32,273	18,229	5,150	1,607	2,683	2,127	4,604	3,437
Under $10,000	1,591	264	658	50	267	248	355	335
$10,000 to $19,999	2,438	590	942	143	306	268	458	413
$20,000 to $29,999	2,871	921	898	168	340	309	546	462
$30,000 to $39,999	3,148	1,164	755	222	375	328	632	548
$40,000 to $49,999	2,974	1,393	534	174	339	287	537	415
$50,000 to $59,999	2,960	1,597	375	206	252	210	527	415
$60,000 to $69,999	2,584	1,659	265	166	179	137	318	205
$70,000 to $79,999	2,375	1,626	212	84	169	119	283	174
$80,000 to $89,999	1,949	1,459	128	93	74	38	195	90
$90,000 to $99,999	1,569	1,201	88	50	91	60	141	78
$100,000 or more	7,809	6,358	298	250	294	123	609	303
Median income	$59,979	$79,275	$31,103	$51,358	$40,913	$36,407	$45,758	$39,351
Total households headed by 30-to-44-year-olds	100.0%	100.0%	100.0%	100.0%	100.0%	100.0%	100.0%	100.0%
Under $10,000	4.9	1.4	12.8	3.1	10.0	11.7	7.7	9.7
$10,000 to $19,999	7.6	3.2	18.3	8.9	11.4	12.6	9.9	12.0
$20,000 to $29,999	8.9	5.1	17.4	10.5	12.7	14.5	11.9	13.4
$30,000 to $39,999	9.8	6.4	14.7	13.8	14.0	15.4	13.7	15.9
$40,000 to $49,999	9.2	7.6	10.4	10.8	12.6	13.5	11.7	12.1
$50,000 to $59,999	9.2	8.8	7.3	12.8	9.4	9.9	11.4	12.1
$60,000 to $69,999	8.0	9.1	5.1	10.3	6.7	6.4	6.9	6.0
$70,000 to $79,999	7.4	8.9	4.1	5.2	6.3	5.6	6.1	5.1
$80,000 to $89,999	6.0	8.0	2.5	5.8	2.8	1.8	4.2	2.6
$90,000 to $99,999	4.9	6.6	1.7	3.1	3.4	2.8	3.1	2.3
$100,000 or more	24.2	34.9	5.8	15.6	11.0	5.8	13.2	8.8

Note: "hh" is short for householder.
Source: Bureau of the Census, 2008 Current Population Survey Annual Social and Economic Supplement, Internet site http://www.census.gov/hhes/www/macro/032008/hhinc/new02_000.htm; calculations by New Strategist

Table 5.8 Income of Households by Household Type, 2007: Aged 30 to 34

(number and percent distribution of households headed by people aged 30 to 34, by income and household type, 2007; households in thousands as of 2008)

| | | family households | | | nonfamily households | | | |
| | | | | | female householder | | male householder | |
	total	married couples	female hh, no spouse present	male hh, no spouse present	total	living alone	total	living alone
Total households headed by 30-to-34-year-olds	**9,825**	**5,240**	**1,599**	**546**	**845**	**648**	**1,595**	**1,116**
Under $10,000	512	85	250	17	58	52	103	95
$10,000 to $19,999	835	210	343	52	85	76	144	128
$20,000 to $29,999	1,016	326	320	77	108	103	184	155
$30,000 to $39,999	1,089	408	236	74	122	106	249	225
$40,000 to $49,999	954	487	113	51	121	101	183	137
$50,000 to $59,999	920	492	104	77	72	58	173	124
$60,000 to $69,999	794	512	58	55	48	38	123	76
$70,000 to $79,999	732	494	47	27	74	51	90	49
$80,000 to $89,999	570	421	33	28	19	5	69	26
$90,000 to $99,999	446	342	34	20	16	12	34	12
$100,000 or more	1,955	1,465	62	66	124	46	239	88
Median income	$55,077	$71,555	$25,804	$50,078	$42,456	$38,497	$46,411	$37,686
Total households headed by 30-to-34-year-olds	**100.0%**	**100.0%**	**100.0%**	**100.0%**	**100.0%**	**100.0%**	**100.0%**	**100.0%**
Under $10,000	5.2	1.6	15.6	3.1	6.9	8.0	6.5	8.5
$10,000 to $19,999	8.5	4.0	21.5	9.5	10.1	11.7	9.0	11.5
$20,000 to $29,999	10.3	6.2	20.0	14.1	12.8	15.9	11.5	13.9
$30,000 to $39,999	11.1	7.8	14.8	13.6	14.4	16.4	15.6	20.2
$40,000 to $49,999	9.7	9.3	7.1	9.3	14.3	15.6	11.5	12.3
$50,000 to $59,999	9.4	9.4	6.5	14.1	8.5	9.0	10.8	11.1
$60,000 to $69,999	8.1	9.8	3.6	10.1	5.7	5.9	7.7	6.8
$70,000 to $79,999	7.5	9.4	2.9	4.9	8.8	7.9	5.6	4.4
$80,000 to $89,999	5.8	8.0	2.1	5.1	2.2	0.8	4.3	2.3
$90,000 to $99,999	4.5	6.5	2.1	3.7	1.9	1.9	2.1	1.1
$100,000 or more	19.9	28.0	3.9	12.1	14.7	7.1	15.0	7.9

Note: "hh" is short for householder.
Source: Bureau of the Census, 2008 Current Population Survey Annual Social and Economic Supplement, Internet site http://www.census.gov/hhes/www/macro/032008/hhinc/new02_000.htm; calculations by New Strategist

Table 5.9 Income of Households by Household Type, 2007: Aged 35 to 39

(number and percent distribution of households headed by people aged 35 to 39, by income and household type, 2007; households in thousands as of 2008)

| | | family households | | | nonfamily households | | | |
| | | | | | female householder | | male householder | |
	total	married couples	female hh, no spouse present	male hh, no spouse present	total	living alone	total	living alone
Total households headed by 35-to-39-year-olds	**10,900**	**6,406**	**1,684**	**515**	**853**	**679**	**1,442**	**1,081**
Under $10,000	485	79	212	9	84	73	103	94
$10,000 to $19,999	784	185	308	45	121	109	125	117
$20,000 to $29,999	947	331	305	48	85	80	177	148
$30,000 to $39,999	989	400	227	73	114	100	176	144
$40,000 to $49,999	981	493	172	55	95	88	167	133
$50,000 to $59,999	1,003	555	142	63	78	64	166	135
$60,000 to $69,999	950	637	84	44	68	51	116	74
$70,000 to $79,999	810	554	66	29	37	30	128	81
$80,000 to $89,999	651	498	43	43	21	12	47	16
$90,000 to $99,999	544	408	19	17	40	21	59	42
$100,000 or more	2,756	2,271	104	89	111	48	180	98
Median income	$61,782	$79,393	$30,612	$52,373	$43,485	$36,534	$47,362	$41,956
Total households headed by 35-to-39-year-olds	**100.0%**	**100.0%**	**100.0%**	**100.0%**	**100.0%**	**100.0%**	**100.0%**	**100.0%**
Under $10,000	4.4	1.2	12.6	1.7	9.8	10.8	7.1	8.7
$10,000 to $19,999	7.2	2.9	18.3	8.7	14.2	16.1	8.7	10.8
$20,000 to $29,999	8.7	5.2	18.1	9.3	10.0	11.8	12.3	13.7
$30,000 to $39,999	9.1	6.2	13.5	14.2	13.4	14.7	12.2	13.3
$40,000 to $49,999	9.0	7.7	10.2	10.7	11.1	13.0	11.6	12.3
$50,000 to $59,999	9.2	8.7	8.4	12.2	9.1	9.4	11.5	12.5
$60,000 to $69,999	8.7	9.9	5.0	8.5	8.0	7.5	8.0	6.8
$70,000 to $79,999	7.4	8.6	3.9	5.6	4.3	4.4	8.9	7.5
$80,000 to $89,999	6.0	7.8	2.6	8.3	2.5	1.8	3.3	1.5
$90,000 to $99,999	5.0	6.4	1.1	3.3	4.7	3.1	4.1	3.9
$100,000 or more	25.3	35.5	6.2	17.3	13.0	7.1	12.5	9.1

Note: "hh" is short for householder.
Source: Bureau of the Census, 2008 Current Population Survey Annual Social and Economic Supplement, Internet site http://www.census.gov/hhes/www/macro/032008/hhinc/new02_000.htm; calculations by New Strategist

Table 5.10 Income of Households by Household Type, 2007: Aged 40 to 44

(number and percent distribution of households headed by people aged 40 to 44, by income and household type, 2007; households in thousands as of 2008)

| | | family households | | | nonfamily households | | | |
| | | | | | female householder | | male householder | |
	total	married couples	female hh, no spouse present	male hh, no spouse present	total	living alone	total	living alone
Total households headed by 40-to-44-year-olds	**11,548**	**6,583**	**1,867**	**546**	**985**	**801**	**1,567**	**1,239**
Under $10,000	594	101	195	24	125	122	149	144
$10,000 to $19,999	821	195	291	46	101	83	189	168
$20,000 to $29,999	909	264	272	43	146	125	185	158
$30,000 to $39,999	1,069	354	293	76	139	122	208	181
$40,000 to $49,999	1,037	413	247	68	122	98	187	143
$50,000 to $59,999	1,037	550	130	66	102	88	189	155
$60,000 to $69,999	841	512	122	65	63	48	79	54
$70,000 to $79,999	834	580	100	29	60	38	68	43
$80,000 to $89,999	729	541	52	24	35	21	79	50
$90,000 to $99,999	580	451	34	13	34	26	49	25
$100,000 or more	3,098	2,622	132	95	59	30	190	117
Median income	$62,578	$85,686	$35,728	$51,630	$38,465	$34,130	$41,983	$37,390
Total households headed by 40-to-44-year-olds	**100.0%**	**100.0%**	**100.0%**	**100.0%**	**100.0%**	**100.0%**	**100.0%**	**100.0%**
Under $10,000	5.1	1.5	10.4	4.4	12.7	15.2	9.5	11.6
$10,000 to $19,999	7.1	3.0	15.6	8.4	10.3	10.4	12.1	13.6
$20,000 to $29,999	7.9	4.0	14.6	7.9	14.8	15.6	11.8	12.8
$30,000 to $39,999	9.3	5.4	15.7	13.9	14.1	15.2	13.3	14.6
$40,000 to $49,999	9.0	6.3	13.2	12.5	12.4	12.2	11.9	11.5
$50,000 to $59,999	9.0	8.4	7.0	12.1	10.4	11.0	12.1	12.5
$60,000 to $69,999	7.3	7.8	6.5	11.9	6.4	6.0	5.0	4.4
$70,000 to $79,999	7.2	8.8	5.4	5.3	6.1	4.7	4.3	3.5
$80,000 to $89,999	6.3	8.2	2.8	4.4	3.6	2.6	5.0	4.0
$90,000 to $99,999	5.0	6.9	1.8	2.4	3.5	3.2	3.1	2.0
$100,000 or more	26.8	39.8	7.1	17.4	6.0	3.7	12.1	9.4

Note: "hh" is short for householder.
Source: Bureau of the Census, 2008 Current Population Survey Annual Social and Economic Supplement, Internet site http://www.census.gov/hhes/www/macro/032008/hhinc/new02_000.htm; calculations by New Strategist

Median Income of Men Aged 35 to 44 Is below the 1990 Level

Women's incomes have grown.

The incomes of men aged 35 to 44 fell slightly between 2000 and 2007, down 1 percent after adjusting for inflation. (Gen Xers were aged 31 to 42 in 2007.) The women of the age group enjoyed a rise, however, as their median income grew by 4 percent during those years.

Behind the income reduction for men was the lackluster economic recovery following the recession of 2001 (these figures do not capture the economic downturn of 2008), but the decline in men's incomes began long before 2000. The median income of men aged 35 to 44 in 2007 was 2 percent less than in 1990, after adjusting for inflation. In contrast, women's incomes soared during the 1990s. The women of the age group saw their median income rise 24 percent between 1990 and 2007, while women of all ages experienced an even greater 35 percent gain.

■ Women's incomes have been rising rapidly because more have joined the workforce.

Women have enjoyed big gains in income

(percent change in median income of people aged 35 to 44 by sex, 1990–2007; in 2007 dollars)

Table 5.11 Median Income of Men Aged 35 to 44, 1990 to 2007

(median income of men aged 15 or older and aged 35 to 44, and index of age group to total, 1990 to 2007; percent change for selected years; in 2007 dollars)

	total men	35 to 44	index, 35–44 to total
2007	$33,196	$45,018	136
2006	33,180	43,847	132
2005	33,217	43,507	131
2004	33,497	44,494	133
2003	33,743	44,187	131
2002	33,698	43,672	130
2001	34,082	44,902	132
2000	34,126	45,659	134
1999	33,963	45,292	133
1998	33,654	44,687	133
1997	32,475	42,314	130
1996	31,363	42,329	135
1995	30,480	42,446	139
1994	30,049	42,482	141
1993	29,817	42,873	144
1992	29,617	42,701	144
1991	30,389	43,501	143
1990	31,208	45,787	147
Percent change			
2000 to 2007	–2.7%	–1.4%	–
1990 to 2007	6.4	–1.7	–

Note: The index is calculated by dividing the median income of the age group by the national median and multiplying by 100. "–" means not applicable.
Source: Bureau of the Census, data from the Current Population Survey Annual Demographic Supplements, Internet site http:// www.census.gov/hhes/www/income/histinc/p08AR.html; calculations by New Strategist

Table 5.12 Median Income of Women Aged 35 to 44, 1990 to 2007

(median income of women aged 15 or older and aged 35 to 44, and index of age group to total, 1990 to 2007; percent change for selected years; in 2007 dollars)

	total women	35 to 44	index, 35–44 to total
2007	$20,922	$27,702	132
2006	20,582	27,116	132
2005	19,729	27,014	137
2004	19,393	26,786	138
2003	19,457	26,461	136
2002	19,376	25,727	133
2001	19,458	26,317	135
2000	19,340	26,581	137
1999	19,044	25,709	135
1998	18,331	25,769	141
1997	17,650	24,095	137
1996	16,863	24,274	144
1995	16,387	23,502	143
1994	15,863	22,397	141
1993	15,608	22,387	143
1992	15,513	22,323	144
1991	15,553	22,455	144
1990	15,486	22,305	144
Percent change			
2000 to 2007	8.2%	4.2%	–
1990 to 2007	35.1	24.2	–

Note: The index is calculated by dividing the median income of the age group by the national median and multiplying by 100. "–" means not applicable.
Source: Bureau of the Census, data from the Current Population Survey Annual Demographic Supplements, Internet site http:// www.census.gov/hhes/www/income/histinc/p08AR.html; calculations by New Strategist

Men's Income Rises above Average in the 30-to-34 Age Group

Asian and Non-Hispanic white men have the highest incomes.

The incomes of men increase sharply during their twenties and thirties as they rise in their career. Men's median income grows from a below-average $30,281 in the 25-to-29 age group to an above-average $37,421 among those aged 30 to 34. It continues to grow, rising to $44,514 for men aged 35 to 39 and inching up even more to $45,235 for those aged 40 to 44. (Gen Xers were aged 31 to 42 in 2007.) Income rises in part because a growing proportion of men work full-time. The figure rises from 76 percent in the 30-to-34 age group to 79 percent in the 35-to-39 age group. It then drops again, however, to 78 percent among men aged 40 to 44.

Among men aged 30 to 44 who work full-time, Asians have the highest median income—$56,479 in 2007. Non-Hispanic white men follow with a median income of $53,356. Black and Hispanic men have the lowest incomes. Among black men aged 30 to 44 who work full-time, median income was $39,276 in 2007. Hispanic men in the age group who work full-time had an even lower median income of $31,631.

■ Black and Hispanic men have lower incomes than Asian or non-Hispanic white men because they are less educated.

Among men aged 30 to 44, Hispanics have the lowest incomes

(median income of men aged 30 to 44 who work full-time, by race and Hispanic origin, 2007)

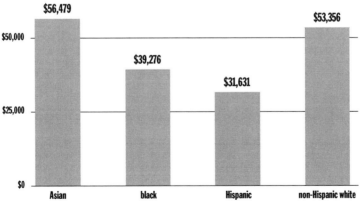

Table 5.13 Income of Men Aged 30 to 44, 2007: Total Men

(number and percent distribution of men aged 15 or older and aged 30 to 44 by income, 2007; median income by work status, and percent working year-round, full-time; men in thousands as of 2008)

| | total | aged 30 to 44 | | | |
		total	30 to 34	35 to 39	40 to 44
TOTAL MEN	**115,678**	**30,369**	**9,489**	**10,291**	**10,589**
Without income	**10,889**	**1,206**	**434**	**371**	**401**
With income	**104,789**	**29,163**	**9,055**	**9,920**	**10,188**
Under $10,000	13,989	1,929	645	542	742
$10,000 to $19,999	16,953	3,137	1,125	1,002	1,010
$20,000 to $29,999	15,483	4,043	1,448	1,374	1,221
$30,000 to $39,999	13,877	4,451	1,551	1,409	1,491
$40,000 to $49,999	10,420	3,622	1,206	1,262	1,154
$50,000 to $59,999	8,291	2,971	889	1,060	1,022
$60,000 to $69,999	5,814	2,113	587	747	779
$70,000 to $79,999	4,677	1,742	490	627	625
$80,000 to $89,999	3,066	1,093	302	372	419
$90,000 to $99,999	2,273	851	201	344	306
$100,000 or more	9,949	3,219	615	1,185	1,419
Median income of men with income	$33,196	$42,549	$37,421	$44,514	$45,235
Median income of full-time workers	46,224	47,879	41,918	49,855	51,146
Percent working full-time	54.5%	77.6%	75.9%	79.1%	77.6%
TOTAL MEN	**100.0%**	**100.0%**	**100.0%**	**100.0%**	**100.0%**
Without income	**9.4**	**4.0**	**4.6**	**3.6**	**3.8**
With income	**90.6**	**96.0**	**95.4**	**96.4**	**96.2**
Under $10,000	12.1	6.4	6.8	5.3	7.0
$10,000 to $19,999	14.7	10.3	11.9	9.7	9.5
$20,000 to $29,999	13.4	13.3	15.3	13.4	11.5
$30,000 to $39,999	12.0	14.7	16.3	13.7	14.1
$40,000 to $49,999	9.0	11.9	12.7	12.3	10.9
$50,000 to $59,999	7.2	9.8	9.4	10.3	9.7
$60,000 to $69,999	5.0	7.0	6.2	7.3	7.4
$70,000 to $79,999	4.0	5.7	5.2	6.1	5.9
$80,000 to $89,999	2.7	3.6	3.2	3.6	4.0
$90,000 to $99,999	2.0	2.8	2.1	3.3	2.9
$100,000 or more	8.6	10.6	6.5	11.5	13.4

Source: Bureau of the Census, 2008 Current Population Survey Annual Social and Economic Supplement, Internet site http:// www.census.gov/hhes/www/macro/032008/perinc/new01_000.htm; calculations by New Strategist

Table 5.14 Income of Men Aged 30 to 44, 2007: Asian Men

(number and percent distribution of Asian men aged 15 or older and aged 30 to 44 by income, 2007; median income by work status, and percent working year-round, full-time; men in thousands as of 2008)

	total	aged 30 to 44			
		total	30 to 34	35 to 39	40 to 44
TOTAL ASIAN MEN	**5,414**	**1,787**	**596**	**645**	**546**
Without income	**705**	**87**	**41**	**20**	**26**
With income	**4,709**	**1,700**	**555**	**625**	**520**
Under $10,000	639	77	22	27	28
$10,000 to $19,999	645	155	52	66	37
$20,000 to $29,999	646	196	61	77	58
$30,000 to $39,999	536	199	68	70	61
$40,000 to $49,999	426	169	69	63	37
$50,000 to $59,999	338	155	51	57	47
$60,000 to $69,999	278	150	64	44	42
$70,000 to $79,999	276	152	46	54	52
$80,000 to $89,999	156	67	29	17	21
$90,000 to $99,999	144	81	21	44	16
$100,000 or more	625	303	72	107	124
Median income of men with income	$36,729	$52,602	$50,433	$50,529	$57,417
Median income of full-time workers	51,001	56,479	56,759	52,387	61,008
Percent working full-time	58.5%	81.2%	75.5%	83.1%	85.2%
TOTAL ASIAN MEN	**100.0%**	**100.0%**	**100.0%**	**100.0%**	**100.0%**
Without income	**13.0**	**4.9**	**6.9**	**3.1**	**4.8**
With income	**87.0**	**95.1**	**93.1**	**96.9**	**95.2**
Under $10,000	11.8	4.3	3.7	4.2	5.1
$10,000 to $19,999	11.9	8.7	8.7	10.2	6.8
$20,000 to $29,999	11.9	11.0	10.2	11.9	10.6
$30,000 to $39,999	9.9	11.1	11.4	10.9	11.2
$40,000 to $49,999	7.9	9.5	11.6	9.8	6.8
$50,000 to $59,999	6.2	8.7	8.6	8.8	8.6
$60,000 to $69,999	5.1	8.4	10.7	6.8	7.7
$70,000 to $79,999	5.1	8.5	7.7	8.4	9.5
$80,000 to $89,999	2.9	3.7	4.9	2.6	3.8
$90,000 to $99,999	2.7	4.5	3.5	6.8	2.9
$100,000 or more	11.5	17.0	12.1	16.6	22.7

Note: Asians include those who identify themselves as being of the race alone and those who identify themselves as being of the race in combination with other races.
Source: Bureau of the Census, 2008 Current Population Survey Annual Social and Economic Supplement, Internet site http:// www.census.gov/hhes/www/macro/032008/perinc/new01_000.htm; calculations by New Strategist

Table 5.15 Income of Men Aged 30 to 44, 2007: Black Men

(number and percent distribution of black men aged 15 or older and aged 30 to 44 by income, 2007; median income by work status, and percent working year-round, full-time; men in thousands as of 2008)

		aged 30 to 44			
	total	total	30 to 34	35 to 39	40 to 44
TOTAL BLACK MEN	13,370	3,563	1,141	1,190	1,232
Without income	2,389	317	147	78	92
With income	10,981	3,246	994	1,112	1,140
Under $10,000	2,307	433	130	114	189
$10,000 to $19,999	2,145	491	165	158	168
$20,000 to $29,999	1,691	506	157	158	191
$30,000 to $39,999	1,559	531	178	194	159
$40,000 to $49,999	997	383	118	151	114
$50,000 to $59,999	747	313	95	104	114
$60,000 to $69,999	482	209	50	74	85
$70,000 to $79,999	345	128	33	57	38
$80,000 to $89,999	196	79	23	28	28
$90,000 to $99,999	122	48	10	24	14
$100,000 or more	390	127	37	50	40
Median income of men with income	$25,792	$32,870	$31,991	$35,858	$30,799
Median income of full-time workers	36,780	39,276	38,179	41,261	38,374
Percent working full-time	46.1%	66.7%	62.0%	70.8%	67.2%
TOTAL BLACK MEN	100.0%	100.0%	100.0%	100.0%	100.0%
Without income	17.9	8.9	12.9	6.6	7.5
With income	82.1	91.1	87.1	93.4	92.5
Under $10,000	17.3	12.2	11.4	9.6	15.3
$10,000 to $19,999	16.0	13.8	14.5	13.3	13.6
$20,000 to $29,999	12.6	14.2	13.8	13.3	15.5
$30,000 to $39,999	11.7	14.9	15.6	16.3	12.9
$40,000 to $49,999	7.5	10.7	10.3	12.7	9.3
$50,000 to $59,999	5.6	8.8	8.3	8.7	9.3
$60,000 to $69,999	3.6	5.9	4.4	6.2	6.9
$70,000 to $79,999	2.6	3.6	2.9	4.8	3.1
$80,000 to $89,999	1.5	2.2	2.0	2.4	2.3
$90,000 to $99,999	0.9	1.3	0.9	2.0	1.1
$100,000 or more	2.9	3.6	3.2	4.2	3.2

Note: Blacks include those who identify themselves as being of the race alone and those who identify themselves as being of the race in combination with other races.
Source: Bureau of the Census, 2008 Current Population Survey Annual Social and Economic Supplement, Internet site http:// www.census.gov/hhes/www/macro/032008/perinc/new01_000.htm; calculations by New Strategist

Table 5.16 Income of Men Aged 30 to 44, 2007: Hispanic Men

(number and percent distribution of Hispanic men aged 15 or older and aged 30 to 44 by income, 2007; median income by work status, and percent working year-round, full-time; men in thousands as of 2008)

		aged 30 to 44			
	total	total	30 to 34	35 to 39	40 to 44
TOTAL HISPANIC MEN	**16,837**	**5,668**	**2,030**	**1,922**	**1,716**
Without income	**2,228**	**258**	**83**	**83**	**92**
With income	**14,609**	**5,410**	**1,947**	**1,839**	**1,624**
Under $10,000	2,135	420	168	119	133
$10,000 to $19,999	3,548	1,080	441	323	316
$20,000 to $29,999	3,168	1,261	476	463	322
$30,000 to $39,999	2,143	963	330	302	331
$40,000 to $49,999	1,209	559	194	215	150
$50,000 to $59,999	809	361	118	133	110
$60,000 to $69,999	513	235	83	84	68
$70,000 to $79,999	330	180	51	68	61
$80,000 to $89,999	201	94	24	32	38
$90,000 to $99,999	127	52	13	25	14
$100,000 or more	425	201	48	76	77
Median income of men with income	$24,451	$29,104	$26,755	$30,241	$30,610
Median income of full-time workers	30,454	31,631	30,661	32,140	32,208
Percent working full-time	58.0%	76.0%	74.8%	77.1%	76.3%
TOTAL HISPANIC MEN	**100.0%**	**100.0%**	**100.0%**	**100.0%**	**100.0%**
Without income	**13.2**	**4.6**	**4.1**	**4.3**	**5.4**
With income	**86.8**	**95.4**	**95.9**	**95.7**	**94.6**
Under $10,000	12.7	7.4	8.3	6.2	7.8
$10,000 to $19,999	21.1	19.1	21.7	16.8	18.4
$20,000 to $29,999	18.8	22.2	23.4	24.1	18.8
$30,000 to $39,999	12.7	17.0	16.3	15.7	19.3
$40,000 to $49,999	7.2	9.9	9.6	11.2	8.7
$50,000 to $59,999	4.8	6.4	5.8	6.9	6.4
$60,000 to $69,999	3.0	4.1	4.1	4.4	4.0
$70,000 to $79,999	2.0	3.2	2.5	3.5	3.6
$80,000 to $89,999	1.2	1.7	1.2	1.7	2.2
$90,000 to $99,999	0.8	0.9	0.6	1.3	0.8
$100,000 or more	2.5	3.5	2.4	4.0	4.5

Source: Bureau of the Census, 2008 Current Population Survey Annual Social and Economic Supplement, Internet site http://www.census.gov/hhes/www/macro/032008/perinc/new01_000.htm; calculations by New Strategist

Table 5.17 Income of Men Aged 30 to 44, 2007: Non-Hispanic White Men

(number and percent distribution of non-Hispanic white men aged 15 or older and aged 30 to 44 by income, 2007; median income by work status, and percent working year-round, full-time; men in thousands as of 2008)

	total	aged 30 to 44 total	30 to 34	35 to 39	40 to 44
TOTAL NON-HISPANIC WHITE MEN	**79,100**	**19,126**	**5,657**	**6,478**	**6,991**
Without income	**5,483**	**531**	**161**	**180**	**190**
With income	**73,617**	**18,595**	**5,496**	**6,298**	**6,801**
Under $10,000	8,760	977	324	274	379
$10,000 to $19,999	10,470	1,395	454	462	479
$20,000 to $29,999	9,834	2,044	744	664	636
$30,000 to $39,999	9,518	2,731	960	839	932
$40,000 to $49,999	7,703	2,470	809	829	832
$50,000 to $59,999	6,323	2,116	621	755	740
$60,000 to $69,999	4,493	1,510	391	544	575
$70,000 to $79,999	3,717	1,282	361	449	472
$80,000 to $89,999	2,491	840	219	294	327
$90,000 to $99,999	1,871	665	155	249	261
$100,000 or more	8,438	2,566	458	940	1,168
Median income of men with income	$37,373	$48,280	$42,070	$50,621	$51,137
Median income of full-time workers	51,465	53,356	46,609	55,172	57,134
Percent working full-time	55.0%	79.8%	79.1%	80.9%	79.4%
TOTAL NON-HISPANIC WHITE MEN	**100.0%**	**100.0%**	**100.0%**	**100.0%**	**100.0%**
Without income	**6.9**	**2.8**	**2.8**	**2.8**	**2.7**
With income	**93.1**	**97.2**	**97.2**	**97.2**	**97.3**
Under $10,000	11.1	5.1	5.7	4.2	5.4
$10,000 to $19,999	13.2	7.3	8.0	7.1	6.9
$20,000 to $29,999	12.4	10.7	13.2	10.3	9.1
$30,000 to $39,999	12.0	14.3	17.0	13.0	13.3
$40,000 to $49,999	9.7	12.9	14.3	12.8	11.9
$50,000 to $59,999	8.0	11.1	11.0	11.7	10.6
$60,000 to $69,999	5.7	7.9	6.9	8.4	8.2
$70,000 to $79,999	4.7	6.7	6.4	6.9	6.8
$80,000 to $89,999	3.1	4.4	3.9	4.5	4.7
$90,000 to $99,999	2.4	3.5	2.7	3.8	3.7
$100,000 or more	10.7	13.4	8.1	14.5	16.7

Note: Non-Hispanic whites are those who identify themselves as being white alone and not Hispanic.
Source: Bureau of the Census, 2008 Current Population Survey Annual Social and Economic Supplement, Internet site http://www.census.gov/hhes/www/macro/032008/perinc/new01_000.htm; calculations by New Strategist

Among Gen X Women, Asians Have the Highest Incomes

Hispanics have the lowest incomes.

The median income of Gen X women ranges from a low of $26,370 among 30-to-34-year-olds to a high of $28,280 among those aged 40 to 44. (Generation Xers were aged 31 to 42 in 2007.) One reason for the relatively flat income trajectory of Generation X women is that only 52 percent of them work full-time. Another reason is that many women choose lower-paying careers that allow them to spend more time with their children.

Among women aged 30 to 44 who work full-time, Asians have the highest median income, $43,474 in 2007. Non-Hispanic white women follow, with a median income of $40,604. Black and Hispanic women have lower incomes. Among black women aged 30 to 44 who work full-time, median income was $33,755 in 2007. Their Hispanic counterparts had an even lower income of $28,803.

■ Black and Hispanic women have lower incomes than Asian or non-Hispanic white women because they are less educated.

Among women aged 30 to 44 who work full-time, Hispanics have the lowest incomes

(median income of women aged 30 to 44 who work full-time, by race and Hispanic origin, 2007)

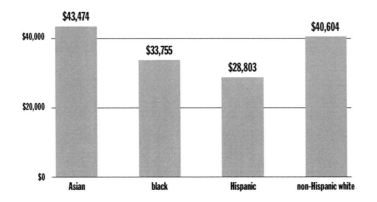

Table 5.18 Income of Women Aged 30 to 44, 2007: Total Women

(number and percent distribution of women aged 15 or older and aged 30 to 44 by income, 2007; median income by work status, and percent working year-round, full-time; women in thousands as of 2008)

| | total | aged 30 to 44 | | | |
		total	30 to 34	35 to 39	40 to 44
TOTAL WOMEN	**122,470**	**30,852**	**9,600**	**10,442**	**10,810**
Without income	**17,240**	**3,702**	**1,274**	**1,319**	**1,109**
With income	**105,230**	**27,150**	**8,326**	**9,123**	**9,701**
Under $10,000	26,931	5,180	1,616	1,821	1,743
$10,000 to $19,999	23,616	4,779	1,493	1,609	1,677
$20,000 to $29,999	16,710	4,550	1,479	1,426	1,645
$30,000 to $39,999	12,457	4,020	1,295	1,270	1,455
$40,000 to $49,999	8,573	2,824	862	943	1,019
$50,000 to $59,999	5,461	1,813	501	635	677
$60,000 to $69,999	3,589	1,303	426	432	445
$70,000 to $79,999	2,317	839	215	288	336
$80,000 to $89,999	1,371	471	142	160	169
$90,000 to $99,999	958	323	73	124	126
$100,000 or more	3,246	1,051	225	416	410
Median income of women with income	$20,922	$27,325	$26,370	$27,213	$28,280
Median income of full-time workers	36,167	37,255	36,233	38,410	37,047
Percent working full-time	37.3%	52.2%	50.3%	51.0%	54.9%
TOTAL WOMEN	**100.0%**	**100.0%**	**100.0%**	**100.0%**	**100.0%**
Without income	**14.1**	**12.0**	**13.3**	**12.6**	**10.3**
With income	**85.9**	**88.0**	**86.7**	**87.4**	**89.7**
Under $10,000	22.0	16.8	16.8	17.4	16.1
$10,000 to $19,999	19.3	15.5	15.6	15.4	15.5
$20,000 to $29,999	13.6	14.7	15.4	13.7	15.2
$30,000 to $39,999	10.2	13.0	13.5	12.2	13.5
$40,000 to $49,999	7.0	9.2	9.0	9.0	9.4
$50,000 to $59,999	4.5	5.9	5.2	6.1	6.3
$60,000 to $69,999	2.9	4.2	4.4	4.1	4.1
$70,000 to $79,999	1.9	2.7	2.2	2.8	3.1
$80,000 to $89,999	1.1	1.5	1.5	1.5	1.6
$90,000 to $99,999	0.8	1.0	0.8	1.2	1.2
$100,000 or more	2.7	3.4	2.3	4.0	3.8

Source: Bureau of the Census, 2008 Current Population Survey Annual Social and Economic Supplement, Internet site http://www.census.gov/hhes/www/macro/032008/perinc/new01_000.htm; calculations by New Strategist

Table 5.19 Income of Women Aged 30 to 44, 2007: Asian Women

(number and percent distribution of Asian women aged 15 or older and aged 30 to 44 by income, 2007; median income by work status, and percent working year-round, full-time; women in thousands as of 2008)

	total	aged 30 to 44			
		total	30 to 34	35 to 39	40 to 44
TOTAL ASIAN WOMEN	**6,029**	**1,941**	**665**	**687**	**589**
Without income	**1,243**	**303**	**122**	**109**	**72**
With income	**4,786**	**1,638**	**543**	**578**	**517**
Under $10,000	1,217	337	95	137	105
$10,000 to $19,999	866	218	61	69	88
$20,000 to $29,999	632	222	67	81	74
$30,000 to $39,999	511	200	81	54	65
$40,000 to $49,999	426	152	56	53	43
$50,000 to $59,999	289	116	49	37	30
$60,000 to $69,999	212	97	41	33	23
$70,000 to $79,999	171	73	18	34	21
$80,000 to $89,999	102	56	23	11	22
$90,000 to $99,999	94	40	14	12	14
$100,000 or more	265	131	38	55	38
Median income of women with income	$24,095	$31,286	$34,238	$30,257	$29,153
Median income of full-time workers	41,254	43,474	46,033	45,927	37,724
Percent working full-time	40.4%	52.0%	49.9%	50.8%	55.5%
TOTAL ASIAN WOMEN	**100.0%**	**100.0%**	**100.0%**	**100.0%**	**100.0%**
Without income	**20.6**	**15.6**	**18.3**	**15.9**	**12.2**
With income	**79.4**	**84.4**	**81.7**	**84.1**	**87.8**
Under $10,000	20.2	17.4	14.3	19.9	17.8
$10,000 to $19,999	14.4	11.2	9.2	10.0	14.9
$20,000 to $29,999	10.5	11.4	10.1	11.8	12.6
$30,000 to $39,999	8.5	10.3	12.2	7.9	11.0
$40,000 to $49,999	7.1	7.8	8.4	7.7	7.3
$50,000 to $59,999	4.8	6.0	7.4	5.4	5.1
$60,000 to $69,999	3.5	5.0	6.2	4.8	3.9
$70,000 to $79,999	2.8	3.8	2.7	4.9	3.6
$80,000 to $89,999	1.7	2.9	3.5	1.6	3.7
$90,000 to $99,999	1.6	2.1	2.1	1.7	2.4
$100,000 or more	4.4	6.7	5.7	8.0	6.5

Note: Asians include those who identify themselves as being of the race alone and those who identify themselves as being of the race in combination with other races.
Source: Bureau of the Census, 2008 Current Population Survey Annual Social and Economic Supplement, Internet site http://www.census.gov/hhes/www/macro/032008/perinc/new01_000.htm; calculations by New Strategist

Table 5.20 Income of Women Aged 30 to 44, 2007: Black Women

(number and percent distribution of black women aged 15 or older and aged 30 to 44 by income, 2007; median income by work status, and percent working year-round, full-time; women in thousands as of 2008)

	total	aged 30 to 44			
		total	30 to 34	35 to 39	40 to 44
TOTAL BLACK WOMEN	**16,097**	**4,371**	**1,378**	**1,489**	**1,504**
Without income	**2,670**	**406**	**128**	**140**	**138**
With income	**13,427**	**3,965**	**1,250**	**1,349**	**1,366**
Under $10,000	3,628	636	259	167	210
$10,000 to $19,999	3,158	823	296	295	232
$20,000 to $29,999	2,295	754	253	234	267
$30,000 to $39,999	1,659	678	198	225	255
$40,000 to $49,999	1,016	402	90	152	160
$50,000 to $59,999	594	210	53	84	73
$60,000 to $69,999	435	195	57	77	61
$70,000 to $79,999	220	100	14	34	52
$80,000 to $89,999	139	54	13	27	14
$90,000 to $99,999	63	23	3	13	7
$100,000 or more	223	91	16	39	36
Median income of women with income	$19,712	$26,598	$22,192	$28,721	$28,532
Median income of full-time workers	31,672	33,755	30,619	35,464	34,937
Percent working full-time	41.2%	59.8%	54.4%	61.8%	62.8%
TOTAL BLACK WOMEN	**100.0%**	**100.0%**	**100.0%**	**100.0%**	**100.0%**
Without income	**16.6**	**9.3**	**9.3**	**9.4**	**9.2**
With income	**83.4**	**90.7**	**90.7**	**90.6**	**90.8**
Under $10,000	22.5	14.6	18.8	11.2	14.0
$10,000 to $19,999	19.6	18.8	21.5	19.8	15.4
$20,000 to $29,999	14.3	17.3	18.4	15.7	17.8
$30,000 to $39,999	10.3	15.5	14.4	15.1	17.0
$40,000 to $49,999	6.3	9.2	6.5	10.2	10.6
$50,000 to $59,999	3.7	4.8	3.8	5.6	4.9
$60,000 to $69,999	2.7	4.5	4.1	5.2	4.1
$70,000 to $79,999	1.4	2.3	1.0	2.3	3.5
$80,000 to $89,999	0.9	1.2	0.9	1.8	0.9
$90,000 to $99,999	0.4	0.5	0.2	0.9	0.5
$100,000 or more	1.4	2.1	1.2	2.6	2.4

Note: Blacks include those who identify themselves as being of the race alone and those who identify themselves as being of the race in combination with other races.
Source: Bureau of the Census, 2008 Current Population Survey Annual Social and Economic Supplement, Internet site http://www.census.gov/hhes/www/macro/032008/perinc/new01_000.htm; calculations by New Strategist

Table 5.21 Income of Women Aged 30 to 44, 2007: Hispanic Women

(number and percent distribution of Hispanic women aged 15 or older and aged 30 to 44 by income, 2007; median income by work status, and percent working year-round, full-time; women in thousands as of 2008)

	total	aged 30 to 44			
		total	30 to 34	35 to 39	40 to 44
TOTAL HISPANIC WOMEN	**15,853**	**5,097**	**1,831**	**1,728**	**1,538**
Without income	**4,588**	**1,237**	**504**	**427**	**306**
With income	**11,265**	**3,860**	**1,327**	**1,301**	**1,232**
Under $10,000	3,397	772	261	270	241
$10,000 to $19,999	2,967	1,017	349	320	348
$20,000 to $29,999	1,973	750	274	248	228
$30,000 to $39,999	1,284	576	202	210	164
$40,000 to $49,999	675	308	95	108	105
$50,000 to $59,999	359	186	51	60	75
$60,000 to $69,999	202	88	41	29	18
$70,000 to $79,999	144	57	22	18	17
$80,000 to $89,999	66	26	4	9	13
$90,000 to $99,999	51	22	8	9	5
$100,000 or more	148	55	16	22	17
Median income of women with income	$16,748	$21,274	$21,081	$21,932	$20,766
Median income of full-time workers	27,154	28,803	29,171	28,985	28,160
Percent working full-time	34.2%	46.3%	41.7%	46.4%	51.7%
TOTAL HISPANIC WOMEN	**100.0%**	**100.0%**	**100.0%**	**100.0%**	**100.0%**
Without income	**28.9**	**24.3**	**27.5**	**24.7**	**19.9**
With income	**71.1**	**75.7**	**72.5**	**75.3**	**80.1**
Under $10,000	21.4	15.1	14.3	15.6	15.7
$10,000 to $19,999	18.7	20.0	19.1	18.5	22.6
$20,000 to $29,999	12.4	14.7	15.0	14.4	14.8
$30,000 to $39,999	8.1	11.3	11.0	12.2	10.7
$40,000 to $49,999	4.3	6.0	5.2	6.3	6.8
$50,000 to $59,999	2.3	3.6	2.8	3.5	4.9
$60,000 to $69,999	1.3	1.7	2.2	1.7	1.2
$70,000 to $79,999	0.9	1.1	1.2	1.0	1.1
$80,000 to $89,999	0.4	0.5	0.2	0.5	0.8
$90,000 to $99,999	0.3	0.4	0.4	0.5	0.3
$100,000 or more	0.9	1.1	0.9	1.3	1.1

Source: Bureau of the Census, 2008 Current Population Survey Annual Social and Economic Supplement, Internet site http://www.census.gov/hhes/www/macro/032008/perinc/new01_000.htm; calculations by New Strategist

Table 5.22 Income of Women Aged 30 to 44, 2007: Non-Hispanic White Women

(number and percent distribution of non-Hispanic white women aged 15 or older and aged 30 to 44 by income, 2007; median income by work status, and percent working year-round, full-time; women in thousands as of 2008)

	total	aged 30 to 44 total	30 to 34	35 to 39	40 to 44
TOTAL NON-HISPANIC WHITE WOMEN	83,534	19,228	5,651	6,473	7,104
Without income	8,632	1,730	513	634	583
With income	74,902	17,498	5,138	5,839	6,521
Under $10,000	18,386	3,377	978	1,226	1,173
$10,000 to $19,999	16,472	2,705	796	912	997
$20,000 to $29,999	11,666	2,782	873	858	1,051
$30,000 to $39,999	8,904	2,538	781	783	974
$40,000 to $49,999	6,403	1,959	620	633	706
$50,000 to $59,999	4,185	1,290	342	446	502
$60,000 to $69,999	2,719	912	283	290	339
$70,000 to $79,999	1,769	605	160	198	247
$80,000 to $89,999	1,053	327	99	107	121
$90,000 to $99,999	746	236	50	89	97
$100,000 or more	2,596	768	154	298	316
Median income of women with income	$21,687	$29,199	$28,474	$28,674	$30,253
Median income of full-time workers	38,678	40,604	39,421	41,685	40,560
Percent working full-time	37.0%	52.2%	52.4%	50.0%	54.0%
TOTAL NON-HISPANIC WHITE WOMEN	100.0%	100.0%	100.0%	100.0%	100.0%
Without income	10.3	9.0	9.1	9.8	8.2
With income	89.7	91.0	90.9	90.2	91.8
Under $10,000	22.0	17.6	17.3	18.9	16.5
$10,000 to $19,999	19.7	14.1	14.1	14.1	14.0
$20,000 to $29,999	14.0	14.5	15.4	13.3	14.8
$30,000 to $39,999	10.7	13.2	13.8	12.1	13.7
$40,000 to $49,999	7.7	10.2	11.0	9.8	9.9
$50,000 to $59,999	5.0	6.7	6.1	6.9	7.1
$60,000 to $69,999	3.3	4.7	5.0	4.5	4.8
$70,000 to $79,999	2.1	3.1	2.8	3.1	3.5
$80,000 to $89,999	1.3	1.7	1.8	1.7	1.7
$90,000 to $99,999	0.9	1.2	0.9	1.4	1.4
$100,000 or more	3.1	4.0	2.7	4.6	4.4

Note: Non-Hispanic whites are those who identify themselves as being of the race alone and those who identify themselves as being of the race in combination with other races.
Source: Bureau of the Census, 2008 Current Population Survey Annual Social and Economic Supplement, Internet site http://www.census.gov/hhes/www/macro/032008/perinc/new01_000.htm; calculations by New Strategist

Earnings Rise with Education

The highest earners are men with a professional degree.

For many years, a college degree has been well worth its cost. The higher the education, the greater the earnings. Among men aged 35 to 44 in 2007 (Generation Xers were aged 31 to 42 in that year), those with a professional degree (such as physicians and lawyers) who worked full-time earned a median of more than $100,000. Among women of the age group who work full-time, median earnings also peak among those with a professional degree, at $71,486.

Among men aged 35 to 44 who did not finish high school, full-time workers earned less than $30,000 in 2007. For their counterparts with at least a bachelor's degree, median earnings are above $65,000. The pattern is the same for women, although the dollar figures are much lower. Among women aged 35 to 44 who dropped out of high school, full-time workers earned less than $21,000 in 2007. Among college graduates in the age group, median earnings were above $48,000.

■ The steeply rising cost of a college degree, combined with competition from well-educated but lower-paid workers in other countries, may reduce the financial return of a college degree.

College bonus is still big

(median earnings of men aged 35 to 44 with earnings, by education, 2007)

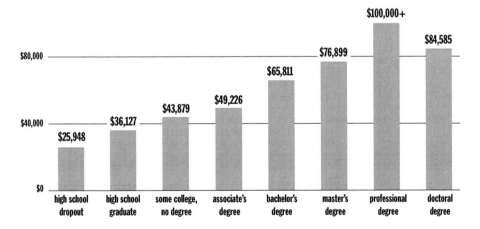

Table 5.23 Earnings of Men by Education, 2007: Aged 35 to 44

(number and percent distribution of men aged 35 to 44 by earnings and education, 2007; men in thousands as of 2008)

	total	less than 9th grade	9th to 12th grade, no degree	high school graduate, incl. GED	some college, no degree	associate's degree	bachelor's degree or more total	bachelor's degree	master's degree	professional degree	doctoral degree
TOTAL MEN AGED 35 TO 44	**20,880**	**1,022**	**1,627**	**6,391**	**3,464**	**1,794**	**6,582**	**4,251**	**1,609**	**398**	**324**
Without earnings	**1,772**	**133**	**333**	**739**	**241**	**102**	**225**	**157**	**40**	**17**	**12**
With earnings	**19,108**	**889**	**1,294**	**5,653**	**3,223**	**1,693**	**6,357**	**4,095**	**1,569**	**382**	**312**
Under $10,000	784	103	147	286	134	35	77	54	15	4	4
$10,000 to $19,999	1,781	320	279	635	232	85	232	165	52	2	11
$20,000 to $29,999	2,582	238	340	1,097	410	168	328	259	53	8	7
$30,000 to $39,999	2,821	129	202	1,160	596	272	461	342	93	10	17
$40,000 to $49,999	2,484	49	135	840	526	296	636	495	106	17	18
$50,000 to $59,999	2,098	27	96	644	380	239	711	482	170	25	34
$60,000 to $69,999	1,482	11	32	353	288	178	621	390	166	30	35
$70,000 to $79,999	1,257	5	22	234	205	159	633	439	162	11	21
$80,000 to $89,999	805	0	18	121	133	90	445	305	118	10	11
$90,000 to $99,999	580	0	10	86	79	57	348	185	106	27	29
$100,000 or more	2,431	7	15	196	238	111	1,864	978	527	236	122
Median earnings of men with earnings	$45,754	$20,588	$25,948	$36,127	$43,879	$49,226	$70,981	$65,811	$76,899	$100,000+	$84,585
Median earnings of full-time workers	50,048	22,874	29,560	38,847	47,145	51,167	72,723	67,490	80,471	100,000+	90,451
Percent working full-time	78.3%	66.0%	59.5%	74.2%	79.1%	83.7%	87.1%	86.9%	88.3%	84.9%	88.0%
TOTAL MEN AGED 35 TO 44	**100.0%**	**100.0%**	**100.0%**	**100.0%**	**100.0%**	**100.0%**	**100.0%**	**100.0%**	**100.0%**	**100.0%**	**100.0%**
Without earnings	**8.5**	**13.0**	**20.5**	**11.6**	**7.0**	**5.7**	**3.4**	**3.7**	**2.5**	**4.3**	**3.7**
With earnings	**91.5**	**87.0**	**79.5**	**88.5**	**93.0**	**94.4**	**96.6**	**96.3**	**97.5**	**96.0**	**96.3**
Under $10,000	3.8	10.1	9.0	4.5	3.9	2.0	1.2	1.3	0.9	1.0	1.2
$10,000 to $19,999	8.5	31.3	17.1	9.9	6.7	4.7	3.5	3.9	3.2	0.5	3.4
$20,000 to $29,999	12.4	23.3	20.9	17.2	11.8	9.4	5.0	6.1	3.3	2.0	2.2
$30,000 to $39,999	13.5	12.6	12.4	18.2	17.2	15.2	7.0	8.0	5.8	2.5	5.2
$40,000 to $49,999	11.9	4.8	8.3	13.1	15.2	16.5	9.7	11.6	6.6	4.3	5.6
$50,000 to $59,999	10.0	2.6	5.9	10.1	11.0	13.3	10.8	11.3	10.6	6.3	10.5
$60,000 to $69,999	7.1	1.1	2.0	5.5	8.3	9.9	9.4	9.2	10.3	7.5	10.8
$70,000 to $79,999	6.0	0.5	1.4	3.7	5.9	8.9	9.6	10.3	10.1	2.8	6.5
$80,000 to $89,999	3.9	0.0	1.1	1.9	3.8	5.0	6.8	7.2	7.3	2.5	3.4
$90,000 to $99,999	2.8	0.0	0.6	1.3	2.3	3.2	5.3	4.4	6.6	6.8	9.0
$100,000 or more	11.6	0.7	0.9	3.1	6.9	6.2	28.3	23.0	32.8	59.3	37.7

Source: Bureau of the Census, 2008 Current Population Survey Annual Social and Economic Supplement, Internet site http:// www.census.gov/hhes/www/macro/032008/perinc/new03_000.htm; calculations by New Strategist

Table 5.24 Earnings of Women by Education, 2007: Aged 35 to 44

(number and percent distribution of women aged 35 to 44 by earnings and education, 2007; women in thousands as of 2008)

	total	less than 9th grade	9th to 12th grade, no degree	high school graduate, incl. GED	some college, no degree	associate's degree	bachelor's degree or more total	bachelor's degree	master's degree	professional degree	doctoral degree
TOTAL WOMEN AGED 35 TO 44	21,252	787	1,357	5,648	3,735	2,365	7,360	4,953	1,898	295	214
Without earnings	4,835	359	545	1,440	772	360	1,358	1,043	266	34	14
With earnings	16,417	427	811	4,208	2,964	2,004	6,002	3,910	1,631	261	200
Under $10,000	2,061	99	194	631	368	208	560	433	110	9	7
$10,000 to $19,999	2,971	182	299	1,068	554	351	515	392	106	13	6
$20,000 to $29,999	2,955	100	188	1,065	648	382	574	429	109	19	18
$30,000 to $39,999	2,673	28	57	730	602	367	889	659	197	15	16
$40,000 to $49,999	1,924	16	38	352	352	277	891	561	272	29	27
$50,000 to $59,999	1,224	0	18	149	205	167	684	411	245	18	10
$60,000 to $69,999	820	0	6	106	97	112	499	279	170	21	30
$70,000 to $79,999	571	0	4	40	51	63	413	225	143	27	16
$80,000 to $89,999	296	0	3	15	30	41	208	113	61	23	11
$90,000 to $99,999	236	0	2	9	20	10	193	119	52	9	13
$100,000 or more	686	1	2	40	38	26	578	288	165	80	44
Median earnings of women with earnings	$30,497	$16,191	$16,840	$23,416	$28,142	$30,945	$44,399	$40,433	$50,450	$71,284	$65,063
Median earnings of full-time workers	36,519	18,717	20,842	27,412	32,414	37,115	51,440	48,066	55,683	71,486	67,369
Percent working full-time	53.0%	36.6%	36.9%	51.0%	55.3%	58.0%	56.4%	53.1%	62.4%	64.1%	69.6%
TOTAL WOMEN AGED 35 TO 44	100.0%	100.0%	100.0%	100.0%	100.0%	100.0%	100.0%	100.0%	100.0%	100.0%	100.0%
Without earnings	22.8	45.6	40.2	25.5	20.7	15.2	18.5	21.1	14.0	11.5	6.5
With earnings	77.2	54.3	59.8	74.5	79.4	84.7	81.5	78.9	85.9	88.5	93.5
Under $10,000	9.7	12.6	14.3	11.2	9.9	8.8	7.6	8.7	5.8	3.1	3.3
$10,000 to $19,999	14.0	23.1	22.0	18.9	14.8	14.8	7.0	7.9	5.6	4.4	2.8
$20,000 to $29,999	13.9	12.7	13.9	18.9	17.3	16.2	7.8	8.7	5.7	6.4	8.4
$30,000 to $39,999	12.6	3.6	4.2	12.9	16.1	15.5	12.1	13.3	10.4	5.1	7.5
$40,000 to $49,999	9.1	2.0	2.8	6.2	9.4	11.7	12.1	11.3	14.3	9.8	12.6
$50,000 to $59,999	5.8	0.0	1.3	2.6	5.5	7.1	9.3	8.3	12.9	6.1	4.7
$60,000 to $69,999	3.9	0.0	0.4	1.9	2.6	4.7	6.8	5.6	9.0	7.1	14.0
$70,000 to $79,999	2.7	0.0	0.3	0.7	1.4	2.7	5.6	4.5	7.5	9.2	7.5
$80,000 to $89,999	1.4	0.0	0.2	0.3	0.8	1.7	2.8	2.3	3.2	7.8	5.1
$90,000 to $99,999	1.1	0.0	0.1	0.2	0.5	0.4	2.6	2.4	2.7	3.1	6.1
$100,000 or more	3.2	0.1	0.1	0.7	1.0	1.1	7.9	5.8	8.7	27.1	20.6

Source: Bureau of the Census, 2008 Current Population Survey Annual Social and Economic Supplement, Internet site http:// www.census.gov/hhes/www/macro/032008/perinc/new03_000.htm; calculations by New Strategist

Poverty Rate Is below Average for Gen Xers

Poverty falls below average in the 30-to-34 age group.

Generation Xers (aged 31 to 42 in 2007) are slightly less likely to be poor than the average American. Overall, 12 percent of Americans lived in poverty in 2007. Among people aged 31 to 42, however, a smaller 10 percent are poor. People under age 30 are more likely than average to be poor, with a poverty rate of 17 percent. In the 35-to-39 age group, the poverty rate falls below 10 percent.

Black and Hispanic Generation Xers are more than twice as likely as Asian and non-Hispanic white Gen Xers to be poor. Eighteen percent of blacks and Hispanics aged 31 to 42 live below the poverty level versus 8 percent of Asians and just 6 percent of non-Hispanic whites. Blacks and Hispanics together account for the 55 percent majority of poor Generation Xers, while non-Hispanic whites account for a 39 percent minority.

■ Blacks are more likely to be poor than Asians or non-Hispanic whites because they are less likely to live in married-couple families, the most affluent household type.

The young are most likely to be poor

(percent of people with incomes below poverty level, by age, 2007)

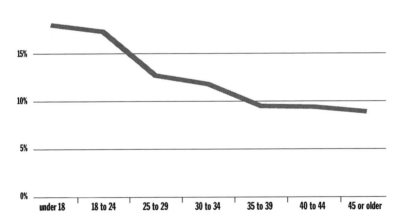

Table 5.25 People below Poverty Level by Age, Race, and Hispanic Origin, 2007

(number, percent, and percent distribution of people below poverty level by age, race, and Hispanic origin, 2007; people in thousands as of 2008)

	total	Asian	black	Hispanic	non-Hispanic white
NUMBER IN POVERTY					
Total people	37,276	1,467	9,668	9,890	16,032
Under age 30	20,908	751	6,013	6,349	7,759
Generation X (31 to 42)	4,900	249	1,155	1,553	1,916
Aged 30 to 34	2,249	109	535	754	850
Aged 35 to 39	1,965	104	448	607	783
Aged 40 to 44	2,007	79	472	547	887
Aged 45 or older	10,154	424	2,202	1,634	2,180
PERCENT IN POVERTY					
Total people	12.5%	10.2%	24.4%	21.5%	8.2%
Under age 30	16.9	12.3	30.6	25.5	10.8
Generation X (31 to 42)	9.9	7.8	17.8	17.6	6.4
Aged 30 to 34	11.8	8.6	21.2	19.5	7.5
Aged 35 to 39	9.5	7.8	16.7	16.6	6.0
Aged 40 to 44	9.4	7.0	17.2	16.8	6.3
Aged 45 or older	8.9	9.2	18.4	16.0	7.4
PERCENT DISTRIBUTION OF POOR BY AGE					
Total people	100.0%	100.0%	100.0%	100.0%	100.0%
Under age 30	56.1	51.2	62.2	64.2	48.4
Generation X (31 to 42)	13.1	17.0	11.9	15.7	12.0
Aged 30 to 34	6.0	7.4	5.5	7.6	5.3
Aged 35 to 39	5.3	7.1	4.6	6.1	4.9
Aged 40 to 44	5.4	5.4	4.9	5.5	5.5
Aged 45 or older	27.2	28.9	22.8	16.5	13.6
PERCENT DISTRIBUTION OF POOR BY RACE AND HISPANIC ORIGIN					
Total people	100.0%	3.9%	25.9%	26.5%	43.0%
Under age 30	100.0	3.6	28.8	30.4	37.1
Generation X (31 to 42)	100.0	5.1	23.6	31.7	39.1
Aged 30 to 34	100.0	4.8	23.8	33.5	37.8
Aged 35 to 39	100.0	5.3	22.8	30.9	39.8
Aged 40 to 44	100.0	3.9	23.5	27.3	44.2
Aged 45 or older	100.0	4.2	21.7	16.1	21.5

Note: Numbers do not add to total because Asians and blacks include those who identify themselves as being of the race alone and those who identify themselves as being of the race in combination with other races, because Hispanics may be of any race, and because not all races are shown. Non-Hispanic whites are those who identify themselves as being white alone and not Hispanic.
Source: Bureau of the Census, 2008 Current Population Survey Annual Social and Economic Supplement, Internet site http:// www.census.gov/hhes/www/macro/032008/pov/new34_100.htm; calculations by New Strategist

6

Labor Force

■ Generation Xers are at the career-building stage of their lives. But their labor force participation rate has fallen, thanks to the weak economy.

■ Eighty-four percent of people aged 30 to 44 were in the labor force in 2008 (Generation Xers were aged 32 to 43 in that year). Among men, from 92 to 93 percent of those aged 30 to 44 are in the labor force. Among women in the age group, the figures range from 74 to 77 percent.

■ Among men aged 30 to 44, Asians are less likely to be unemployed than others. In 2008, only 3.5 percent of Asian men aged 30 to 44 were unemployed, a lower rate than the 6.1 percent average for all men in the age group.

■ Sixty-nine percent of married couples aged 30 to 44 are dual earners, while the husband is the only one in the labor force in another 26 percent.

■ Long-term employment has fallen among both male and female workers in their thirties and forties. Among men aged 40 to 44, the percentage who had been with their current employer for 10 or more years fell from 40 to 36 percent between 2000 and 2008.

■ Between 2006 and 2016, the small Generation X will fill the 40-to-49 age group (Gen Xers will be aged 40 to 51 in 2016). Consequently, the total number of workers in the broad 35 to 54 age group will decline by more than 2 million.

Fewer Gen Xers Are Working

Labor force participation rate has declined slightly for both men and women.

Generation Xers are at the career-building stage of their lives. But their labor force participation rate has fallen because of the weak economy.

Men in their thirties typically have a higher labor force participation rate than men in any other age group, and that is still true today. The labor force participation rate of men peaks in the 30-to-44 age group (Gen Xers were aged 32 to 43 in 2008) at 92 to 93 percent. But the peak today is lower than it was a few years ago. Among men in the 30-to-44 age group, the labor force participation rate fell by 0.3 to 1.3 percentage points between 2000 and 2008. Among their female counterparts, the decline ranged from 0.6 to 1.6 percentage points.

■ Although labor force participation has declined among Generation Xers, the great majority of both men and women either have a job or are looking for work.

The labor force participation rate of men aged 30 to 44 has fallen

(percent of men aged 30 to 44 in the labor force, 2000 and 2008)

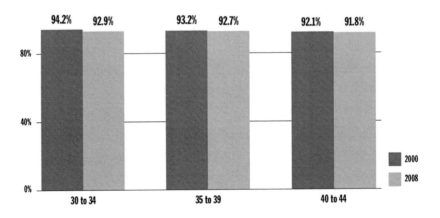

Table 6.1 Labor Force Participation Rate by Sex and Age, 2000 and 2008

(civilian labor force participation rate of people aged 16 or older, by sex and age, 2000 and 2008; percentage point change, 2000–2008)

	2008	2000	percentage point change
Men aged 16 or older	**73.0%**	**74.8%**	**–1.8**
Aged 16 to 17	26.8	40.9	–14.1
Aged 18 to 19	55.4	65.0	–9.6
Aged 20 to 24	78.7	82.6	–3.9
Aged 25 to 29	90.2	92.5	–2.3
Aged 30 to 34	92.9	94.2	–1.3
Aged 35 to 39	92.7	93.2	–0.5
Aged 40 to 44	91.8	92.1	–0.3
Aged 45 to 49	89.7	90.2	–0.5
Aged 50 to 54	86.2	86.8	–0.6
Aged 55 to 59	78.8	77.0	1.8
Aged 60 to 64	59.9	54.9	5.0
Aged 65 or older	21.5	17.7	3.8
Women aged 16 or older	**59.5**	**59.9**	**–0.4**
Aged 16 to 17	29.2	40.8	–11.6
Aged 18 to 19	53.0	61.3	–8.3
Aged 20 to 24	70.0	73.1	–3.1
Aged 25 to 29	75.9	76.7	–0.8
Aged 30 to 34	74.4	75.5	–1.1
Aged 35 to 39	75.2	75.7	–0.5
Aged 40 to 44	77.1	78.7	–1.6
Aged 45 to 49	77.2	79.1	–1.9
Aged 50 to 54	74.8	74.1	0.7
Aged 55 to 59	67.7	61.4	6.3
Aged 60 to 64	48.7	40.2	8.5
Aged 65 or older	13.3	9.4	3.9

Source: Bureau of Labor Statistics, Public Query Data Tool, Internet site http://www.bls.gov/data; and 2008 Current Population Survey, Internet site http://www.bls.gov/cps/tables.htm#empstat; calculations by New Strategist

More than 80 Percent of Generation Xers Are in the Labor Force

Among men, labor force participation is over 90 percent.

Eighty-four percent of people aged 30 to 44 were in the labor force in 2008 (Generation Xers were aged 32 to 43 in that year). The labor force participation rate varies little within the age group. Among men, from 92 to 93 percent of those aged 30 to 44 are in the labor force. Among women in the age group, the figures range from 74 to 77 percent.

Generation X men are slightly less likely to be unemployed than the average male worker—4.8 percent of men aged 30 to 44 versus 6.1 percent of all male workers. The unemployment rate among Gen X women is also slightly below the average for all women, at 4.7 percent compared with a rate of 5.4 percent for all women. Gen Xers are less likely to be unemployed than workers under age 30, but more likely to be job hunting than those aged 45 or older.

■ Workers aged 30 to 44 account for 33 percent of the employed and 27 percent of the unemployed.

Most men and women of Generation X are in the labor force

(percent of people aged 30 to 44 in the labor force, by sex, 2008)

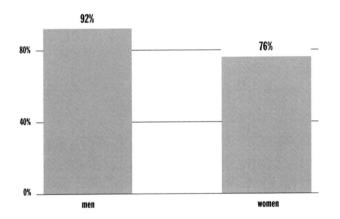

Table 6.2 Employment Status by Sex and Age, 2008

(number and percent of people aged 16 or older in the civilian labor force by sex and age, 2008; numbers in thousands)

	civilian noninstitutional population	civilian labor force			unemployed	
		total	percent of population	employed	number	percent of labor force
Total aged 16 or older	**233,788**	**154,287**	**66.0%**	**145,362**	**8,924**	**5.8%**
Under age 25	37,484	22,032	58.8	19,202	2,830	12.8
Aged 25 to 29	20,815	17,293	83.1	16,171	1,122	6.5
Aged 30 to 44	60,878	51,100	83.9	48,669	2,432	4.8
Aged 30 to 34	19,179	16,039	83.6	15,212	827	5.2
Aged 35 to 39	20,537	17,218	83.8	16,408	810	4.7
Aged 40 to 44	21,162	17,843	84.3	17,049	795	4.5
Aged 45 to 64	77,451	57,618	74.4	55,341	2,277	4.0
Aged 65 or older	37,161	6,243	16.8	5,979	264	4.2
Men aged 16 or older	**113,113**	**82,520**	**73.0**	**77,486**	**5,033**	**6.1**
Under age 25	18,909	11,537	61.0	9,881	1,656	14.4
Aged 25 to 29	10,451	9,431	90.2	8,774	657	7.0
Aged 30 to 44	30,115	27,843	92.5	26,506	1,337	4.8
Aged 30 to 34	9,548	8,871	92.9	8,409	462	5.2
Aged 35 to 39	10,142	9,404	92.7	8,971	433	4.6
Aged 40 to 44	10,425	9,568	91.8	9,126	442	4.6
Aged 45 to 64	37,635	30,273	80.4	29,042	1,229	4.1
Aged 65 or older	16,002	3,436	21.5	3,282	153	4.5
Women aged 16 or older	**120,675**	**71,767**	**59.5**	**67,876**	**3,891**	**5.4**
Under age 25	18,575	10,494	56.5	9,321	1,174	11.2
Aged 25 to 29	10,363	7,862	75.9	7,397	466	5.9
Aged 30 to 44	30,763	23,257	75.6	22,162	1,095	4.7
Aged 30 to 34	9,631	7,168	74.4	6,803	365	5.1
Aged 35 to 39	10,395	7,814	75.2	7,437	377	4.8
Aged 40 to 44	10,737	8,275	77.1	7,922	353	4.3
Aged 45 to 64	39,815	27,345	68.7	26,299	1,047	3.8
Aged 65 or older	21,160	2,808	13.3	2,697	111	3.9

Source: Bureau of Labor Statistics, 2008 Current Population Survey, Internet site http://www.bls.gov/cps/tables.htm#empstat; calculations by New Strategist

Asians Are Least Likely to Be Unemployed

More than 8 percent of black men aged 30 to 44 were looking for work in 2008.

Most men of Generation X are in the labor force, but there are differences in labor force participation and unemployment by race and Hispanic origin. Among Asian, Hispanic, and white men aged 30 to 44, fully 93 to 94 percent are in the labor force. Among black men the figure is 87 percent.

Asian men aged 30 to 44 are less likely to be unemployed than others. In 2008, only 3.5 percent were unemployed, lower than the 4.1 percent average for all Asian men and less than the 4.3 percent rate among white men in the age group. A larger 5.8 percent of Hispanic men aged 30 to 44 were unemployed. Among blacks in the age group, 8.5 percent were unemployed in 2008.

■ Higher unemployment among black men contributes to their lower labor force participation rate. Discouraged by the prospects for work in their communities, some black men give up looking for jobs.

Unemployment rate differs by race and Hispanic origin

(percent of men aged 30 to 44 who are unemployed, by race and Hispanic origin, 2008)

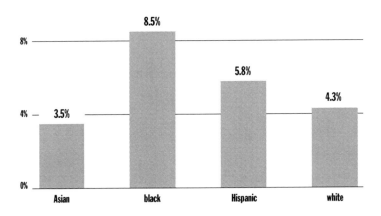

Table 6.3 Employment Status of Men by Race, Hispanic Origin, and Age, 2008

(number and percent of men aged 16 or older in the civilian labor force by race, Hispanic origin, and age, 2008; numbers in thousands)

	civilian noninstitutional population	civilian labor force			unemployed	
		total	percent of population	employed	number	percent of labor force
ASIAN MEN						
Total aged 16 or older	**5,112**	**3,852**	**75.3%**	**3,692**	**160**	**4.1%**
Under age 25	753	353	46.9	322	31	8.8
Aged 25 to 29	519	448	86.2	432	16	3.5
Aged 30 to 44	1,751	1,637	93.5	1,580	58	3.5
Aged 30 to 34	592	548	92.6	521	27	4.9
Aged 35 to 39	641	599	93.5	582	18	3.0
Aged 40 to 44	518	490	94.5	477	13	2.6
Aged 45 to 64	1,534	1,293	84.3	1,244	49	3.8
Aged 65 or older	553	120	21.8	114	6	5.1
BLACK MEN						
Total aged 16 or older	**12,516**	**8,347**	**66.7**	**7,398**	**949**	**11.4**
Under age 25	2,706	1,369	50.6	1,041	328	24.0
Aged 25 to 29	1,311	1,102	84.0	956	146	13.3
Aged 30 to 44	3,400	2,953	86.9	2,703	250	8.5
Aged 30 to 34	1,087	945	86.9	849	96	10.1
Aged 35 to 39	1,132	1,000	88.3	920	80	8.0
Aged 40 to 44	1,181	1,008	85.3	934	74	7.3
Aged 45 to 64	3,854	2,698	70.0	2,494	204	7.6
Aged 65 or older	1,245	225	18.1	204	21	9.5
HISPANIC MEN						
Total aged 16 or older	**16,524**	**13,255**	**80.2**	**12,248**	**1,007**	**7.6**
Under age 25	3,443	2,220	64.5	1,885	335	15.1
Aged 25 to 29	2,260	2,110	93.4	1,958	152	7.2
Aged 30 to 44	5,834	5,488	94.1	5,172	316	5.8
Aged 30 to 34	2,178	2,063	94.7	1,939	124	6.0
Aged 35 to 39	1,957	1,845	94.3	1,745	100	5.4
Aged 40 to 44	1,699	1,580	93.0	1,488	92	5.8
Aged 45 to 64	3,866	3,195	82.6	3,008	186	5.8
Aged 65 or older	1,121	243	21.7	224	19	7.8
WHITE MEN						
Total aged 16 or older	**92,725**	**68,351**	**73.7**	**64,624**	**3,727**	**5.5**
Under age 25	14,741	9,394	63.7	8,178	1,216	12.9
Aged 25 to 29	8,289	7,591	91.6	7,125	466	6.1
Aged 30 to 44	24,196	22,562	93.2	21,582	980	4.3
Aged 30 to 34	7,596	7,125	93.8	6,807	318	4.5
Aged 35 to 39	8,131	7,595	93.4	7,276	319	4.2
Aged 40 to 44	8,469	7,842	92.6	7,499	343	4.4
Aged 45 to 64	31,528	25,760	81.7	24,818	942	3.7
Aged 65 or older	13,972	3,046	21.8	2,922	124	4.1

Note: Race is shown only for those selecting that race group only. People who selected more than one race are not included. Hispanics may be of any race.
Source: Bureau of Labor Statistics, 2008 Current Population Survey, Internet site http://www.bls.gov/cps/tables.htm#empstat; calculations by New Strategist

Labor Force Participation of Gen X Women Varies by Race and Ethnicity

Asian and Hispanic women are least likely to be in the labor force.

Black women aged 30 to 44 are more likely than Asian, Hispanic, or white women to be in the labor force. Eighty percent of black women in the age group were working or looking for work in 2008. This figure compares with 75 percent of white women, 72 percent of Asian women, and just 68 percent of Hispanic women in the age group.

Unemployment is greater among black and Hispanic women than among Asian or white women. Among black women aged 30 to 44, 7.2 percent were unemployed in 2008. For their Hispanic counterparts, the figure was 6.1 percent. Among white women aged 30 to 44, unemployment stood at 4.4 percent, while for Asian women it was just 2.8 percent.

■ Among young adults, Hispanic women are less likely to work than black or white women because a larger proportion of them are married and caring for young children.

Labor force participation rate is highest among black women

(labor force participation rate of women aged 30 to 44, by race and Hispanic origin, 2008)

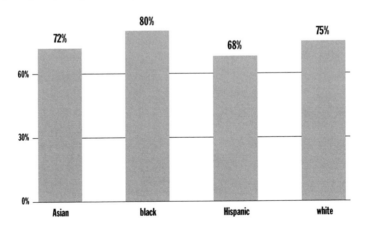

Table 6.4 Employment Status of Women by Race, Hispanic Origin, and Age, 2008

(number and percent of women aged 16 or older in the civilian labor force by race, Hispanic origin, and age, 2008; numbers in thousands)

| | civilian noninstitutional population | civilian labor force | | | unemployed | |
		total	percent of population	employed	number	percent of labor force
ASIAN WOMEN						
Total aged 16 or older	**5,639**	**3,350**	**59.4%**	**3,225**	**125**	**3.7%**
Under age 25	749	330	44.1	305	25	7.6
Aged 25 to 29	543	376	69.2	354	21	5.7
Aged 30 to 44	1,868	1,339	71.7	1,303	37	2.8
Aged 30 to 34	624	439	70.4	430	10	2.2
Aged 35 to 39	662	469	70.9	453	16	3.5
Aged 40 to 44	582	431	74.0	420	11	2.5
Aged 45 to 64	1,741	1,206	69.3	1,166	40	3.3
Aged 65 or older	738	99	13.4	97	2	2.2
BLACK WOMEN						
Total aged 16 or older	**15,328**	**9,393**	**61.3**	**8,554**	**839**	**8.9**
Under age 25	2,884	1,399	48.5	1,125	274	19.6
Aged 25 to 29	1,511	1,209	80.0	1,090	119	9.9
Aged 30 to 44	4,238	3,380	79.8	3,136	244	7.2
Aged 30 to 34	1,353	1,072	79.2	975	97	9.1
Aged 35 to 39	1,426	1,145	80.3	1,060	85	7.4
Aged 40 to 44	1,459	1,163	79.7	1,101	62	5.3
Aged 45 to 64	4,758	3,155	66.3	2,967	188	6.0
Aged 65 or older	1,937	251	13.0	236	15	5.8
HISPANIC WOMEN						
Total aged 16 or older	**15,616**	**8,769**	**56.2**	**8,098**	**672**	**7.7**
Under age 25	3,219	1,569	48.7	1,346	223	14.2
Aged 25 to 29	1,866	1,175	63.0	1,089	86	7.3
Aged 30 to 44	5,134	3,483	67.8	3,271	212	6.1
Aged 30 to 34	1,844	1,209	65.6	1,133	76	6.3
Aged 35 to 39	1,741	1,183	67.9	1,112	71	6.0
Aged 40 to 44	1,549	1,091	70.4	1,026	65	5.9
Aged 45 to 64	3,909	2,368	60.6	2,232	136	5.7
Aged 65 or older	1,488	174	11.7	161	13	7.7
WHITE WOMEN						
Total aged 16 or older	**96,814**	**57,284**	**59.2**	**54,501**	**2,782**	**4.9**
Under age 25	14,256	8,392	58.9	7,574	818	9.7
Aged 25 to 29	7,979	6,043	75.7	5,738	305	5.1
Aged 30 to 44	23,863	17,948	75.2	17,166	781	4.4
Aged 30 to 34	7,370	5,452	74.0	5,205	246	4.5
Aged 35 to 39	8,042	5,999	74.6	5,733	266	4.4
Aged 40 to 44	8,451	6,497	76.9	6,228	269	4.1
Aged 45 to 64	32,522	22,484	69.1	21,697	787	3.5
Aged 65 or older	18,193	2,417	13.3	2,325	92	3.8

Note: Race is shown only for those selecting that race group only. People who selected more than one race are not included. Hispanics may be of any race.
Source: Bureau of Labor Statistics, 2008 Current Population Survey, Internet site http://www.bls.gov/cps/tables.htm#empstat; calculations by New Strategist

Most Generation X Couples Are Dual Earners

The husband is the sole support for only about one in four couples.

Dual incomes are by far the norm among married couples. Both husband and wife are in the labor force in 55 percent of the nation's couples. In another 22 percent, the husband is the only worker. Not far behind are the 16 percent of couples in which neither spouse is in the labor force. The wife is the sole worker in 7 percent of couples.

Sixty-nine percent of couples aged 30 to 44 are dual earners, while the husband is the only one in the labor force in another 26 percent. The dual-earner share of couples peaks at 71 percent in the 40-to-44 age group because at that age children usually are grown and wives are more likely to work. The dual-earner share falls to just 49 percent among couples aged 55 to 64 as workers begin to retire.

■ The dual-earner share of couples will rise in the older age groups as early retirement becomes less common.

Few Generation X couples are supported solely by the husband

(percent distribution of married couples aged 30 to 44 by labor force status of husband and wife, 2008)

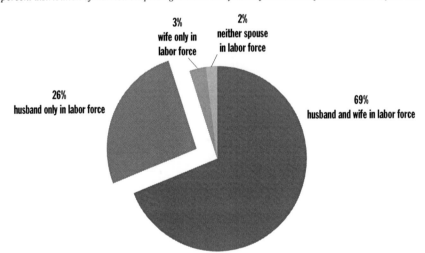

Table 6.5 Labor Force Status of Married-Couple Family Groups by Age, 2008

(number and percent distribution of married-couple family groups by age of reference person and labor force status of husband and wife, 2008; numbers in thousands)

	total	husband and wife in labor force	husband only in labor force	wife only in labor force	neither husband nor wife in labor force
Total married-couple family groups	**60,129**	**32,988**	**13,141**	**4,118**	**9,882**
Under age 25	1,417	763	543	60	49
Aged 25 to 29	3,962	2,615	1,136	138	73
Aged 30 to 44	18,695	12,912	4,860	576	347
Aged 30 to 34	5,408	3,680	1,490	138	99
Aged 35 to 39	6,532	4,456	1,782	197	99
Aged 40 to 44	6,755	4,776	1,588	241	149
Aged 45 to 54	14,210	9,922	3,000	796	491
Aged 55 to 64	11,399	5,613	2,426	1,446	1,915
Aged 65 or older	10,446	1,163	1,176	1,102	7,007
PERCENT DISTRIBUTION					
Total married-couple family groups	**100.0%**	**54.9%**	**21.9%**	**6.8%**	**16.4%**
Under age 25	100.0	53.8	38.3	4.2	3.5
Aged 25 to 29	100.0	66.0	28.7	3.5	1.8
Aged 30 to 44	100.0	69.1	26.0	3.1	1.9
Aged 30 to 34	100.0	68.0	27.6	2.6	1.8
Aged 35 to 39	100.0	68.2	27.3	3.0	1.5
Aged 40 to 44	100.0	70.7	23.5	3.6	2.2
Aged 45 to 54	100.0	69.8	21.1	5.6	3.5
Aged 55 to 64	100.0	49.2	21.3	12.7	16.8
Aged 65 or older	100.0	11.1	11.3	10.5	67.1

Source: Bureau of the Census, America's Families and Living Arrangements: 2008, Internet site http://www.census.gov/ population/www/socdemo/hh-fam/cps2008.html; calculations by New Strategist

Generation Xers Are Overrepresented in Some Jobs

They are more than one-third of computer and information system managers.

Only about 23 percent of workers were aged 35 to 44 in 2008 (Generation X was aged 32 to 43 in that year), but the share varies widely by occupation. Workers in the 35-to-44 age group tend to be underrepresented in leadership positions and overrepresented in jobs requiring technical skills. The 35-to-44 age group accounts for only 17 percent of legislators and 24 percent of chief executives. But 30 percent of computer software engineers and 31 percent of medical scientists are aged 35 to 44.

Generation Xers make up a large share of employees in jobs requiring physical stamina. Thirty-six percent of firefighters and police are in the 35-to-44 age group. The age group also accounts for 36 percent of physical therapists.

■ Generation X was raised on computers, which explains their disproportionate presence in high-tech jobs.

People aged 35 to 44 account for more than one-third of some occupations

(percent of workers in the 35-to-44 age group, by occupation, 2008)

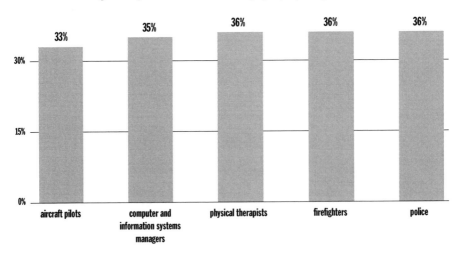

Table 6.6 Occupations of Workers Aged 35 to 44, 2008

(number of employed workers aged 16 or older and median age, number and percent distribution of workers aged 35 to 44, and 35-to-44-year-olds as share of total, by occupation, 2008; numbers in thousands)

| | | | aged 35 to 44 | | |
	total	median age	number	percent distribution	share of total
TOTAL WORKERS	**145,362**	**41.3**	**33,457**	**100.0%**	**23.0%**
Management and professional occupations	**52,761**	**43.5**	**13,284**	**39.7**	**25.2**
Management, business and financial operations	22,059	44.8	5,706	17.1	25.9
Management	15,852	45.6	4,146	12.4	26.2
Business and financial operations	6,207	42.8	1,560	4.7	25.1
Professional and related occupations	30,702	42.5	7,578	22.6	24.7
Computer and mathematical	3,676	39.9	1,107	3.3	30.1
Architecture and engineering	2,931	43.1	731	2.2	24.9
Life, physical, and social sciences	1,307	41.4	331	1.0	25.3
Community and social services	2,293	44.1	488	1.5	21.3
Legal	1,671	44.7	440	1.3	26.3
Education, training, and library	8,605	42.8	1,997	6.0	23.2
Arts, design, entertainment, sports, and media	2,820	40.5	621	1.9	22.0
Health care practitioner and technician	7,399	43.3	1,865	5.6	25.2
Service occupations	**24,451**	**37.1**	**4,982**	**14.9**	**20.4**
Health care support	3,212	38.5	693	2.1	21.6
Protective service	3,047	40.6	835	2.5	27.4
Food preparation and serving	7,824	28.9	1,200	3.6	15.3
Building and grounds cleaning and maintenance	5,445	42.4	1,251	3.7	23.0
Personal care and service	4,923	39.0	1,002	3.0	20.4
Sales and office occupations	**35,544**	**40.6**	**7,326**	**21.9**	**20.6**
Sales and related occupations	16,295	39.5	3,298	9.9	20.2
Office and administrative support	19,249	41.4	4,029	12.0	20.9
Natural resources, construction, maintenance occupations	**14,806**	**39.9**	**3,626**	**10.8**	**24.5**
Farming, fishing, and forestry	988	37.7	193	0.6	19.5
Construction and extraction	8,667	39.0	2,158	6.5	24.9
Installation, maintenance, and repair	5,152	41.7	1,275	3.8	24.7
Production, transportation, material-moving occupations	**17,800**	**41.9**	**4,238**	**12.7**	**23.8**
Production	8,973	42.3	2,185	6.5	24.4
Transportation and material moving	8,827	41.4	2,052	6.1	23.2

Source: Bureau of Labor Statistics, unpublished data from the 2008 Current Population Survey; calculations by New Strategist

Table 6.7 Workers Aged 35 to 44 by Detailed Occupation, 2008

(number of employed workers aged 16 or older, median age, and number and percent aged 35 to 44, by selected detailed occupation, 2008; numbers in thousands)

	total workers	median age	aged 35 to 44 number	aged 35 to 44 percent of total
TOTAL WORKERS	**145,362**	**41.3**	**33,457**	**23.0%**
Chief executives	1,655	49.9	405	24.5
Legislators	23	54.5	4	17.4
Marketing and sales managers	922	41.5	293	31.8
Computer and information systems managers	475	42.5	168	35.4
Financial managers	1,168	42.9	322	27.6
Human resources managers	293	44.1	90	30.7
Farmers and ranchers	751	55.5	103	13.7
Construction managers	1,244	44.7	339	27.3
Education administrators	829	47.7	206	24.8
Food service managers	1,039	40.0	266	25.6
Medical and health services managers	561	46.8	152	27.1
Accountants and auditors	1,762	41.6	449	25.5
Computer scientists and systems analysts	837	41.0	237	28.3
Computer programmers	534	40.3	151	28.3
Computer software engineers	1,034	39.5	313	30.3
Architects	233	44.2	60	25.8
Civil engineers	346	42.9	74	21.4
Electrical engineers	350	44.7	89	25.4
Mechanical engineers	318	43.6	83	26.1
Medical scientists	132	39.7	41	31.1
Economists	19	47.3	6	31.6
Market researchers	134	38.8	37	27.6
Psychologists	176	48.9	37	21.0
Social workers	729	42.3	174	23.9
Clergy	441	51.3	71	16.1
Lawyers	1,014	45.8	281	27.7
Postsecondary teachers	1,218	43.7	253	20.8
Preschool and kindergarten teachers	685	39.2	161	23.5
Elementary and middle school teachers	2,958	42.6	729	24.6
Secondary school teachers	1,210	43.4	290	24.0
Librarians	197	51.2	36	18.3
Teacher assistants	1,020	43.1	245	24.0
Artists	213	46.2	43	20.2
Designers	834	40.8	173	20.7
Actors	30	32.6	6	20.0
Athletes, coaches, umpires	252	31.4	56	22.2
Musicians	186	44.0	40	21.5
Editors	171	40.9	41	24.0
Writers and authors	186	46.9	46	24.7
Dentists	152	48.2	35	23.0
Pharmacists	243	42.2	67	27.6

	total workers	median age	aged 35 to 44	
			number	percent of total
Physicians and surgeons	877	45.7	254	29.0%
Registered nurses	2,778	45.0	662	23.8
Physical therapists	197	40.9	70	35.5
Emergency medical technicians and paramedics	138	32.8	33	23.9
Licensed practical nurses	566	43.7	139	24.6
Nursing, psychiatric, and home health aides	1,889	39.8	398	21.1
Firefighters	293	39.3	105	35.8
Police and sheriff's patrol officers	674	38.7	242	35.9
Security guards and gaming surveillance officers	867	42.0	164	18.9
Chefs and head cooks	351	37.3	100	28.5
Cooks	1,997	32.2	382	19.1
Food preparation workers	724	27.9	102	14.1
Waiters and waitresses	2,010	24.8	235	11.7
Janitors and building cleaners	2,125	45.5	417	19.6
Maids and housekeeping cleaners	1,434	43.6	386	26.9
Grounds maintenance workers	1,262	35.5	278	22.0
Hairdressers, hair stylists, and cosmetologists	773	39.0	195	25.2
Child care workers	1,314	36.3	237	18.0
Cashiers	3,031	27.1	387	12.8
Retail salespersons	3,416	34.9	493	14.4
Insurance sales agents	573	44.8	126	22.0
Securities, commodities, and financial services sales agents	388	40.0	104	26.8
Sales representatives, wholesale/manufacturing	1,343	42.8	368	27.4
Real estate brokers and sales agents	962	47.9	229	23.8
Bookkeeping, accounting, and auditing clerks	1,434	46.5	316	22.0
Customer service representatives	1,908	35.3	402	21.1
Receptionists and information clerks	1,413	37.2	231	16.3
Stock clerks and order fillers	1,481	33.0	246	16.6
Secretaries and administrative assistants	3,296	45.7	708	21.5
Miscellaneous agricultural workers	723	34.1	125	17.3
Carpenters	1,562	39.4	371	23.8
Construction laborers	1,651	35.9	391	23.7
Automotive service technicians and mechanics	852	38.8	202	23.7
Miscellaneous assemblers and fabricators	1,050	40.8	267	25.4
Machinists	409	44.8	92	22.5
Aircraft pilots and flight engineers	141	43.6	46	32.6
Driver/sales workers and truck drivers	3,388	43.5	906	26.7
Laborers and freight, stock, and material movers	1,889	34.3	358	19.0

Source: Bureau of Labor Statistics, unpublished tables from the 2008 Current Population Survey; calculations by New Strategist

Few Gen Xers Work Part-Time

Part-time work is the rule only among teenagers aged 16 to 19.

Among employed men ranging in age from 25 to 54 in 2008, a tiny 7 percent had part-time jobs. Among the part-time workers, the 57 percent majority would have preferred full-time work but could not find it.

Among employed women aged 25 to 54, a larger 19 percent worked part-time. Only 20 percent of the part-time workers were doing so for economic reasons—meaning they could not find a full-time job.

Older workers are more likely to work part-time. Among workers aged 55 or older, 16 percent of employed men and 28 percent of employed women had part-time jobs. The percentage of workers with part-time jobs peaks at 71 percent among 16-to-19-year-olds.

■ The percentage of workers who have part-time jobs because they cannot find full-time employment has been rising during the economic downturn.

Some part-time workers want full-time jobs

(percent of employed men who work part-time but would prefer a full-time job, by age, 2008)

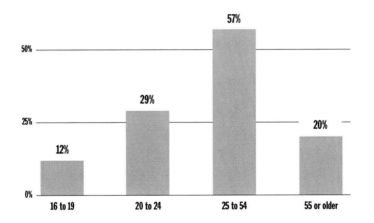

Table 6.8 Full-Time and Part-Time Workers by Age and Sex, 2008

(number and percent distribution of people aged 16 or older at work in nonagricultural industries by age, employment status, and sex, 2008; numbers in thousands)

	total			men			women		
	total	full-time	part-time	total	full-time	part-time	total	full-time	part-time
Total at work	**137,739**	**112,961**	**24,778**	**73,471**	**64,375**	**9,095**	**64,268**	**48,586**	**15,682**
Aged 16 to 19	5,252	1,526	3,727	2,556	875	1,681	2,696	650	2,046
Aged 20 to 24	13,091	9,058	4,033	6,866	5,067	1,798	6,225	3,990	2,235
Aged 25 to 54	94,577	82,960	11,617	50,972	47,468	3,504	43,605	35,492	8,112
Aged 55 or older	24,819	19,418	5,401	13,077	10,964	2,112	11,742	8,454	3,288

PERCENT DISTRIBUTION BY EMPLOYMENT STATUS

	total			men			women		
Total at work	**100.0%**	**82.0%**	**18.0%**	**100.0%**	**87.6%**	**12.4%**	**100.0%**	**75.6%**	**24.4%**
Aged 16 to 19	100.0	29.1	71.0	100.0	34.2	65.8	100.0	24.1	75.9
Aged 20 to 24	100.0	69.2	30.8	100.0	73.8	26.2	100.0	64.1	35.9
Aged 25 to 54	100.0	87.7	12.3	100.0	93.1	6.9	100.0	81.4	18.6
Aged 55 or older	100.0	78.2	21.8	100.0	83.8	16.2	100.0	72.0	28.0

PERCENT DISTRIBUTION BY AGE

	total			men			women		
Total at work	**100.0%**	**100.0%**	**100.0%**	**100.0%**	**100.0%**	**100.0%**	**100.0%**	**100.0%**	**100.0%**
Aged 16 to 19	3.8	1.4	15.0	3.5	1.4	18.5	4.2	1.3	13.0
Aged 20 to 24	9.5	8.0	16.3	9.3	7.9	19.8	9.7	8.2	14.3
Aged 25 to 54	68.7	73.4	46.9	69.4	73.7	38.5	67.8	73.0	51.7
Aged 55 or older	18.0	17.2	21.8	17.8	17.0	23.2	18.3	17.4	21.0

Note: Part-time work is less than 35 hours per week. Part-time workers exclude those who worked less than 35 hours in the previous week because of vacation, holidays, child care problems, weather issues, and other temporary, noneconomic reasons.
Source: Bureau of Labor Statistics, Current Population Survey, Internet site http://www.bls.gov/cps/tables.htm#empstat; calculations by New Strategist

Table 6.9 Part-Time Workers by Sex, Age, and Reason, 2008

(total number of people aged 16 or older who work in nonagricultural industries part-time, and number and percent working part-time for economic reasons, by sex and age, 2008; numbers in thousands)

| | total | working part-time for economic reasons | |
		number	share of total
Men working part-time	**9,095**	**3,162**	**34.8%**
Aged 16 to 19	1,681	209	12.4
Aged 20 to 24	1,798	526	29.3
Aged 25 to 54	3,504	2,014	57.5
Aged 55 or older	2,112	412	19.5
Women working part-time	**15,682**	**2,611**	**16.6**
Aged 16 to 19	2,046	173	8.5
Aged 20 to 24	2,235	412	18.4
Aged 25 to 54	8,112	1,637	20.2
Aged 55 or older	3,288	388	11.8

Note: Part-time work is less than 35 hours per week. Part-time workers exclude those who worked less than 35 hours in the previous week because of vacation, holidays, child care problems, weather issues, and other temporary, noneconomic reasons. "Economic reasons" means a worker's hours have been reduced or workers cannot find full-time employment.
Source: Bureau of Labor Statistics, Current Population Survey, Internet site http://www.bls.gov/cps/tables.htm#empstat; calculations by New Strategist

Self-Employment Is Uncommon among Gen Xers

Men are more likely than women to be self-employed.

Despite plenty of media hype about America's entrepreneurial spirit, few Americans are self-employed. Only 7 percent of the nation's workers were self-employed in 2008.

Men are more likely than women to be self-employed, and self-employment rises with age. Among 35-to-44-year-olds, 8 percent of men and 6 percent of women are self-employed. The figures peak among men and women aged 65 or older at 20 and 13 percent, respectively.

■ Self-employment is becoming a more difficult proposition for Americans because the cost of buying private health insurance has become prohibitive.

Few Generation Xers are self-employed

(percent of workers who are self-employed, by age, 2008)

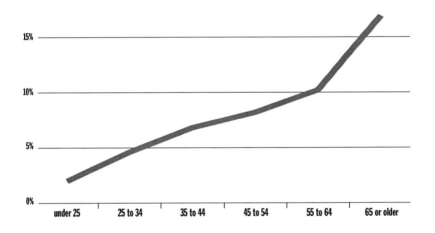

Table 6.10 Self-Employed Workers by Sex and Age, 2008

(number of employed workers aged 16 or older, number and percent who are self-employed, and percent distribution of self-employed, by age, 2008; numbers in thousands)

	total	self-employed number	self-employed percent	percent distribution of self-employed by age
Total aged 16 or older	**145,362**	**10,079**	**6.9%**	**100.0%**
Under age 25	19,202	386	2.0	3.8
Aged 25 to 34	31,383	1,447	4.6	14.4
Aged 35 to 44	33,457	2,286	6.8	22.7
Aged 45 to 54	34,529	2,832	8.2	28.1
Aged 55 to 64	20,812	2,120	10.2	21.0
Aged 65 or older	5,979	1,009	16.9	10.0
Total men	**77,486**	**6,373**	**8.2**	**100.0**
Under age 25	9,881	264	2.7	4.1
Aged 25 to 34	17,183	921	5.4	14.5
Aged 35 to 44	18,097	1,407	7.8	22.1
Aged 45 to 54	18,124	1,769	9.8	27.8
Aged 55 to 64	10,919	1,341	12.3	21.0
Aged 65 or older	3,283	670	20.4	10.5
Total women	**67,876**	**3,707**	**5.5**	**100.0**
Under age 25	9,320	118	1.3	3.2
Aged 25 to 34	14,200	525	3.7	14.2
Aged 35 to 44	15,360	879	5.7	23.7
Aged 45 to 54	16,405	1,063	6.5	28.7
Aged 55 to 64	9,893	779	7.9	21.0
Aged 65 or older	2,697	340	12.6	9.2

Source: Bureau of Labor Statistics, Current Population Survey, Internet site http://www.bls.gov/cps/tables.htm#empstat; calculations by New Strategist

Job Tenure Has Decreased Slightly for Men Aged 35 to 44

Long-term employment has fallen more sharply.

Job tenure (the median number of years a worker has been with his current employer) has been declining among middle-aged men over the past few years. Among men aged 35 to 44, median job tenure fell by 0.1 years between 2000 and 2008. Among women in the age group, in contrast, job tenure climbed by 0.4 years.

Long-term employment has fallen among both male and female workers in their thirties and forties. The percentage of men aged 35 to 39 who had been with their current employer for 10 or more years fell from 29 to 25 percent between 2000 and 2008. Among men aged 40 to 44, the figure fell from 40 to 36 percent. Their female counterparts saw a 1 to 2 percentage point decline in long-term employment during those years.

■ The decline in long-term employment is due to massive job cuts in many sectors.

Fewer men aged 35 to 44 have long-term jobs

(percent of men aged 35 to 44 who have worked for their current employer for 10 or more years, 2000 and 2008)

Table 6.11 Job Tenure by Sex and Age, 2000 and 2008

(median number of years workers aged 25 or older have been with their current employer by sex and age, and change in years, 2000 and 2008)

	2008	2000	change in years 2000–08
Total aged 25 or older	**5.1**	**4.7**	**0.4**
Aged 25 to 34	2.7	2.6	0.1
Aged 35 to 44	4.9	4.8	0.1
Aged 45 to 54	7.6	8.2	−0.6
Aged 55 to 64	9.9	10.0	−0.1
Aged 65 or older	10.2	9.4	0.8
Men aged 25 or older	**5.2**	**4.9**	**0.3**
Aged 25 to 34	2.8	2.7	0.1
Aged 35 to 44	5.2	5.3	−0.1
Aged 45 to 54	8.2	9.5	−1.3
Aged 55 to 64	10.1	10.2	−0.1
Aged 65 or older	10.4	9.0	1.4
Women aged 25 or older	**4.9**	**4.4**	**0.5**
Aged 25 to 34	2.6	2.5	0.1
Aged 35 to 44	4.7	4.3	0.4
Aged 45 to 54	7.0	7.3	−0.3
Aged 55 to 64	9.8	9.9	−0.1
Aged 65 or older	9.9	9.7	0.2

Source: Bureau of Labor Statistics, Employee Tenure, Internet site http://www.bls.gov/news.release/tenure.toc.htm; calculations by New Strategist

Table 6.12 Long-Term Employment by Sex and Age, 2000 and 2008

(percent of employed wage and salary workers aged 25 or older who have been with their current employer for 10 or more years, by sex and age, 2000 and 2008; percentage point change in share, 2000–08)

	2008	2000	percentage point change 2000–08
TOTAL AGED 25 OR OLDER	**31.5%**	**31.5%**	**0.0**
Men aged 25 or older	**32.9**	**33.4**	**−0.5**
Aged 25 to 29	2.4	3.0	−0.6
Aged 30 to 34	11.3	15.1	−3.8
Aged 35 to 39	25.4	29.4	−4.0
Aged 40 to 44	35.8	40.2	−4.4
Aged 45 to 49	43.5	49.0	−5.5
Aged 50 to 54	50.4	51.6	−1.2
Aged 55 to 59	54.9	53.7	1.2
Aged 60 to 64	52.4	52.4	0.0
Aged 65 or older	58.9	48.6	10.3
Women aged 25 or older	**30.0**	**29.5**	**0.5**
Aged 25 to 29	2.1	1.9	0.2
Aged 30 to 34	8.7	12.5	−3.8
Aged 35 to 39	20.3	22.3	−2.0
Aged 40 to 44	29.9	31.2	−1.3
Aged 45 to 49	36.7	41.4	−4.7
Aged 50 to 54	45.0	45.8	−0.8
Aged 55 to 59	50.0	52.5	−2.5
Aged 60 to 64	54.8	53.6	1.2
Aged 65 or older	53.8	51.0	2.8

Source: Bureau of Labor Statistics, Employee Tenure, Internet site http://www.bls.gov/news.release/tenure.toc.htm; calculations by New Strategist

More than One in 10 Generation Xers Have Alternative Work Arrangements

Most of those with alternative jobs are independent contractors.

Among the nation's 15 million alternative workers, nearly 4 million (25 percent) are aged 35 to 44. According to the Bureau of Labor Statistics, alternative workers are defined as independent contractors, on-call workers (such as substitute teachers), temporary-help agency workers, and people who work for contract firms (such as lawn or janitorial service companies).

The most popular alternative work arrangement is independent contracting—which includes most of the self-employed. Among the 15 million alternative workers, 10 million are independent contractors—or 70 percent. Eight percent of workers aged 35 to 44 are independent contractors.

The percentage of workers with alternative work arrangements rises with age as independent contracting becomes more popular. Ten percent of workers aged 45 or older are independent contractors.

■ Older workers have more skills and experience, which makes it easier for them to earn a living by self-employment.

The percentage of workers who are independent contractors rises with age

(percent of employed workers who are independent contractors, by age, 2005)

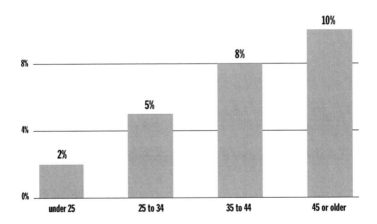

Table 6.13 Alternative Work Arrangements by Age, 2005

(number and percent distribution of employed people aged 16 or older by age and work arrangement, 2005; numbers in thousands)

			alternative workers				
	total employed	traditional arrangements	total	independent contractors	on-call workers	temporary-help agency workers	workers provided by contract firms
Total people	138,952	123,843	14,826	10,342	2,454	1,217	813
Under age 25	18,624	17,249	1,262	445	488	235	94
Aged 25 to 34	30,103	27,427	2,622	1,520	535	362	205
Aged 35 to 44	34,481	30,646	3,774	2,754	571	253	196
Aged 45 or older	55,744	48,521	7,168	5,623	859	368	318
PERCENT DISTRIBUTION BY ALTERNATIVE WORK STATUS							
Total people	100.0%	89.1%	10.7%	7.4%	1.8%	0.9%	0.6%
Under age 25	100.0	92.6	6.8	2.4	2.6	1.3	0.5
Aged 25 to 34	100.0	91.1	8.7	5.0	1.8	1.2	0.7
Aged 35 to 44	100.0	88.9	10.9	8.0	1.7	0.7	0.6
Aged 45 or older	100.0	87.0	12.9	10.1	1.5	0.7	0.6
PERCENT DISTRIBUTION BY AGE							
Total people	100.0%	100.0%	100.0%	100.0%	100.0%	100.0%	100.0%
Under age 25	13.4	13.9	8.5	4.3	19.9	19.3	11.6
Aged 25 to 34	21.7	22.1	17.7	14.7	21.8	29.7	25.2
Aged 35 to 44	24.8	24.7	25.5	26.6	23.3	20.8	24.1
Aged 45 or older	40.1	39.2	48.3	54.4	35.0	30.2	39.1

Note: Numbers may not add to total because "total employed" includes day laborers, an alternative arrangement not shown separately, and a small number of workers were both on call and provided by contract firms. Independent contractors are workers who obtain customers on their own to provide a product or service, and include the self-employed. On-call workers are in a pool of workers who are called to work only as needed, such as substitute teachers and construction workers supplied by a union hiring hall. Temporary-help agency workers are those who said they are paid by a temporary-help agency. Workers provided by contract firms are those employed by a company that provides employees or their services under contract, such as security, landscaping, and computer programming.

Source: Bureau of Labor Statistics, Contingent and Alternative Employment Arrangements, February 2005, Internet site http:// www.bls.gov/news.release/conemp.t05.htm; calculations by New Strategist

Few Gen Xers Work for Minimum Wage

Only 2 percent of workers aged 30 to 44 earn minimum wage or less.

Among the nation's 75 million workers who were paid hourly rates in 2008, only 2.2 million (3 percent) made minimum wage or less, according to the Bureau of Labor Statistics. Half of minimum-wage workers are under age 25.

Among workers aged 30 to 44 (Gen Xers were aged 32 to 43 in 2008) only 431,000 made minimum wage or less. The 30-to-44 age group accounts for 19 percent of all minimum wage workers.

■ Younger workers are most likely to earn minimum wage or less because many hold entry-level jobs.

Half of minimum wage workers are under age 25

(percent distribution of workers who make minimum wage or less, by age, 2008)

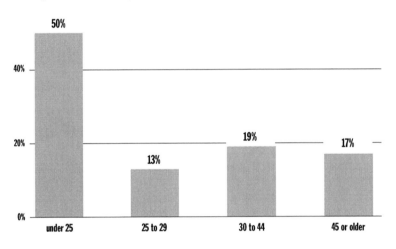

Table 6.14 Workers Earning Minimum Wage by Age, 2008

(number, percent, and percent distribution of workers aged 16 or older paid hourly rates at or below minimum wage, by age, 2008; numbers in thousands)

	total paid hourly rates	at or below minimum wage		
		number	share of total	percent distribution
Total aged 16 or older	**75,305**	**2,226**	**3.0%**	**100.0%**
Under age 25	15,680	1,122	7.2	50.4
Aged 25 to 29	9,309	292	3.1	13.1
Aged 30 to 44	23,062	431	1.9	19.4
Aged 30 to 34	7,584	190	2.5	8.5
Aged 35 to 39	7,683	127	1.7	5.7
Aged 40 to 44	7,795	114	1.5	5.1
Aged 45 to 54	15,625	201	1.3	9.0
Aged 55 to 64	8,987	106	1.2	4.8
Aged 65 or older	2,642	72	2.7	3.2

Source: Bureau of Labor Statistics, Characteristics of Minimum Wage Workers, 2008, Internet site http://www.bls.gov/cps/ minwage2008.htm; calculations by New Strategist

Few 35-to-44-Year-Olds Are Represented by Unions

Men are more likely than women to be represented by a union.

Union representation has fallen sharply over the past few decades. In 2008, only 14 percent of employed wage and salary workers were represented by a union.

The percentage of workers who are represented by a union peaks in the 55-to-64 age group at 19 percent for men and 17 percent for women. Men are more likely than women to be represented by unions because men are more likely to work in manufacturing—the traditional stronghold of labor unions. In fact, the decline of labor unions is partly the result of the shift in jobs from manufacturing to services. Among 35-to-44-year-olds, 16 percent of men and 13 percent of women are represented by a union.

■ Union representation may rise along with workers' concerns about job security and the cost of health care coverage.

Few workers are represented by a union

(percent of employed wage and salary workers who are represented by unions, by age, 2008)

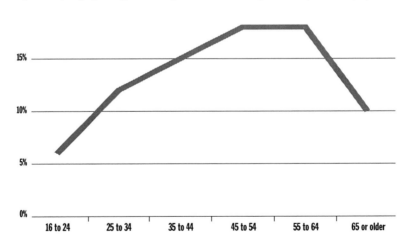

Table 6.15 Union Representation by Sex and Age, 2008

(number and percent of employed wage and salary workers aged 16 or older by union representation status, sex, and age, 2008; numbers in thousands)

		represented by unions	
	total employed	number	percent
Total aged 16 or older	**129,377**	**17,761**	**13.7%**
Aged 16 to 24	18,705	1,062	5.7
Aged 25 to 34	29,276	3,443	11.8
Aged 35 to 44	29,708	4,365	14.7
Aged 45 to 54	29,787	5,228	17.6
Aged 55 to 64	17,430	3,209	18.4
Aged 65 or older	4,471	454	10.2
Men aged 16 or older	**66,846**	**9,724**	**14.5**
Aged 16 to 24	9,537	617	6.5
Aged 25 to 34	15,780	1,909	12.1
Aged 35 to 44	15,653	2,491	15.9
Aged 45 to 54	14,988	2,812	18.8
Aged 55 to 64	8,657	1,682	19.4
Aged 65 or older	2,230	213	9.6
Women aged 16 or older	**62,532**	**8,036**	**12.9**
Aged 16 to 24	9,168	445	4.8
Aged 25 to 34	13,496	1,534	11.4
Aged 35 to 44	14,055	1,874	13.3
Aged 45 to 54	14,799	2,416	16.3
Aged 55 to 64	8,773	1,527	17.4
Aged 65 or older	2,241	241	10.7

Note: Workers represented by unions are either members of a labor union or similar employee association or workers who report no union affiliation but whose jobs are covered by a union or an employee association contract.
Source: Bureau of Labor Statistics, 2008 Current Population Survey, Internet site http://www.bls.gov/cps/tables.htm#empstat; calculations by New Strategist

Number of Workers Aged 35 to 54 Will Decline

The number of workers aged 25 to 34 will grow.

Between 2006 and 2016, the small Generation X will fill the 40-to-49 age group (Gen Xers will be aged 40 to 51 in 2016). Consequently, the total number of workers in the broad 35-to-54 age group will decline by more than 2 million. The 25-to-34 age group, in contrast, will be filling with the larger Millennial generation, and the total number of workers aged 25 to 34 will expand by nearly 5 million during those years.

The number of older workers is projected to soar between 2006 and 2016 as Boomers enter the age group and many postpone retirement. The Bureau of Labor Statistics projects a 78 percent increase in the number of male workers aged 65 or older during those years. The number of older female workers is projected to increase by an even greater 91 percent.

■ Generation X may find it difficult to advance on the job as Boomers, working well into their sixties, clog the ranks of upper management.

The number of workers aged 35 to 54 will decline

(percent change in number of workers aged 25 to 54, by sex and age, 2006–16)

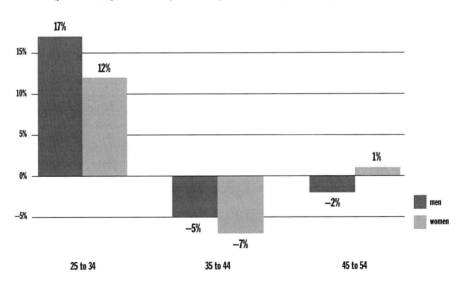

Table 6.16 Projections of the Labor Force by Sex and Age, 2006 and 2016

(number and percent of people aged 16 or older in the civilian labor force by sex and age, 2006 and 2016; percent change in number and percentage point change in participation rate, 2006–16; numbers in thousands)

	number			participation rate		
	2006	2016	percent change 2006–16	2006	2016	percentage point change 2006–16
TOTAL LABOR FORCE	**151,428**	**164,232**	**8.5%**	**66.2%**	**65.5%**	**–0.7**
Total men in labor force	**81,255**	**87,781**	**8.0**	**73.5**	**72.3**	**–1.2**
Aged 16 to 19	3,693	2,923	–20.9	43.7	36.8	–6.9
Aged 20 to 24	8,116	7,992	–1.5	79.6	76.4	–3.2
Aged 25 to 34	17,944	20,913	16.5	91.7	95.7	4.0
Aged 35 to 44	19,407	18,373	–5.3	92.1	91.7	–0.4
Aged 45 to 54	18,489	18,205	–1.5	88.1	86.6	–1.5
Aged 55 to 64	10,509	13,865	31.9	69.6	70.1	0.5
Aged 65 or older	3,096	5,511	78.0	20.3	27.1	6.8
Total women in labor force	**70,173**	**76,450**	**8.9**	**59.4**	**59.2**	**–0.2**
Aged 16 to 19	3,588	2,974	–17.1	43.7	38.3	–5.4
Aged 20 to 24	6,997	6,963	–0.5	69.5	67.2	–2.3
Aged 25 to 34	14,628	16,376	11.9	74.4	75.0	0.6
Aged 35 to 44	16,441	15,281	–7.1	75.9	75.1	–0.8
Aged 45 to 54	16,656	16,877	1.3	76.0	77.8	1.8
Aged 55 to 64	9,475	13,423	41.7	58.2	63.5	5.3
Aged 65 or older	2,388	4,556	90.8	11.7	17.5	5.8

Source: Bureau of Labor Statistics, Labor Force Projections to 2016: More Workers in Their Golden Years, Monthly Labor Review, November 2007, Internet site http://www.bls.gov/opub/mlr/2007/11/contents.htm; calculations by New Strategist

Living Arrangements

■ The lives of Gen Xers revolve around marriage and children. Overall, 56 percent of households headed by 30-to-44-year-olds were married couples in 2008 (Gen Xers were aged 32 to 43 in that year).

■ Among all households headed by people aged 30 to 44, non-Hispanic whites head the 63 percent majority. But the figure varies greatly by type of household.

■ The average American household was home to 2.56 people in 2008. Household size peaks among householders aged 35 to 39, at 3.31 people.

■ More than half the households headed by people aged 30 to 44 include children under age 18. The proportion of households with children does not vary much within the age group.

■ Overall, 54 percent of men aged 30 to 44 were married and living with their spouse in 2008. Among their female counterparts, an even larger 64 percent were married.

Married Couples Become the Norm among 30-to-34-Year-Olds

As they enter middle age, Gen Xers are in a stable lifestage.

As people age through their thirties and into their forties, life gets serious. Gen Xers are now at the stage of life when work, marriage, children, and home are the central focus.

Overall, 56 percent of households headed by 30-to-44-year-olds were married couples in 2008 (Gen Xers were aged 32 to 43 in that year). Among householders aged 30 to 34, the 53 percent majority are married couples. The figure rises to 59 percent in the 35-to-39 age group and remains above 50 percent until people are in their seventies.

Sixteen percent of householders in the 30-to-44 age group are women heading families without a spouse, making it the second-most-common household type. Men who live alone rank third, and account for 11 percent of householders aged 30 to 44. Women who live alone account for only 7 percent of householders in the age group, and men heading families without a spouse are just 5 percent.

■ People in their thirties are looking for stability as they raise their children.

Married couples dominate Gen X households

(married couples as a percent of householders aged 30 to 44, by age, 2008)

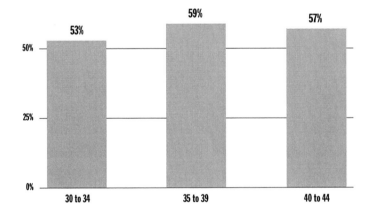

Table 7.1 Households Headed by People Aged 30 to 44 by Household Type, 2008: Total Households

(number and percent distribution of total households and households headed by people aged 30 to 44, by household type, 2008; numbers in thousands)

	total	aged 30 to 44			
		total	30 to 34	35 to 39	40 to 44
TOTAL HOUSEHOLDS	**116,783**	**32,273**	**9,825**	**10,900**	**11,548**
Family households	**77,873**	**24,985**	**7,384**	**8,605**	**8,996**
Married couples	58,370	18,229	5,240	6,406	6,583
Female householder, no spouse present	14,404	5,150	1,599	1,684	1,867
Male householder, no spouse present	5,100	1,607	546	515	546
Nonfamily households	**38,910**	**7,287**	**2,440**	**2,295**	**2,552**
Female householder	21,038	2,683	845	853	985
Living alone	18,297	2,128	648	679	801
Male householder	17,872	4,604	1,595	1,442	1,567
Living alone	13,870	3,436	1,116	1,081	1,239
Percent distribution by type					
TOTAL HOUSEHOLDS	**100.0%**	**100.0%**	**100.0%**	**100.0%**	**100.0%**
Family households	**66.7**	**77.4**	**75.2**	**78.9**	**77.9**
Married couples	50.0	56.5	53.3	58.8	57.0
Female householder, no spouse present	12.3	16.0	16.3	15.4	16.2
Male householder, no spouse present	4.4	5.0	5.6	4.7	4.7
Nonfamily households	**33.3**	**22.6**	**24.8**	**21.1**	**22.1**
Female householder	18.0	8.3	8.6	7.8	8.5
Living alone	15.7	6.6	6.6	6.2	6.9
Male householder	15.3	14.3	16.2	13.2	13.6
Living alone	11.9	10.6	11.4	9.9	10.7
Percent distribution by age					
TOTAL HOUSEHOLDS	**100.0%**	**27.6%**	**8.4%**	**9.3%**	**9.9%**
Family households	100.0	32.1	9.5	11.1	11.6
Married couples	100.0	31.2	9.0	11.0	11.3
Female householder, no spouse present	100.0	35.8	11.1	11.7	13.0
Male householder, no spouse present	100.0	31.5	10.7	10.1	10.7
Nonfamily households	**100.0**	**18.7**	**6.3**	**5.9**	**6.6**
Female householder	100.0	12.8	4.0	4.1	4.7
Living alone	100.0	11.6	3.5	3.7	4.4
Male householder	100.0	25.8	8.9	8.1	8.8
Living alone	100.0	24.8	8.0	7.8	8.9

Source: Bureau of the Census, 2008 Current Population Survey, Annual Social and Economic Supplement, Internet site http://www.census.gov/hhes/www/macro/032008/hhinc/new02_000.htm; calculations by New Strategist

Hispanics and Blacks Head Many Gen X Households

Non-Hispanic whites head fewer than half of female-headed families.

Among all households headed by people aged 30 to 44, non-Hispanic whites head the 63 percent majority. But the figure varies greatly by type of household. Non-Hispanic whites account for only 45 percent of female-headed families in the 30-to-44 age group, for example, but they account for 68 percent of married couples.

Married couples dominate households headed by Asian Gen Xers and account for nearly 64 percent of the total. The figure is 61 percent among non-Hispanic whites and 58 percent among Hispanics. Among households headed by black Gen Xers, however, only 32 percent are married couples. A larger 35 percent are female-headed families.

■ The non-Hispanic white share of households will continue to shrink as the more diverse younger generations replace older people in the population.

Seventeen percent of Gen X couples are Hispanic

(percent distribution of married couples aged 30 to 44 by race and Hispanic origin, 2008)

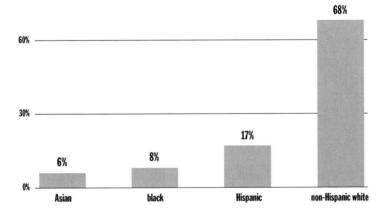

Table 7.2 Households Headed by People Aged 30 to 44 by Household Type, Race, and Hispanic Origin, 2008

(number and percent distribution of households headed by people aged 30 to 44, by household type, race, and Hispanic origin, 2008; numbers in thousands)

	total	Asian	black	Hispanic	non-Hispanic white
TOTAL HOUSEHOLDERS 30 TO 44	**32,273**	**1,768**	**4,623**	**5,185**	**20,466**
Family households	**24,985**	**1,386**	**3,405**	**4,384**	**15,640**
Married couples	18,229	1,129	1,496	3,013	12,427
Female householder, no spouse present	5,150	160	1,637	1,035	2,323
Male householder, no spouse present	1,607	97	272	335	889
Nonfamily households	**7,287**	**383**	**1,218**	**800**	**4,826**
Female householder	2,683	146	545	212	1,756
Living alone	2,128	111	474	165	1,352
Male householder	4,604	237	671	589	3,069
Living alone	3,436	164	553	385	2,303
Percent distribution by race and Hispanic origin					
TOTAL HOUSEHOLDERS 30 TO 44	**100.0%**	**5.5%**	**14.3%**	**16.1%**	**63.4%**
Family households	**100.0**	**5.5**	**13.6**	**17.5**	**62.6**
Married couples	100.0	6.2	8.2	16.5	68.2
Female householder, no spouse present	100.0	3.1	31.8	20.1	45.1
Male householder, no spouse present	100.0	6.0	16.9	20.8	55.3
Nonfamily households	**100.0**	**5.3**	**16.7**	**11.0**	**66.2**
Female householder	100.0	5.4	20.3	7.9	65.4
Living alone	100.0	5.2	22.3	7.8	63.5
Male householder	100.0	5.1	14.6	12.8	66.7
Living alone	100.0	4.8	16.1	11.2	67.0

Note: Numbers do not add to total because Asian and black include those who identify themselves as being of the race alone as well as those who identify themselves as being of the race in combination with other races and because Hispanics may be of any race. Non-Hispanic whites are those who identify themselves as being white alone and not Hispanic.
Source: Bureau of the Census, 2008 Current Population Survey, Annual Social and Economic Supplement, Internet site http:// www.census.gov/hhes/www/macro/032008/hhinc/new02_000.htm; calculations by New Strategist

Table 7.3 Households Headed by People Aged 30 to 44 by Household Type, 2008: Asian Households

(number and percent distribution of total households headed by Asians and households headed by Asians aged 30 to 44, by household type, 2008; numbers in thousands)

	total	aged 30 to 44 total	30 to 34	35 to 39	40 to 44
TOTAL ASIAN HOUSEHOLDS	**4,715**	**1,768**	**620**	**628**	**520**
Family households	**3,451**	**1,386**	**447**	**485**	**454**
Married couples	2,757	1,129	368	395	366
Female householder, no spouse present	452	160	50	57	53
Male householder, no spouse present	242	97	29	33	35
Nonfamily households	**1,256**	**383**	**173**	**144**	**66**
Female householder	662	146	73	54	19
Living alone	545	111	50	47	14
Male householder	602	237	100	90	47
Living alone	420	164	66	65	33
Percent distribution by type					
TOTAL ASIAN HOUSEHOLDS	**100.0%**	**100.0%**	**100.0%**	**100.0%**	**100.0%**
Family households	**73.2**	**78.4**	**72.1**	**77.2**	**87.3**
Married couples	58.5	63.9	59.4	62.9	70.4
Female householder, no spouse present	9.6	9.0	8.1	9.1	10.2
Male householder, no spouse present	5.1	5.5	4.7	5.3	6.7
Nonfamily households	**26.6**	**21.7**	**27.9**	**22.9**	**12.7**
Female householder	14.0	8.3	11.8	8.6	3.7
Living alone	11.6	6.3	8.1	7.5	2.7
Male householder	12.8	13.4	16.1	14.3	9.0
Living alone	8.9	9.3	10.6	10.4	6.3
Percent distribution by age					
TOTAL ASIAN HOUSEHOLDS	**100.0%**	**37.5%**	**13.1%**	**13.3%**	**11.0%**
Family households	**100.0**	**40.2**	**13.0**	**14.1**	**13.2**
Married couples	100.0	41.0	13.3	14.3	13.3
Female householder, no spouse present	100.0	35.4	11.1	12.6	11.7
Male householder, no spouse present	100.0	40.1	12.0	13.6	14.5
Nonfamily households	**100.0**	**30.5**	**13.8**	**11.5**	**5.3**
Female householder	100.0	22.1	11.0	8.2	2.9
Living alone	100.0	20.4	9.2	8.6	2.6
Male householder	100.0	39.4	16.6	15.0	7.8
Living alone	100.0	39.0	15.7	15.5	7.9

Note: Asians include those who identify themselves as being of the race alone and those who identify themselves as being of the race in combination with other races.
Source: Bureau of the Census, 2008 Current Population Survey, Annual Social and Economic Supplement, Internet site http:// www.census.gov/hhes/www/macro/032008/hhinc/new02_000.htm; calculations by New Strategist

Table 7.4 Households Headed by People Aged 30 to 44 by Household Type, 2008: Black Households

(number and percent distribution of total households headed by blacks and households headed by blacks aged 30 to 44, by household type, 2008; numbers in thousands)

	total	aged 30 to 44			
		total	30 to 34	35 to 39	40 to 44
TOTAL BLACK HOUSEHOLDS	14,976	4,623	1,421	1,621	1,581
Family households	9,503	3,405	1,025	1,203	1,177
Married couples	4,461	1,496	370	549	577
Female householder, no spouse present	4,218	1,637	559	567	511
Male householder, no spouse present	824	272	96	87	89
Nonfamily households	5,474	1,218	396	418	404
Female householder	3,064	545	158	200	187
Living alone	2,748	474	136	175	163
Male householder	2,410	671	238	217	216
Living alone	2,012	553	189	191	173
Percent distribution by age					
TOTAL BLACK HOUSEHOLDS	100.0%	100.0%	100.0%	100.0%	100.0%
Family households	63.5	73.7	72.1	74.2	74.4
Married couples	29.8	32.4	26.0	33.9	36.5
Female householder, no spouse present	28.2	35.4	39.3	35.0	32.3
Male householder, no spouse present	5.5	5.9	6.8	5.4	5.6
Nonfamily households	36.6	26.3	27.9	25.8	25.6
Female householder	20.5	11.8	11.1	12.3	11.8
Living alone	18.3	10.3	9.6	10.8	10.3
Male householder	16.1	14.5	16.7	13.4	13.7
Living alone	13.4	12.0	13.3	11.8	10.9
Percent distribution by type					
TOTAL BLACK HOUSEHOLDS	100.0%	30.9%	9.5%	10.8%	10.6%
Family households	100.0	35.8	10.8	12.7	12.4
Married couples	100.0	33.5	8.3	12.3	12.9
Female householder, no spouse present	100.0	38.8	13.3	13.4	12.1
Male householder, no spouse present	100.0	33.0	11.7	10.6	10.8
Nonfamily households	100.0	22.3	7.2	7.6	7.4
Female householder	100.0	17.8	5.2	6.5	6.1
Living alone	100.0	17.2	4.9	6.4	5.9
Male householder	100.0	27.8	9.9	9.0	9.0
Living alone	100.0	27.5	9.4	9.5	8.6

Note: Blacks include those who identify themselves as being of the race alone and those who identify themselves as being of the race in combination with other races.
Source: Bureau of the Census, 2008 Current Population Survey, Annual Social and Economic Supplement, Internet site http:// www.census.gov/hhes/www/macro/032008/hhinc/new02_000.htm; calculations by New Strategist

Table 7.5 Households Headed by People Aged 30 to 44 by Household Type, 2008: Hispanic Households

(number and percent distribution of total households headed by Hispanics and households headed by Hispanics aged 30 to 44, by household type, 2008; numbers in thousands)

		aged 30 to 44			
	total	total	30 to 34	35 to 39	40 to 44
TOTAL HISPANIC HOUSEHOLDS	**13,339**	**5,185**	**1,800**	**1,789**	**1,596**
Family households	**10,394**	**4,384**	**1,510**	**1,526**	**1,347**
Married couples	6,888	3,013	1,024	1,091	898
Female householder, no spouse present	2,522	1,035	329	341	365
Male householder, no spouse present	983	335	156	94	85
Nonfamily households	**2,945**	**800**	**290**	**262**	**248**
Female householder	1,291	212	78	56	78
Living alone	1,065	165	55	44	66
Male householder	1,654	589	212	206	171
Living alone	1,138	385	143	131	111
Percent distribution by age					
TOTAL HISPANIC HOUSEHOLDS	**100.0%**	**100.0%**	**100.0%**	**100.0%**	**100.0%**
Family households	**77.9**	**84.6**	**83.9**	**85.3**	**84.4**
Married couples	51.6	58.1	56.9	61.0	56.3
Female householder, no spouse present	18.9	20.0	18.3	19.1	22.9
Male householder, no spouse present	7.4	6.5	8.7	5.3	5.3
Nonfamily households	**22.1**	**15.4**	**16.1**	**14.6**	**15.5**
Female householder	9.7	4.1	4.3	3.1	4.9
Living alone	8.0	3.2	3.1	2.5	4.1
Male householder	12.4	11.4	11.8	11.5	10.7
Living alone	8.5	7.4	7.9	7.3	7.0
Percent distribution by type					
TOTAL HISPANIC HOUSEHOLDS	**100.0%**	**38.9%**	**13.5%**	**13.4%**	**12.0%**
Family households	**100.0**	**42.2**	**14.5**	**14.7**	**13.0**
Married couples	100.0	43.7	14.9	15.8	13.0
Female householder, no spouse present	100.0	41.0	13.0	13.5	14.5
Male householder, no spouse present	100.0	34.1	15.9	9.6	8.6
Nonfamily households	**100.0**	**27.2**	**9.8**	**8.9**	**8.4**
Female householder	100.0	16.4	6.0	4.3	6.0
Living alone	100.0	15.5	5.2	4.1	6.2
Male householder	100.0	35.6	12.8	12.5	10.3
Living alone	100.0	33.8	12.6	11.5	9.8

Source: Bureau of the Census, 2008 Current Population Survey, Annual Social and Economic Supplement, Internet site http:// www.census.gov/hhes/www/macro/032008/hhinc/new02_000.htm; calculations by New Strategist

Table 7.6 Households Headed by People Aged 30 to 44 by Household Type, 2008: Non-Hispanic White Households

(number and percent distribution of total households headed by non-Hispanic whites and households headed by non-Hispanic whites aged 30 to 44, by household type, 2008; numbers in thousands)

	total	aged 30 to 44			
		total	30 to 34	35 to 39	40 to 44
TOTAL NON-HISPANIC WHITE HOUSEHOLDS	**82,765**	**20,466**	**5,937**	**6,786**	**7,743**
Family households	**53,902**	**15,640**	**4,360**	**5,337**	**5,943**
Married couples	43,739	12,427	3,431	4,327	4,669
Female householder, no spouse present	7,171	2,323	665	716	942
Male householder, no spouse present	2,991	889	264	294	331
Nonfamily households	**28,863**	**4,826**	**1,577**	**1,449**	**1,800**
Female householder	15,844	1,756	539	534	683
Living alone	13,771	1,352	406	404	542
Male householder	13,019	3,069	1,038	914	1,117
Living alone	10,151	2,303	716	681	906
Percent distribution by age					
TOTAL NON-HISPANIC WHITE HOUSEHOLDS	**100.0%**	**100.0%**	**100.0%**	**100.0%**	**100.0%**
Family households	**65.1**	**76.4**	**73.4**	**78.6**	**76.8**
Married couples	52.8	60.7	57.8	63.8	60.3
Female householder, no spouse present	8.7	11.4	11.2	10.6	12.2
Male householder, no spouse present	3.6	4.3	4.4	4.3	4.3
Nonfamily households	**34.9**	**23.6**	**26.6**	**21.4**	**23.2**
Female householder	19.1	8.6	9.1	7.9	8.8
Living alone	16.6	6.6	6.8	6.0	7.0
Male householder	15.7	15.0	17.5	13.5	14.4
Living alone	12.3	11.3	12.1	10.0	11.7
Percent distribution by type					
TOTAL NON-HISPANIC WHITE HOUSEHOLDS	**100.0%**	**24.7%**	**7.2%**	**8.2%**	**9.4%**
Family households	**100.0**	**29.0**	**8.1**	**9.9**	**11.0**
Married couples	100.0	28.4	7.8	9.9	10.7
Female householder, no spouse present	100.0	32.4	9.3	10.0	13.1
Male householder, no spouse present	100.0	29.7	8.8	9.8	11.1
Nonfamily households	**100.0**	**16.7**	**5.5**	**5.0**	**6.2**
Female householder	100.0	11.1	3.4	3.4	4.3
Living alone	100.0	9.8	2.9	2.9	3.9
Male householder	100.0	23.6	8.0	7.0	8.6
Living alone	100.0	22.7	7.1	6.7	8.9

Note: Non-Hispanic whites are those who identify themselves as being white alone and not Hispanic.
Source: Bureau of the Census, 2008 Current Population Survey, Annual Social and Economic Supplement, Internet site http://www.census.gov/hhes/www/macro/032008/hhinc/new02_000.htm; calculations by New Strategist

Gen X Households Are Crowded

Household size peaks in the 35-to-39 age group.

The average American household was home to 2.56 people in 2008. Household size peaks among householders aged 35 to 39, at 3.31 people. As householders age into their forties and fifties, the nest empties. Average household size falls below two in the 65-to-74 age group.

Householders aged 30 to 44 average more than one child per household, the figure peaking at 1.43 children in households headed by 35-to-39-year-olds. As people reach their late forties, the nest empties, and the average number of children per household falls below one.

■ The nest may empty more slowly for Gen Xers if the economic downturn is prolonged.

The nest is crowded for householders in their thirties

(average household size by age of householder, 2008)

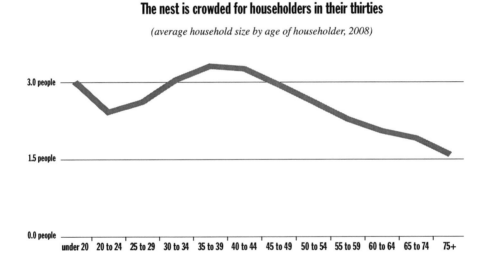

Table 7.7 Average Size of Household by Age of Householder, 2008

(number of households, average number of people per household, and average number of people under age 18 per household, by age of householder, 2008; number of households in thousands)

	number	average number of people	average number of people under age 18
Total households	**116,783**	**2.56**	**0.64**
Under age 20	862	3.01	0.84
Aged 20 to 24	5,691	2.42	0.51
Aged 25 to 29	9,400	2.62	0.80
Aged 30 to 34	9,825	3.05	1.25
Aged 35 to 39	10,900	3.31	1.43
Aged 40 to 44	11,548	3.26	1.25
Aged 45 to 49	12,685	2.95	0.81
Aged 50 to 54	11,851	2.62	0.44
Aged 55 to 59	10,813	2.28	0.23
Aged 60 to 64	9,096	2.05	0.14
Aged 65 to 74	12,284	1.91	0.09
Aged 75 or older	11,829	1.59	0.04

Source: Bureau of the Census, Current Population Survey Annual Social and Economic Supplement, America's Families and Living Arrangements: 2008, detailed tables, Internet site http://www.census.gov/population/www/socdemo/hh-fam/cps2008.html

The Majority of Gen Xers Have Children at Home

Female-headed families are most likely to have children.

More than half the households headed by people aged 30 to 44 (Generation X was aged 32 to 43 in 2008) include children under age 18. The proportion of households with children does not vary much within the age group.

Seventy-nine percent of married couples aged 30 to 44 have children at home. Families headed by women in the age group are even more likely to have children, at 87 percent. Among families headed by men, a smaller 67 percent include children under age 18.

■ The spending of householders aged 30 to 44 is determined by children's wants and needs.

Male-headed families are least likely to include children, but most do

(percent of households headed by people aged 30 to 44 with children under age 18 at home, by household type, 2008)

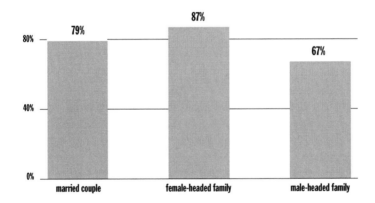

Table 7.8 Households by Type, Age of Householder, and Presence of Children, 2008: Total Households

(total number of households and number and percent with own children under age 18 at home, by household type and age of householder, 2008; numbers in thousands)

		with own children under age 18	
	total	number	percent
TOTAL HOUSEHOLDS	116,783	35,709	30.6%
Under age 30	15,954	5,801	36.4
Aged 30 to 44	32,273	20,015	62.0
Aged 30 to 34	9,825	5,820	59.2
Aged 35 to 39	10,900	7,248	66.5
Aged 40 to 44	11,548	6,947	60.2
Aged 45 or older	68,558	9,894	14.4
Married couples	58,370	25,173	43.1
Under age 30	4,977	3,161	63.5
Aged 30 to 44	18,229	14,458	79.3
Aged 30 to 34	5,240	4,005	76.4
Aged 35 to 39	6,406	5,326	83.1
Aged 40 to 44	6,583	5,127	77.9
Aged 45 or older	35,164	7,553	21.5
Female family householder, no spouse present	14,404	8,374	58.1
Under age 30	2,784	2,167	77.8
Aged 30 to 44	5,150	4,487	87.1
Aged 30 to 34	1,599	1,480	92.6
Aged 35 to 39	1,684	1,546	91.8
Aged 40 to 44	1,867	1,461	78.3
Aged 45 or older	6,471	1,720	26.6
Male family householder, no spouse present	5,100	2,162	42.4
Under age 30	1,467	473	32.2
Aged 30 to 44	1,607	1,070	66.6
Aged 30 to 34	546	334	61.2
Aged 35 to 39	515	377	73.2
Aged 40 to 44	546	359	65.8
Aged 45 or older	2,027	620	30.6

Source: Bureau of the Census, Current Population Survey Annual Social and Economic Supplement, America's Families and Living Arrangements: 2008, detailed tables, Internet site http://www.census.gov/population/www/socdemo/hh-fam/cps2008 .html; calculations by New Strategist

Hispanic Gen X Households Are Most Likely to include Children

More than 70 percent have children at home.

Seventy-two percent of Hispanic households headed by 30-to-44-year-olds include children under age 18. The proportion is a smaller 59 to 60 percent for Asian, black, and non-Hispanic white households in the age group.

Regardless of race or Hispanic origin, the majority of households headed by married couples aged 30 to 44 include children under age 18, with the proportion peaking at 86 percent among Hispanics. Most Gen X families headed by women also include children, with the proportion peaking at 89 percent among Hispanics.

■ Children dominate Gen X households, regardless of race or Hispanic origin.

Most Gen X households include children

(percent of households headed by people aged 30 to 44 with children under age 18 at home, by race and Hispanic origin, 2008)

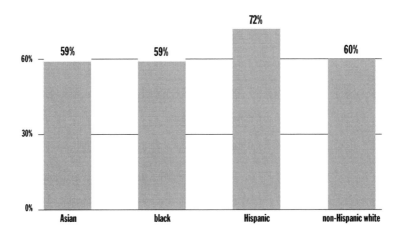

Table 7.9 Households by Type, Age of Householder, and Presence of Children, 2008: Asian Households

(total number of Asian households and number and percent with own children under age 18 at home, by household type and age of householder, 2008; numbers in thousands)

	total	with own children under age 18	
		number	percent
TOTAL ASIAN HOUSEHOLDS	**4,715**	**1,743**	**37.0%**
Under age 30	696	123	17.7
Aged 30 to 44	1,768	1,038	58.7
Aged 30 to 34	620	297	47.9
Aged 35 to 39	628	374	59.6
Aged 40 to 44	520	367	70.6
Aged 45 or older	2,252	581	25.8
Married couples	**2,757**	**1,482**	**53.8**
Under age 30	179	78	43.6
Aged 30 to 44	1,129	883	78.2
Aged 30 to 34	368	257	69.8
Aged 35 to 39	395	316	80.0
Aged 40 to 44	366	310	84.7
Aged 45 or older	1,449	519	35.8
Female family householder, no spouse present	**452**	**202**	**44.7**
Under age 30	96	39	40.6
Aged 30 to 44	160	117	73.1
Aged 30 to 34	50	35	70.0
Aged 35 to 39	57	46	80.7
Aged 40 to 44	53	36	67.9
Aged 45 or older	196	48	24.5
Male family householder, no spouse present	**242**	**60**	**24.8**
Under age 30	71	7	9.9
Aged 30 to 44	97	38	39.2
Aged 30 to 34	29	5	17.2
Aged 35 to 39	33	12	36.4
Aged 40 to 44	35	21	60.0
Aged 45 or older	73	15	20.5

Note: Asians include those who identify themselves as being of the race alone and those who identify themselves as being of the race in combination with other races.
Source: Bureau of the Census, Current Population Survey Annual Social and Economic Supplement, America's Families and Living Arrangements: 2008, detailed tables, Internet site http://www.census.gov/population/www/socdemo/hh-fam/cps2008 .html; calculations by New Strategist

Table 7.10 Households by Type, Age of Householder, and Presence of Children, 2008: Black Households

(total number of black households and number and percent with own children under age 18 at home, by household type and age of householder, 2008; numbers in thousands)

	total	with own children under age 18	
		number	percent
TOTAL BLACK HOUSEHOLDS	**14,976**	**5,078**	**33.9%**
Under age 30	2,518	1,158	46.0
Aged 30 to 44	4,623	2,743	59.3
Aged 30 to 34	1,421	882	62.1
Aged 35 to 39	1,621	1,014	62.6
Aged 40 to 44	1,581	847	53.6
Aged 45 or older	7,835	1,178	15.0
Married couples	**4,461**	**2,070**	**46.4**
Under age 30	358	246	68.7
Aged 30 to 44	1,496	1,161	77.6
Aged 30 to 34	370	298	80.5
Aged 35 to 39	549	446	81.2
Aged 40 to 44	577	417	72.3
Aged 45 or older	2,607	664	25.5
Female family householder, no spouse present	**4,218**	**2694**	**63.9**
Under age 30	971	840	86.5
Aged 30 to 44	1,637	1420	86.7
Aged 30 to 34	559	530	94.8
Aged 35 to 39	567	513	90.5
Aged 40 to 44	511	377	73.8
Aged 45 or older	1,609	434	27.0
Male family householder, no spouse present	**824**	**314**	**38.1**
Under age 30	250	72	28.8
Aged 30 to 44	272	162	59.6
Aged 30 to 34	96	54	56.3
Aged 35 to 39	87	55	63.2
Aged 40 to 44	89	53	59.6
Aged 45 or older	303	79	26.1

Note: Blacks include those who identify themselves as being of the race alone and those who identify themselves as being of the race in combination with other races.
Source: Bureau of the Census, Current Population Survey Annual Social and Economic Supplement, America's Families and Living Arrangements: 2008, detailed tables, Internet site http://www.census.gov/population/www/socdemo/hh-fam/cps2008 .html; calculations by New Strategist

Table 7.11 Households by Type, Age of Householder, and Presence of Children, 2008: Hispanic Households

(total number of Hispanic households and number and percent with own children under age 18 at home, by household type and age of householder, 2008; numbers in thousands)

	total	with own children under age 18	
		number	percent
TOTAL HISPANIC HOUSEHOLDS	**13,339**	**6,431**	**48.2%**
Under age 30	2,783	1,425	51.2
Aged 30 to 44	5,185	3,719	71.7
Aged 30 to 34	1,800	1,272	70.7
Aged 35 to 39	1,789	1,354	75.7
Aged 40 to 44	1,596	1,093	68.5
Aged 45 or older	5,371	1,288	24.0
Married couples	**6,888**	**4,425**	**64.2**
Under age 30	1,101	864	78.5
Aged 30 to 44	3,013	2,604	86.4
Aged 30 to 34	1,024	874	85.4
Aged 35 to 39	1,091	981	89.9
Aged 40 to 44	898	749	83.4
Aged 45 or older	2,775	959	34.6
Female family householder, no spouse present	**2,522**	**1,642**	**65.1**
Under age 30	616	454	73.7
Aged 30 to 44	1,035	924	89.3
Aged 30 to 34	329	314	95.4
Aged 35 to 39	341	317	93.0
Aged 40 to 44	365	293	80.3
Aged 45 or older	872	265	30.4
Male family householder, no spouse present	**983**	**365**	**37.1**
Under age 30	416	108	26.0
Aged 30 to 44	335	193	57.6
Aged 30 to 34	156	85	54.5
Aged 35 to 39	94	57	60.6
Aged 40 to 44	85	51	60.0
Aged 45 or older	231	64	27.7

Source: Bureau of the Census, Current Population Survey Annual Social and Economic Supplement, America's Families and Living Arrangements: 2008, detailed tables, Internet site http://www.census.gov/population/www/socdemo/hh-fam/cps2008 .html; calculations by New Strategist

Table 7.12 Households by Type, Age of Householder, and Presence of Children, 2008: Non-Hispanic White Households

(total number of non-Hispanic white households and number and percent with own children under age 18 at home, by household type and age of householder, 2008; numbers in thousands)

	total	with own children under age 18	
		number	percent
TOTAL NON-HISPANIC WHITE HOUSEHOLDS	**82,765**	**22,221**	**26.8%**
Under age 30	9,860	3,066	31.1
Aged 30 to 44	20,466	12,377	60.5
Aged 30 to 34	5,937	3,329	56.1
Aged 35 to 39	6,786	4,463	65.8
Aged 40 to 44	7,743	4,585	59.2
Aged 45 or older	52,440	6,778	12.9
Married couples	**43,739**	**16,998**	**38.9**
Under age 30	3,301	1,954	59.2
Aged 30 to 44	12,427	9,678	77.9
Aged 30 to 34	3,431	2,535	73.9
Aged 35 to 39	4,327	3,546	82.0
Aged 40 to 44	4,669	3,597	77.0
Aged 45 or older	28,011	5,366	19.2
Female family householder, no spouse present	**7,171**	**3,830**	**53.4**
Under age 30	1,094	834	76.2
Aged 30 to 44	2,323	2,034	87.6
Aged 30 to 34	665	609	91.6
Aged 35 to 39	716	669	93.4
Aged 40 to 44	942	756	80.3
Aged 45 or older	3,753	962	25.6
Male family householder, no spouse present	**2,991**	**1,393**	**46.6**
Under age 30	719	278	38.7
Aged 30 to 44	889	664	74.7
Aged 30 to 34	264	185	70.1
Aged 35 to 39	294	247	84.0
Aged 40 to 44	331	232	70.1
Aged 45 or older	1,382	450	32.6

Note: Non-Hispanic whites are those who identify themselves as being white alone and not Hispanic.
Source: Bureau of the Census, Current Population Survey Annual Social and Economic Supplement, America's Families and Living Arrangements: 2008, detailed tables, Internet site http://www.census.gov/population/www/socdemo/hh-fam/cps2008 .html; calculations by New Strategist

Many Households Headed by Gen Xers include Preschoolers

Gen Xers head half of all households with infants.

During their twenties and early thirties, most people become parents. Among householders under age 30, only 36 percent have children under age 18 at home. The proportion rises to the 59 percent majority in the 30-to-34 age group.

Twenty-nine percent of householders ranging in age from 30 to 44 have preschoolers (children under age 6) at home. This age group accounts for the 60 percent majority of all households with preschoolers. Nine percent of householders aged 30 to 44 have teenagers (aged 12 to 17) in their home, although the figure is a much larger 38 percent among householders aged 40 to 44.

■ As people have children, their priorities shift from pursuing their own wants and needs to meeting the needs of their children.

Children are the norm for householders aged 30 to 44

(percent of households headed by people aged 30 to 44 with children at home, by age of child, 2008)

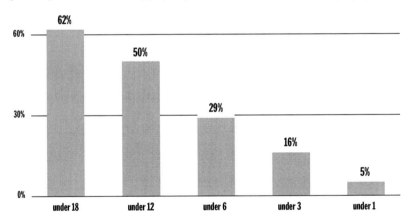

Table 7.13 Households by Presence and Age of Children and Age of Householder, 2008

(number and percent distribution of households by presence and age of own children at home, by age of children and age of householder, 2008; numbers in thousands)

	total	under 30	aged 30 to 44 total	30 to 34	35 to 39	40 to 44	45 or older
Total households	**116,783**	**15,954**	**32,273**	**9,825**	**10,900**	**11,548**	**68,558**
With children of any age	46,995	5,802	20,914	5,841	7,370	7,703	20,278
Under age 25	41,647	5,802	20,868	5,841	7,370	7,657	14,976
Under age 18	35,709	5,801	20,015	5,820	7,248	6,947	9,894
Under age 12	26,125	5,755	16,264	5,496	6,054	4,714	4,106
Under age 6	15,733	5,136	9,429	3,948	3,633	1,848	1,169
Under age 3	9,192	3,721	5,027	2,505	1,806	716	444
Under age 1	3,401	1,557	1,713	918	600	195	131
Aged 12 to 17	16,907	260	2,763	1,486	3,206	4,377	7,576

PERCENT DISTRIBUTION BY AGE OF CHILD

Total households	**100.0%**	**100.0%**	**100.0%**	**100.0%**	**100.0%**	**100.0%**	**100.0%**
With children of any age	40.2	36.4	64.8	59.5	67.6	66.7	29.6
Under age 25	35.7	36.4	64.7	59.5	67.6	66.3	21.8
Under age 18	30.6	36.4	62.0	59.2	66.5	60.2	14.4
Under age 12	22.4	36.1	50.4	55.9	55.5	40.8	6.0
Under age 6	13.5	32.2	29.2	40.2	33.3	16.0	1.7
Under age 3	7.9	23.3	15.6	25.5	16.6	6.2	0.6
Under age 1	2.9	9.8	5.3	9.3	5.5	1.7	0.2
Aged 12 to 17	14.5	1.6	8.6	15.1	29.4	37.9	11.1

PERCENT DISTRIBUTION BY AGE OF HOUSEHOLDER

Total households	**100.0%**	**13.7%**	**27.6%**	**8.4%**	**9.3%**	**9.9%**	**58.7%**
With children of any age	100.0	12.3	44.5	12.4	15.7	16.4	43.1
Under age 25	100.0	13.9	50.1	14.0	17.7	18.4	36.0
Under age 18	100.0	16.2	56.1	16.3	20.3	19.5	27.7
Under age 12	100.0	22.0	62.3	21.0	23.2	18.0	15.7
Under age 6	100.0	32.6	59.9	25.1	23.1	11.7	7.4
Under age 3	100.0	40.5	54.7	27.3	19.6	7.8	4.8
Under age 1	100.0	45.8	50.4	27.0	17.6	5.7	3.9
Aged 12 to 17	100.0	1.5	16.3	8.8	19.0	25.9	44.8

Source: Bureau of the Census, Current Population Survey Annual Social and Economic Supplement, America's Families and Living Arrangements: 2008, detailed tables, Internet site http://www.census.gov/population/www/socdemo/hh-fam/cps2008 .html; calculations by New Strategist

Two-Child Families Are Most Common

Many Gen X couples have more than two children, however.

Many Americans consider two children to be the ideal number. But many Gen X couples have three or more.

Among all married couples aged 30 to 44 with children at home, 44 percent have two children under age 18. Another 28 percent have only one child at home, and an equal 28 percent share has three or more children living with them.

Among both female- and male-headed families with children in the Gen X age group, one child is the most common number. Forty-two percent of the female-headed families have only one child under age 18. Among their male counterparts, the figure is an even higher 53 percent.

■ The growing Hispanic population, with its preference for larger families, is boosting the proportion of couples with three or more children.

Most Gen X couples have one or two children at home

(percent distribution of married couples aged 30 to 44 with children under age 18 at home, by number of children, 2008)

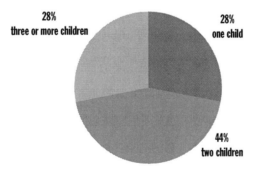

28%
three or more children

28%
one child

44%
two children

Table 7.14 Married Couples with Children by Number of Children and Age of Householder, 2008

(number and percent distribution of married couples with own children under age 18 at home, by number of children and age of householder, 2008; numbers in thousands)

	total	under 30	aged 30 to 44 total	30 to 34	35 to 39	40 to 44	45 or older
Married couples with children under 18	**25,173**	**3,161**	**14,458**	**4,005**	**5,326**	**5,127**	**7,553**
One	9,733	1,526	4,100	1,255	1,334	1,511	4,106
Two	9,886	1,076	6,342	1,673	2,406	2,263	2,467
Three	3,953	392	2,863	762	1,123	978	698
Four or more	1,602	168	1,151	315	462	374	281

PERCENT DISTRIBUTION BY NUMBER OF CHILDREN

	total	under 30	aged 30 to 44 total	30 to 34	35 to 39	40 to 44	45 or older
Married couples with children under 18	**100.0%**	**100.0%**	**100.0%**	**100.0%**	**100.0%**	**100.0%**	**100.0%**
One	38.7	48.3	28.4	31.3	25.0	29.5	54.4
Two	39.3	34.0	43.9	41.8	45.2	44.1	32.7
Three	15.7	12.4	19.8	19.0	21.1	19.1	9.2
Four or more	6.4	5.3	8.0	7.9	8.7	7.3	3.7

Source: Bureau of the Census, Current Population Survey Annual Social and Economic Supplement, America's Families and Living Arrangements: 2008, detailed tables, Internet site http://www.census.gov/population/www/socdemo/hh-fam/cps2008 .html; calculations by New Strategist

Table 7.15 Female-headed Families with Children by Number of Children and Age of Householder, 2008

(number and percent distribution of female-headed families with own children under age 18 at home, by number of children and age of householder, 2008; numbers in thousands)

	total	under 30	aged 30 to 44 total	30 to 34	35 to 39	40 to 44	45 or older
Female-headed families with children under 18	**8,374**	**2,167**	**4,487**	**1,480**	**1,546**	**1,461**	**1,720**
One	4,104	1,066	1,883	511	614	758	1,155
Two	2,675	681	1,566	488	549	529	428
Three	1,107	290	701	320	258	123	115
Four or more	487	130	336	161	124	51	21

PERCENT DISTRIBUTION

	total	under 30	aged 30 to 44 total	30 to 34	35 to 39	40 to 44	45 or older
Female-headed families with children under 18	**100.0%**	**100.0%**	**100.0%**	**100.0%**	**100.0%**	**100.0%**	**100.0%**
One	49.0	49.2	42.0	34.5	39.7	51.9	67.2
Two	31.9	31.4	34.9	33.0	35.5	36.2	24.9
Three	13.2	13.4	15.6	21.6	16.7	8.4	6.7
Four or more	5.8	6.0	7.5	10.9	8.0	3.5	1.2

Source: Bureau of the Census, Current Population Survey Annual Social and Economic Supplement, America's Families and Living Arrangements: 2008, detailed tables, Internet site http://www.census.gov/population/www/socdemo/hh-fam/cps2008 .html; calculations by New Strategist

Table 7.16 Male-headed Families with Children by Number of Children and Age of Householder, 2008

(number and percent distribution of male-headed families with own children under age 18 at home, by number of children and age of householder, 2008; numbers in thousands)

	total	under 30	aged 30 to 44			40 to 44	45 or older
			total	30 to 34	35 to 39		
Male-headed families with children under 18	**2,162**	**473**	**1,070**	**334**	**377**	**359**	**620**
One	1,323	327	571	172	198	201	424
Two	597	126	331	108	121	102	140
Three	174	18	115	41	34	40	40
Four or more	68	3	51	13	23	15	14
PERCENT DISTRIBUTION							
Male-headed families with children under 18	**100.0%**	**100.0%**	**100.0%**	**100.0%**	**100.0%**	**100.0%**	**100.0%**
One	61.2	69.1	53.4	51.5	52.5	56.0	68.4
Two	27.6	26.6	30.9	32.3	32.1	28.4	22.6
Three	8.0	3.8	10.7	12.3	9.0	11.1	6.5
Four or more	3.1	0.6	4.8	3.9	6.1	4.2	2.3

Source: Bureau of the Census, Current Population Survey Annual Social and Economic Supplement, America's Families and Living Arrangements: 2008, detailed tables, Internet site http://www.census.gov/population/www/socdemo/hh-fam/cps2008 .html; calculations by New Strategist

Gen Xers Account for Few People Who Live Alone

The percentage of people who live alone bottoms out in the 35-to-39 age group.

Among the 32 million Americans who live alone, Gen Xers (roughly aged 30 to 44 in 2008) accounted for only 17 percent. Among men who live alone, Gen Xers are a larger 25 percent of the total. Among women who live alone, Gen Xers are a smaller 12 percent.

Gen X men are more likely than Gen X women to live alone. Among men aged 30 to 44, 11 percent live by themselves. The figure is only 7 percent for women in the age group. As they age, the pattern will reverse, and living alone will become more common for Gen X women than Gen X men.

■ Because of the higher mortality rate of men, a growing share of Gen X women will become widows and live by themselves in the decades ahead.

Gen X men are more likely than Gen X women to live alone

(percent of people aged 30 to 44 who live alone, by age and sex, 2008)

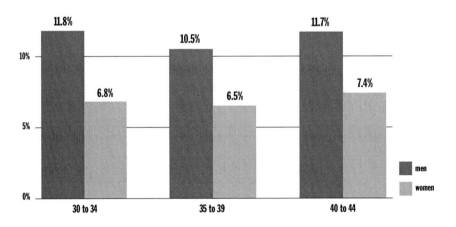

Table 7.17 People Who Live Alone by Age, 2008

(number of people aged 15 or older and number, percent, and percent distribution of people who live alone by sex and age, 2008; numbers in thousands)

		living alone		
	total	number	percent	percent distribution
Total people	**238,148**	**32,167**	**13.5%**	**100.0%**
Under age 30	62,901	3,816	6.1	11.9
Aged 30 to 44	61,221	5,564	9.1	17.3
Aged 30 to 34	19,089	1,764	9.2	5.5
Aged 35 to 39	20,733	1,760	8.5	5.5
Aged 40 to 44	21,399	2,040	9.5	6.3
Aged 45 or older	114,027	22,788	20.0	70.8
Total men	**115,678**	**13,870**	**12.0**	**100.0**
Under age 30	31,929	2,089	6.5	15.1
Aged 30 to 44	30,369	3,436	11.3	24.8
Aged 30 to 34	9,489	1,116	11.8	8.0
Aged 35 to 39	10,291	1,081	10.5	7.8
Aged 40 to 44	10,589	1,239	11.7	8.9
Aged 45 or older	53,380	8,344	15.6	60.2
Total women	**122,470**	**18,297**	**14.9**	**100.0**
Under age 30	30,972	1,727	5.6	9.4
Aged 30 to 44	30,852	2,128	6.9	11.6
Aged 30 to 34	9,600	648	6.8	3.5
Aged 35 to 39	10,442	679	6.5	3.7
Aged 40 to 44	10,810	801	7.4	4.4
Aged 45 or older	60,647	14,444	23.8	78.9

Source: Bureau of the Census, 2008 Current Population Survey, Annual Social and Economic Supplement, Internet sites http://www.census.gov/hhes/www/macro/032008/perinc/new01_000.htm and http://www.census.gov/hhes/www/macro/032008/hhinc/new02_000.htm; calculations by New Strategist

Most Gen Xers Are Married

Many in the 40-to-44 age group are divorced, however.

Overall, 60 percent of men aged 30 to 44 were married and living with their spouse in 2008 (Gen Xers were aged 32 to 43 in that year). Among their female counterparts, an even larger 64 percent were married. A substantial 26 percent of Gen X men are not yet married. Among Gen X women, a smaller 18 percent have not married yet.

Divorce becomes a significant factor in the Gen X age group. Twelve percent of men aged 40 to 44 are currently divorced. Among women, 11 percent in the 35-to-39 age group and 15 percent in the 40-to-44 age group are currently divorced.

■ As Gen Xers age, a growing share of women will become widows.

Divorce climbs in the Gen X age group

(percent of people aged 30 to 44 who are currently divorced, by sex, 2008)

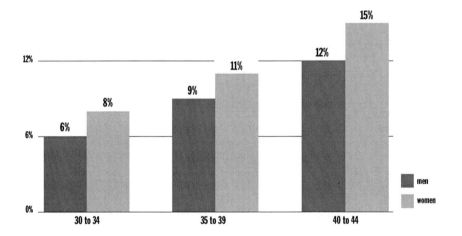

Table 7.18 Marital Status by Sex and Age, 2008: Total People

(number and percent distribution of people aged 15 or older by sex, age, and current marital status, 2008; numbers in thousands)

	total	never married	married spouse present	married spouse absent	separated	divorced	widowed
NUMBER							
Total men	**115,599**	**38,685**	**60,129**	**1,944**	**2,144**	**9,782**	**2,916**
Under age 30	31,905	25,986	4,738	371	375	407	27
Aged 30 to 44	30,339	7,745	18,177	793	729	2,802	95
Aged 30 to 34	9,471	3,270	5,108	243	230	603	17
Aged 35 to 39	10,283	2,387	6,474	242	222	935	24
Aged 40 to 44	10,585	2,088	6,595	308	277	1,264	54
Aged 45 or older	53,356	4,954	37,214	780	1,040	6,575	2,794
Total women	**122,394**	**32,794**	**60,129**	**1,470**	**3,039**	**13,564**	**11,398**
Under age 30	30,937	22,839	6,520	299	563	646	73
Aged 30 to 44	30,840	5,641	19,687	444	1,138	3,613	316
Aged 30 to 34	9,596	2,504	5,776	143	336	780	57
Aged 35 to 39	10,438	1,675	6,910	166	400	1,193	94
Aged 40 to 44	10,806	1,462	7,001	135	402	1,640	165
Aged 45 or older	60,617	4,315	33,923	728	1,338	9,305	11,008
PERCENT DISTRIBUTION							
Total men	**100.0%**	**33.5%**	**52.0%**	**1.7%**	**1.9%**	**8.5%**	**2.5%**
Under age 30	100.0	81.4	14.9	1.2	1.2	1.3	0.1
Aged 30 to 44	100.0	25.5	59.9	2.6	2.4	9.2	0.3
Aged 30 to 34	100.0	34.5	53.9	2.6	2.4	6.4	0.2
Aged 35 to 39	100.0	23.2	63.0	2.4	2.2	9.1	0.2
Aged 40 to 44	100.0	19.7	62.3	2.9	2.6	11.9	0.5
Aged 45 or older	100.0	9.3	69.7	1.5	1.9	12.3	5.2
Total women	**100.0**	**26.8**	**49.1**	**1.2**	**2.5**	**11.1**	**9.3**
Under age 30	100.0	73.8	21.1	1.0	1.8	2.1	0.2
Aged 30 to 44	100.0	18.3	63.8	1.4	3.7	11.7	1.0
Aged 30 to 34	100.0	26.1	60.2	1.5	3.5	8.1	0.6
Aged 35 to 39	100.0	16.0	66.2	1.6	3.8	11.4	0.9
Aged 40 to 44	100.0	13.5	64.8	1.2	3.7	15.2	1.5
Aged 45 or older	100.0	7.1	56.0	1.2	2.2	15.4	18.2

Source: Bureau of the Census, Current Population Survey Annual Social and Economic Supplement, America's Families and Living Arrangements: 2008, detailed tables, Internet site http://www.census.gov/population/www/socdemo/hh-fam/cps2008 .html; calculations by New Strategist

Black Gen Xers Are Least Likely to Be Married

The single outnumber the married among blacks aged 30 to 34.

The percentage of Asians, Hispanics, and non-Hispanic whites aged 30 to 44 who are currently married and living with their spouse ranges from 55 to 64 percent among men and from 63 to 74 percent among women. Blacks in the age group are far less likely to be currently married—only 36 percent of black women and 42 percent of black men are currently married. Forty percent have not yet married.

Asian Gen Xers are least likely to be currently divorced. Only 3 percent of Asian men aged 30 to 44 are currently divorced compared with 7 to 11 percent of Hispanic, non-Hispanic white, and black men in the age group. Among Asian women aged 30 to 44, only 5 percent are currently divorced compared with 9 to 13 percent of Hispanic, black, and non-Hispanic white women.

■ As the nation has become more diverse racially and ethnically, it has also become more diverse in its living arrangements.

Among 30-to-44-year-olds, Asian women are most likely to be married

(percent of people aged 30 to 44 who are currently married and living with their spouse, by race, Hispanic origin, and sex, 2008)

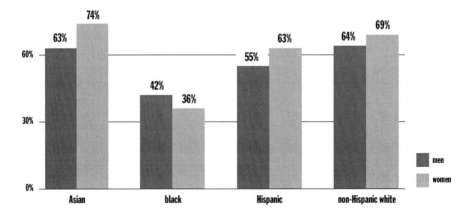

Table 7.19 Marital Status by Sex and Age, 2008: Asians

(number and percent distribution of Asians aged 15 or older by sex, age, and current marital status, 2008; numbers in thousands)

	total	never married	married spouse present	married spouse absent	separated	divorced	widowed
NUMBER							
Total Asian men	**5,408**	**1,922**	**2,968**	**202**	**79**	**155**	**83**
Under age 30	1,526	1,303	177	28	10	8	1
Aged 30 to 44	1785	465	1,122	97	36	62	4
Aged 30 to 34	594	210	340	33	7	4	1
Aged 35 to 39	645	180	406	27	8	24	–
Aged 40 to 44	546	75	376	37	21	34	3
Aged 45 or older	2,095	153	1,669	76	34	83	78
Total Asian women	**6,022**	**1,596**	**3,413**	**158**	**105**	**325**	**424**
Under age 30	1,563	1,136	348	36	24	16	4
Aged 30 to 44	1,941	311	1,441	52	29	97	12
Aged 30 to 34	665	159	457	14	7	23	5
Aged 35 to 39	687	91	513	24	9	44	6
Aged 40 to 44	589	61	471	14	13	30	1
Aged 45 or older	2,517	149	1,625	69	53	215	408
PERCENT DISTRIBUTION							
Total Asian men	**100.0%**	**35.5%**	**54.9%**	**3.7%**	**1.5%**	**2.9%**	**1.5%**
Under age 30	100.0	85.4	11.6	1.8	0.7	0.5	0.1
Aged 30 to 44	100.0	26.1	62.9	5.4	2.0	3.5	0.2
Aged 30 to 34	100.0	35.4	57.2	5.6	1.2	0.7	0.2
Aged 35 to 39	100.0	27.9	62.9	4.2	1.2	3.7	–
Aged 40 to 44	100.0	13.7	68.9	6.8	3.8	6.2	0.5
Aged 45 to or older	100.0	7.3	79.7	3.6	1.6	4.0	3.7
Total Asian women	**100.0**	**26.5**	**56.7**	**2.6**	**1.7**	**5.4**	**7.0**
Under age 30	100.0	72.7	22.3	2.3	1.5	1.0	0.3
Aged 30 to 44	100.0	16.0	74.2	2.7	1.5	5.0	0.6
Aged 30 to 34	100.0	23.9	68.7	2.1	1.1	3.5	0.8
Aged 35 to 39	100.0	13.2	74.7	3.5	1.3	6.4	0.9
Aged 40 to 44	100.0	10.4	80.0	2.4	2.2	5.1	0.2
Aged 45 to or older	100.0	5.9	64.6	2.7	2.1	8.5	16.2

Note: Asians include those who identify themselves as being of the race alone and those who identify themselves as being of the race in combination with other races. "–" means number is less than 500 or sample is too small to make a reliable estimate. Source: Bureau of the Census, Current Population Survey Annual Social and Economic Supplement, America's Families and Living Arrangements: 2008, detailed tables, Internet site http://www.census.gov/population/www/socdemo/hh-fam/cps2008 .html; calculations by New Strategist

Table 7.20 Marital Status by Sex and Age, 2008: Blacks

(number and percent distribution of blacks aged 15 or older by sex, age, and current marital status, 2008; numbers in thousands)

	total	never married	married spouse present	married spouse absent	separated	divorced	widowed
NUMBER							
Total black men	**13,360**	**6,412**	**4,636**	**241**	**517**	**1,219**	**335**
Under age 30	4,612	4,107	321	46	82	53	–
Aged 30 to 44	3,559	1,427	1,477	101	156	374	24
Aged 30 to 34	1,138	624	365	40	49	56	4
Aged 35 to 39	1,189	386	559	32	55	151	6
Aged 40 to 44	1,232	417	553	29	52	167	14
Aged 45 or older	5,188	878	2,837	95	279	792	311
Total black women	**16,094**	**7,136**	**4,439**	**261**	**820**	**2,034**	**1,404**
Under age 30	4,952	4,238	467	40	99	96	12
Aged 30 to 44	4,371	1,742	1,573	107	310	574	66
Aged 30 to 34	1,378	734	403	39	87	108	7
Aged 35 to 39	1,489	556	551	34	119	197	32
Aged 40 to 44	1,504	452	619	34	104	269	27
Aged 45 or older	6,773	1,156	2,400	114	411	1,365	1,326
PERCENT DISTRIBUTION							
Total black men	**100.0%**	**48.0%**	**34.7%**	**1.8%**	**3.9%**	**9.1%**	**2.5%**
Under age 30	100.0	89.1	7.0	1.0	1.8	1.1	–
Aged 30 to 44	100.0	40.1	41.5	2.8	4.4	10.5	0.7
Aged 30 to 34	100.0	54.8	32.1	3.5	4.3	4.9	0.4
Aged 35 to 39	100.0	32.5	47.0	2.7	4.6	12.7	0.5
Aged 40 to 44	100.0	33.8	44.9	2.4	4.2	13.6	1.1
Aged 45 to or older	100.0	16.9	54.7	1.8	5.4	15.3	6.0
Total black women	**100.0**	**44.3**	**27.6**	**1.6**	**5.1**	**12.6**	**8.7**
Under age 30	100.0	85.6	9.4	0.8	2.0	1.9	0.2
Aged 30 to 44	100.0	39.9	36.0	2.4	7.1	13.1	1.5
Aged 30 to 34	100.0	53.3	29.2	2.8	6.3	7.8	0.5
Aged 35 to 39	100.0	37.3	37.0	2.3	8.0	13.2	2.1
Aged 40 to 44	100.0	30.1	41.2	2.3	6.9	17.9	1.8
Aged 45 to or older	100.0	17.1	35.4	1.7	6.1	20.2	19.6

Note: Blacks include those who identify themselves as being of the race alone and those who identify themselves as being of the race in combination with other races. "–" means number is less than 500 or sample is too small to make a reliable estimate.
Source: Bureau of the Census, Current Population Survey Annual Social and Economic Supplement, America's Families and Living Arrangements: 2008, detailed tables, Internet site http://www.census.gov/population/www/socdemo/hh-fam/cps2008 .html; calculations by New Strategist

Table 7.21 Marital Status by Sex and Age, 2008: Hispanics

(number and percent distribution of Hispanics aged 15 or older by sex, age, and current marital status, 2008; numbers in thousands)

	total	never married	married spouse present	married spouse absent	separated	divorced	widowed
NUMBER							
Total Hispanic men	**16,832**	**6,955**	**7,445**	**820**	**438**	**945**	**228**
Under age 30	6,254	4,762	1,176	185	89	34	10
Aged 30 to 44	5,665	1,545	3,134	406	175	396	9
Aged 30 to 34	2,028	709	1,031	130	45	111	1
Aged 35 to 39	1,921	485	1,136	110	72	119	–
Aged 40 to 44	1,716	351	967	166	58	166	8
Aged 45 or older	4,913	648	3,136	229	175	515	208
Total Hispanic women	**15,845**	**5,066**	**7,557**	**288**	**709**	**1,385**	**839**
Under age 30	5,435	3,644	1,490	71	119	100	11
Aged 30 to 44	5,094	941	3,234	111	301	465	42
Aged 30 to 34	1,831	443	1,147	43	90	105	3
Aged 35 to 39	1,728	260	1,150	29	107	164	18
Aged 40 to 44	1,535	238	937	39	104	196	21
Aged 45 or older	5,316	482	2,833	106	289	819	786
PERCENT DISTRIBUTION							
Total Hispanic men	**100.0%**	**41.3%**	**44.2%**	**4.9%**	**2.6%**	**5.6%**	**1.4%**
Under age 30	100.0	76.1	18.8	3.0	1.4	0.5	0.2
Aged 30 to 44	100.0	27.3	55.3	7.2	3.1	7.0	0.2
Aged 30 to 34	100.0	35.0	50.8	6.4	2.2	5.5	0.0
Aged 35 to 39	100.0	25.2	59.1	5.7	3.7	6.2	–
Aged 40 to 44	100.0	20.5	56.4	9.7	3.4	9.7	0.5
Aged 45 to or older	100.0	13.2	63.8	4.7	3.6	10.5	4.2
Total Hispanic women	**100.0**	**32.0**	**47.7**	**1.8**	**4.5**	**8.7**	**5.3**
Under age 30	100.0	67.0	27.4	1.3	2.2	1.8	0.2
Aged 30 to 44	100.0	18.5	63.5	2.2	5.9	9.1	0.8
Aged 30 to 34	100.0	24.2	62.6	2.3	4.9	5.7	0.2
Aged 35 to 39	100.0	15.0	66.6	1.7	6.2	9.5	1.0
Aged 40 to 44	100.0	15.5	61.0	2.5	6.8	12.8	1.4
Aged 45 to or older	100.0	9.1	53.3	2.0	5.4	15.4	14.8

Note: "–" means number is less than 500 or sample is too small to make a reliable estimate.
Source: Bureau of the Census, Current Population Survey Annual Social and Economic Supplement, America's Families and Living Arrangements: 2008, detailed tables, Internet site http://www.census.gov/population/www/socdemo/hh-fam/cps2008 .html; calculations by New Strategist

Table 7.22 Marital Status by Sex and Age, 2008: Non-Hispanic Whites

(number and percent distribution of non-Hispanic whites aged 15 or older by sex, age, and current marital status, 2008; numbers in thousands)

	total	never married	married spouse present	married spouse absent	separated	divorced	widowed
NUMBER							
Total non-Hispanic white men	**79,043**	**23,142**	**44,570**	**681**	**1,099**	**7,309**	**2,242**
Under age 30	19,290	15,632	3,028	113	193	307	16
Aged 30 to 44	19,105	4,272	12,302	187	358	1,932	56
Aged 30 to 34	5,646	1,710	3,334	42	133	416	11
Aged 35 to 39	6,473	1,323	4,334	71	89	640	17
Aged 40 to 44	6,986	1,239	4,634	74	136	876	28
Aged 45 or older	40,648	3,239	29,240	381	547	5,070	2,170
Total non-Hispanic white women	**83,479**	**18,794**	**44,246**	**757**	**1,401**	**9,642**	**8,639**
Under age 30	18,773	13,660	4,177	147	320	423	46
Aged 30 to 44	19,220	2,621	13,305	178	503	2,422	192
Aged 30 to 34	5,648	1,156	3,715	50	154	535	38
Aged 35 to 39	6,469	755	4,660	80	172	765	37
Aged 40 to 44	7,103	710	4,930	48	177	1,122	117
Aged 45 or older	45,487	2515	26,765	433	579	6,796	8,400
PERCENT DISTRIBUTION							
Total non-Hispanic white men	**100.0%**	**29.3%**	**56.4%**	**0.9%**	**1.4%**	**9.2%**	**2.8%**
Under age 30	100.0	81.0	15.7	0.6	1.0	1.6	0.1
Aged 30 to 44	100.0	22.4	64.4	1.0	1.9	10.1	0.3
Aged 30 to 34	100.0	30.3	59.1	0.7	2.4	7.4	0.2
Aged 35 to 39	100.0	20.4	67.0	1.1	1.4	9.9	0.3
Aged 40 to 44	100.0	17.7	66.3	1.1	1.9	12.5	0.4
Aged 45 to or older	100.0	8.0	71.9	0.9	1.3	12.5	5.3
Total non-Hispanic white women	**100.0**	**22.5**	**53.0**	**0.9**	**1.7**	**11.6**	**10.3**
Under age 30	100.0	72.8	22.3	0.8	1.7	2.3	0.2
Aged 30 to 44	100.0	13.6	69.2	0.9	2.6	12.6	1.0
Aged 30 to 34	100.0	20.5	65.8	0.9	2.7	9.5	0.7
Aged 35 to 39	100.0	11.7	72.0	1.2	2.7	11.8	0.6
Aged 40 to 44	100.0	10.0	69.4	0.7	2.5	15.8	1.6
Aged 45 to or older	100.0	58.8	1.0	1.3	14.9	18.5	18.5

Note: Non-Hispanic whites are those who identify themselves as being white alone and not Hispanic.
Source: Bureau of the Census, Current Population Survey Annual Social and Economic Supplement, America's Families and Living Arrangements: 2008, detailed tables, Internet site http://www.census.gov/population/www/socdemo/hh-fam/cps2008 .html; calculations by New Strategist

Divorce Is Highest among Men and Women in Their Fifties

Few Gen Xers have experienced divorce, according to a 2004 study.

The experience of divorce is most common among men and women aged 50 to 59. Among men in the age group in 2004, 37.5 percent had ever divorced, according to a Census Bureau study of marriage and divorce. The percentage of women in the age group who had ever divorced was an even higher 40.7 percent.

Among all Americans aged 15 or older, 41 percent of women and 44 percent of men had married once and were still married. The figure topped 50 percent for men aged 30 or older and for women aged 30 to 39.

■ Because many Gen Xers had only recently married in 2004, few had yet to experience divorce. The percentage of Gen Xers who have ever divorced will rise as they get older.

More than one in five adults have experienced divorce

(percent of people aged 15 or older, by selected marital history and sex, 2004)

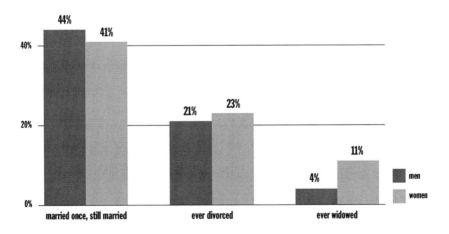

Table 7.23 Marital History of Men by Age, 2004

(number of men aged 15 or older and percent distribution by marital history and age, 2004; numbers in thousands)

	total	15–19	20–24	25–29	30–34	35–39	40–49	50–59	60–69	70+
TOTAL MEN, NUMBER	109,830	10,473	10,022	9,511	9,848	10,121	21,857	17,352	10,571	10,075
TOTAL MEN, PERCENT	100.0%	100.0%	100.0%	100.0%	100.0%	100.0%	100.0%	100.0%	100.0%	100.0%
Never married	31.2	98.1	84.0	53.6	30.3	20.2	14.1	8.7	4.8	3.2
Ever married	68.8	1.9	16.0	46.4	69.7	79.8	85.9	91.3	95.2	96.8
Married once	54.0	1.9	15.9	44.3	62.4	68.1	66.8	63.4	66.8	74.9
Still married	43.8	1.5	14.4	39.7	54.4	56.6	52.8	50.3	54.7	55.1
Married twice	11.8	0.0	0.1	2.0	6.7	10.3	15.7	21.3	20.6	17.0
Still married	9.2	0.0	0.1	1.9	6.0	8.5	12.5	16.1	16.1	12.6
Married three or more times	3.1	0.0	0.0	0.1	0.6	1.4	3.3	6.6	7.7	4.9
Still married	2.3	0.0	0.0	0.0	0.4	1.2	2.7	5.1	5.6	3.1
Ever divorced	20.7	0.1	0.8	5.1	13.1	20.7	30.3	37.5	34.1	20.6
Currently divorced	9.3	0.1	0.7	3.2	6.6	10.9	14.7	16.2	13.0	6.2
Ever widowed	3.6	0.2	0.0	0.1	0.1	0.6	1.1	2.8	7.1	23.8
Currently widowed	2.5	0.2	0.0	0.0	0.1	0.4	0.6	1.4	4.2	18.9

Source: Bureau of the Census, Number, Timing, and Duration of Marriages and Divorces: 2004, Detailed Tables, Internet site http://www.census.gov/population/www/socdemo/marr-div/2004detailed_tables.html

Table 7.24 Marital History of Women by Age, 2004

(number of women aged 15 or older and percent distribution by marital history and age, 2004; numbers in thousands)

	total	15–19	20–24	25–29	30–34	35–39	40–49	50–59	60–69	70+
TOTAL WOMEN, NUMBER	117,677	10,082	10,027	9,484	10,097	10,319	22,818	18,412	11,852	14,586
TOTAL WOMEN, PERCENT	100.0%	100.0%	100.0%	100.0%	100.0%	100.0%	100.0%	100.0%	100.0%	100.0%
Never married	25.8	97.3	73.3	41.3	22.3	16.2	11.9	7.6	4.3	4.9
Ever married	74.2	2.7	26.7	58.7	77.7	83.8	88.1	92.4	95.7	95.1
Married once	57.9	2.7	25.8	55.5	68.4	67.5	65.3	62.8	71.1	77.4
Still married	40.6	2.4	23.0	48.6	57.6	54.6	49.7	44.4	46.2	29.0
Married twice	13.2	0.1	0.8	3.1	8.2	14.1	18.9	22.6	18.7	14.9
Still married	8.8	0.0	0.7	2.8	6.6	11.3	14.0	15.5	11.3	5.3
Married three or more times	3.1	0.0	0.0	0.1	1.2	2.2	3.9	7.0	5.9	2.8
Still married	1.9	0.0	0.0	0.1	0.8	1.6	2.8	4.4	3.6	1.0
Ever divorced	22.9	0.2	2.5	7.0	17.1	25.6	33.9	40.7	32.3	17.8
Currently divorced	10.9	0.1	1.7	4.1	9.1	11.7	16.4	19.4	15.0	7.2
Ever widowed	10.8	0.1	0.1	0.3	0.7	1.1	2.5	7.8	21.2	54.5
Currently widowed	9.6	0.1	0.1	0.2	0.5	0.9	1.6	5.7	18.0	51.6

Source: Bureau of the Census, Number, Timing, and Duration of Marriages and Divorces: 2004, Detailed Tables, Internet site http://www.census.gov/population/www/socdemo/marr-div/2004detailed_tables.html

8

Population

■ Generation X numbers 50 million, a figure that includes all those born between 1965 and 1976 (aged 32 to 43 in 2008). Generation Xers account for 16 percent of the population.

■ Between 2008 and 2015, the number of people aged 35 to 54 (Generation Xers will be aged 39 to 50 in 2015) will shrink by 2.5 percent—a loss of more than 2 million people.

■ Sixty-two percent of Generation Xers are non-Hispanic white. Within Generation X, Hispanics outnumber blacks. Eighteen percent of Gen Xers are Hispanic, 13 percent are black, and 6 percent are Asian.

■ Twenty percent of 30-to-44-year-olds were born in another country—much greater than the 13 percent of all U.S. residents who are foreign-born.

■ The diversity of Generation X varies greatly by region. In the West, only 51 percent of 30-to-44-year-olds were non-Hispanic white in 2008. In the Midwest, non-Hispanic whites were a much larger 77 percent of the region's 30-to-44-year-olds.

Generation X Is Sandwiched between Larger Generations

Age groups shrink when Generation X moves in.

Generation X numbers 50 million, a figure that includes all those born between 1965 and 1976 (aged 32 to 43 in 2008). Generation Xers account for 16 percent of the total population. They are surrounded by the two largest generations: the Boomers (25 percent of the population) and the Millennials (also 25 percent).

As Generation X moves through the age structure, age groups shrink. Between 2000 and 2008, the number of 35-to-39-year-olds fell by nearly 8 percent as Generation Xers replaced Boomers in the age group. The number of 30-to-34-year-olds fell 4 percent during those years.

Between 2008 and 2015, the number of people aged 35 to 54 (Generation Xers will be aged 39 to 50 in 2015) will shrink by 2.5 percent—a loss of more than 2 million people. In 2015, Generation X will account for 15 percent of the population, a share that will fall to 14 percent by 2025.

■ Because Generation X is small, attention focuses more on Boomers and Millennials. But Generation X is about to enter its peak earning and spending years and should not be ignored.

The middle-aged population will shrink during the next decade

(percent change in number of people by age, 2008–15)

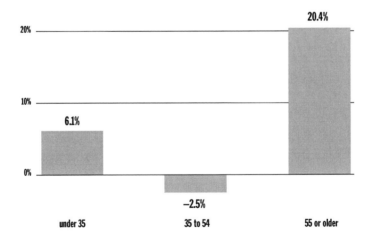

Table 8.1 Population by Age and Generation, 2008

(number and percent distribution of people by age and generation, 2008; numbers in thousands)

	number	percent distribution
Total people	**304,060**	**100.0%**
Under age 5	21,006	6.9
Aged 5 to 9	20,065	6.6
Aged 10 to 14	20,055	6.6
Aged 15 to 19	21,514	7.1
Aged 20 to 24	21,059	6.9
Aged 25 to 29	21,334	7.0
Aged 30 to 44	62,099	20.4
Aged 30 to 34	19,598	6.4
Aged 35 to 39	20,994	6.9
Aged 40 to 44	21,507	7.1
Aged 45 to 49	22,880	7.5
Aged 50 to 54	21,492	7.1
Aged 55 to 59	18,583	6.1
Aged 60 to 64	15,103	5.0
Aged 65 to 69	11,349	3.7
Aged 70 to 74	8,774	2.9
Aged 75 to 79	7,275	2.4
Aged 80 to 84	5,750	1.9
Aged 85 or older	5,722	1.9
Total people	**304,060**	**100.0**
iGeneration (under age 14)	57,115	18.8
Millennial (aged 14 to 31)	75,757	24.9
Generation X (aged 32 to 43)	49,958	16.4
Baby Boom (aged 44 to 62)	76,319	25.1
Older Americans (aged 63 or older)	44,911	14.8

Source: Bureau of the Census, Population Estimates, Internet site http://www.census.gov/popest/national/asrh/ NC-EST2008-sa.html; calculations by New Strategist

Table 8.2 Population by Age and Sex, 2008

(number of people by age and sex, and sex ratio by age, 2008; numbers in thousands)

	total	female	male	sex ratio
Total people	**304,060**	**154,135**	**149,925**	**97**
Under age 5	21,006	10,258	10,748	105
Aged 5 to 9	20,065	9,806	10,259	105
Aged 10 to 14	20,055	9,792	10,262	105
Aged 15 to 19	21,514	10,487	11,027	105
Aged 20 to 24	21,059	10,214	10,845	106
Aged 25 to 29	21,334	10,393	10,941	105
Aged 30 to 44	62,099	30,826	31,273	101
Aged 30 to 34	19,598	9,639	9,959	103
Aged 35 to 39	20,994	10,425	10,569	101
Aged 40 to 44	21,507	10,762	10,746	100
Aged 45 to 49	22,880	11,566	11,314	98
Aged 50 to 54	21,492	10,954	10,539	96
Aged 55 to 59	18,583	9,569	9,015	94
Aged 60 to 64	15,103	7,867	7,236	92
Aged 65 to 69	11,349	6,042	5,306	88
Aged 70 to 74	8,774	4,816	3,959	82
Aged 75 to 79	7,275	4,178	3,097	74
Aged 80 to 84	5,750	3,510	2,239	64
Aged 85 or older	5,722	3,858	1,864	48

Note: The sex ratio is the number of males per 100 females.
Source: Bureau of the Census, Population Estimates, Internet site http://www.census.gov/popest/national/asrh/NC-EST2008-sa.html; calculations by New Strategist

Table 8.3 Population by Age, 2000 and 2008

(number of people by age, 2000 and 2008; percent change, 2000–08)

	2008	2000	percent change 2000–08
Total people	**304,060**	**281,422**	**8.0%**
Under age 5	21,006	19,176	9.5
Aged 5 to 9	20,065	20,550	–2.4
Aged 10 to 14	20,055	20,528	–2.3
Aged 15 to 19	21,514	20,220	6.4
Aged 20 to 24	21,059	18,964	11.0
Aged 25 to 29	21,334	19,381	10.1
Aged 30 to 34	19,598	20,510	–4.4
Aged 35 to 39	20,994	22,707	–7.5
Aged 40 to 44	21,507	22,442	–4.2
Aged 45 to 49	22,880	20,092	13.9
Aged 50 to 54	21,492	17,586	22.2
Aged 55 to 59	18,583	13,469	38.0
Aged 60 to 64	15,103	10,805	39.8
Aged 65 to 69	11,349	9,534	19.0
Aged 70 to 74	8,774	8,857	–0.9
Aged 75 to 79	7,275	7,416	–1.9
Aged 80 to 84	5,750	4,945	16.3
Aged 85 or older	5,722	4,240	35.0
Aged 18 to 24	29,757	27,143	9.6
Aged 18 or older	230,118	209,128	10.0
Aged 65 or older	38,870	34,992	11.1

Source: Bureau of the Census, National Population Estimates, Internet site http://www.census.gov/popest/national/asrh/NC-EST2008-asrh.html; calculations by New Strategist

Table 8.4 Population by Age, 2008 to 2025

(number of people by age, 2008 to 2025; percent change for selected years; numbers in thousands)

	2008	2010	2015	2025	percent change 2008–10	percent change 2008–15	percent change 2008–25
Total people	**304,060**	**310,233**	**325,540**	**357,452**	**2.0%**	**7.1%**	**17.6%**
Under age 5	21,006	21,100	22,076	23,484	0.4	5.1	11.8
Aged 5 to 9	20,065	20,886	21,707	23,548	4.1	8.2	17.4
Aged 10 to 14	20,055	20,395	21,658	23,677	1.7	8.0	18.1
Aged 15 to 19	21,514	21,770	21,209	23,545	1.2	−1.4	9.4
Aged 20 to 24	21,059	21,779	22,342	23,168	3.4	6.1	10.0
Aged 25 to 29	21,334	21,418	22,400	22,417	0.4	5.0	5.1
Aged 30 to 34	19,598	20,400	22,099	23,699	4.1	12.8	20.9
Aged 35 to 39	20,994	20,267	20,841	23,645	−3.5	−0.7	12.6
Aged 40 to 44	21,507	21,010	20,460	22,851	−2.3	−4.9	6.2
Aged 45 to 49	22,880	22,596	21,001	21,154	−1.2	−8.2	−7.5
Aged 50 to 54	21,492	22,109	22,367	20,404	2.9	4.1	−5.1
Aged 55 to 59	18,583	19,517	21,682	20,575	5.0	16.7	10.7
Aged 60 to 64	15,103	16,758	18,861	21,377	11.0	24.9	41.5
Aged 65 to 69	11,349	12,261	15,812	19,957	8.0	39.3	75.9
Aged 70 to 74	8,774	9,202	11,155	16,399	4.9	27.1	86.9
Aged 75 to 79	7,275	7,282	7,901	12,598	0.1	8.6	73.2
Aged 80 to 84	5,750	5,733	5,676	7,715	−0.3	−1.3	34.2
Aged 85 or older	5,722	5,751	6,292	7,239	0.5	10.0	26.5

Source: Bureau of the Census, 2008 National Population Projections, Internet site http://www.census.gov/population/www/ projections/2008projections.html; calculations by New Strategist

Table 8.5 Population by Generation, 2008 to 2025

(number and percent distribution of people by generation, 2008 to 2025; numbers in thousands)

	number	percent distribution
2008		
Total people	**304,060**	**100.0%**
iGeneration (under age 14)	57,115	18.8
Millennial (aged 14 to 31)	75,757	24.9
Generation X (aged 32 to 43)	49,958	16.4
Baby Boom (aged 44 to 62)	76,319	25.1
Older Americans (aged 63 or older)	44,911	14.8
2010		
Total people	**310,233**	**100.0**
iGeneration (under age 16)	66,594	21.5
Millennial (aged 16 to 33)	77,248	24.9
Generation X (aged 34 to 45)	49,651	16.0
Baby Boom (aged 46 to 64)	76,511	24.7
Older Americans (aged 65 or older)	40,229	13.0
2015		
Total people	**325,540**	**100.0**
iGeneration (under age 21)	91,002	28.0
Millennial (aged 21 to 38)	79,357	24.4
Generation X (aged 39 to 50)	49,872	15.3
Baby Boom (aged 51 to 69)	74,284	22.8
Older Americans (aged 70 or older)	31,025	9.5
2025		
Total people	**357,452**	**100.0**
iGeneration (under age 31)	144,444	40.4
Millennial (aged 31 to 48)	82,736	23.1
Generation X (aged 49 to 60)	49,278	13.8
Baby Boom (aged 61 to 79)	66,041	18.5
Older Americans (aged 80 or older)	14,953	4.2

Source: Bureau of the Census, 2008 National Population Projections, Internet site http://www.census.gov/population/www/projections/2008projections.html; calculations by New Strategist"

Generation X Is More Diverse than Average

The generation is less diverse than children and young adults, however.

Sixty-two percent of Generation Xers are non-Hispanic white, according to 2008 estimates by the Census Bureau. This figure is smaller than the 66 percent for the population as a whole, but larger than the share among the youngest Americans—only 53 percent of children under age 5 are non-Hispanic white. Older generations of Americans are much less diverse than Generation X. Among Boomers, 72 percent are non-Hispanic white. Among older Americans (aged 63 or older), the proportion is 80 percent.

Within Generation X, Hispanics outnumber blacks. Eighteen percent of Gen Xers are Hispanic, 13 percent are black, and 6 percent are Asian. Generation Xers account for only 16 percent of the non-Hispanic white and black populations. They account for a larger 19 percent of Hispanics and 20 percent of Asians. Among Hispanics, Generation Xers outnumber Boomers.

■ The differing racial and ethnic makeup of older versus younger generations of Americans may

Fewer than two-thirds of Generation Xers are non-Hispanic white

(non-Hispanic white share of population by generation, 2008)

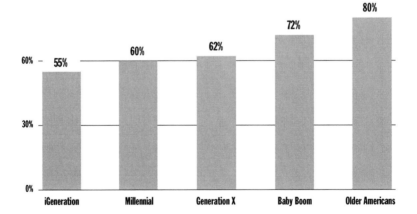

Table 8.6 Population by Age, Race, and Hispanic Origin, 2008

(number and percent distribution of people by age, race, and Hispanic origin, 2008; numbers in thousands)

	total	Asian	black	Hispanic	non-Hispanic white
Total people	**304,060**	**15,480**	**41,127**	**46,944**	**199,491**
Under age 5	21,006	1,242	3,573	5,288	11,065
Aged 5 to 9	20,065	1,107	3,298	4,464	11,222
Aged 10 to 14	20,055	1,033	3,363	3,989	11,660
Aged 15 to 19	21,514	1,018	3,667	3,850	12,903
Aged 20 to 24	21,059	1,027	3,307	3,663	12,949
Aged 25 to 29	21,334	1,206	3,166	4,141	12,740
Aged 30 to 44	62,099	3,948	8,394	11,050	38,522
Aged 30 to 34	19,598	1,334	2,724	4,041	11,456
Aged 35 to 39	20,994	1,404	2,823	3,730	12,981
Aged 40 to 44	21,507	1,210	2,847	3,279	14,085
Aged 45 to 49	22,880	1,107	2,882	2,795	15,964
Aged 50 to 54	21,492	986	2,563	2,187	15,615
Aged 55 to 59	18,583	829	2,068	1,650	13,907
Aged 60 to 64	15,103	612	1,471	1,204	11,706
Aged 65 to 69	11,349	443	1,075	853	8,899
Aged 70 to 74	8,774	339	829	653	6,899
Aged 75 to 79	7,275	255	614	496	5,871
Aged 80 to 84	5,750	176	438	346	4,763
Aged 85 or older	5,722	154	419	313	4,807

PERCENT DISTRIBUTION BY RACE AND HISPANIC ORIGIN

Total people	**100.0%**	**5.1%**	**13.5%**	**15.4%**	**65.6%**
Under age 5	100.0	5.9	17.0	25.2	52.7
Aged 5 to 9	100.0	5.5	16.4	22.2	55.9
Aged 10 to 14	100.0	5.1	16.8	19.9	58.1
Aged 15 to 19	100.0	4.7	17.0	17.9	60.0
Aged 20 to 24	100.0	4.9	15.7	17.4	61.5
Aged 25 to 29	100.0	5.7	14.8	19.4	59.7
Aged 30 to 44	100.0	6.4	13.5	17.8	62.0
Aged 30 to 34	100.0	6.8	13.9	20.6	58.5
Aged 35 to 39	100.0	6.7	13.4	17.8	61.8
Aged 40 to 44	100.0	5.6	13.2	15.2	65.5
Aged 45 to 49	100.0	4.8	12.6	12.2	69.8
Aged 50 to 54	100.0	4.6	11.9	10.2	72.7
Aged 55 to 59	100.0	4.5	11.1	8.9	74.8
Aged 60 to 64	100.0	4.1	9.7	8.0	77.5
Aged 65 to 69	100.0	3.9	9.5	7.5	78.4
Aged 70 to 74	100.0	3.9	9.5	7.4	78.6
Aged 75 to 79	100.0	3.5	8.4	6.8	80.7
Aged 80 to 84	100.0	3.1	7.6	6.0	82.8
Aged 85 or older	100.0	2.7	7.3	5.5	84.0

Note: Numbers do not add to total because Asians and blacks include those who identified themselves as being of the race alone and those who identified themselves as being of the race in combination with other races, and because Hispanics may be of any race. Non-Hispanic whites include those who identified themselves as being white alone and not Hispanic.
Source: Bureau of the Census, Population Estimates, Internet site http://www.census.gov/popest/national/asrh/ NC-EST2008-sa.html; calculations by New Strategis

Table 8.7 Population by Generation, Race, and Hispanic Origin, 2008

(number and percent distribution of people by generation, race, and Hispanic origin, 2008; numbers in thousands)

	total	Asian	black	Hispanic	non-Hispanic white
Total people	**304,060**	**15,480**	**41,127**	**46,944**	**199,491**
iGeneration (under age 14)	57,115	3,174	9,562	12,944	31,615
Millennial (aged 14 to 31)	75,757	3,991	11,902	14,068	45,506
Generation X (aged 32 to 43)	49,958	3,172	6,735	8,778	31,123
Baby Boom (aged 44 to 62)	76,319	3,531	8,965	8,011	55,326
Older Americans (aged 63 or older)	44,911	1,612	3,964	3,143	35,920
PERCENT DISTRIBUTION BY RACE AND HISPANIC ORIGIN					
Total people	**100.0%**	**5.1%**	**13.5%**	**15.4%**	**65.6%**
iGeneration (under age 14)	100.0	5.6	16.7	22.7	55.4
Millennial (aged 14 to 31)	100.0	5.3	15.7	18.6	60.1
Generation X (aged 32 to 43)	100.0	6.3	13.5	17.6	62.3
Baby Boom (aged 44 to 62)	100.0	4.6	11.7	10.5	72.5
Older Americans (aged 63 or older)	100.0	3.6	8.8	7.0	80.0
PERCENT DISTRIBUTION BY GENERATION					
Total people	**100.0%**	**100.0%**	**100.0%**	**100.0%**	**100.0%**
iGeneration (under age 14)	18.8	20.5	23.2	27.6	15.8
Millennial (aged 14 to 31)	24.9	25.8	28.9	30.0	22.8
Generation X (aged 32 to 43)	16.4	20.5	16.4	18.7	15.6
Baby Boom (aged 44 to 62)	25.1	22.8	21.8	17.1	27.7
Older Americans (aged 63 or older)	14.8	10.4	9.6	6.7	18.0

Note: Numbers do not add to total because Asians and blacks include those who identified themselves as being of the race alone and those who identified themselves as being of the race in combination with other races, and because Hispanics may be of any race. Non-Hispanic whites are those who identified themselves as being white alone and not Hispanic.
Source: Bureau of the Census, Population Estimates, Internet site http://www.census.gov/popest/national/asrh/ NC-EST2008-sa.html; calculations by New Strategist

Many Gen Xers Live in Their State of Birth

One in five is foreign-born.

According to the 2007 American Community Survey, 49 percent of people aged 35 to 44 (Gen Xers were aged 31 to 42 in that year) were born in their state of current residence—a figure nearly identical to the one among U.S. residents aged 45 or older. Thirty percent of Gen Xers were born in the United States, but in a different state. Twenty percent were born in another country—much greater than the 13 percent of all U.S. residents who are foreign-born.

Among the foreign-born in the broad 25-to-44 age group, 60 percent were born in Latin America—including 37 percent who were born in Mexico. Twenty-six percent were born in Asia, and only 8 percent are from Europe.

■ The foreign-born population adds to the multicultural mix, which is becoming a significant factor in American business and politics.

Sixty percent of the foreign-born in the 25-to-44 age group are from Latin America

(percent distribution of the foreign-born aged 25 to 44 by region of birth, 2008)

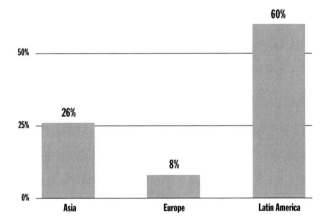

Table 8.8 Population by Age and Place of Birth, 2007

(number and percent distribution of people by age and place of birth, 2007; numbers in thousands)

| | total | born in the United States | | citizen born outside United states | foreign-born |
		in state of current residence	outside state of current residence		
Total people	**301,621**	**177,509**	**82,253**	**3,799**	**38,060**
Under age 18	73,908	59,667	10,643	625	2,973
Aged 18 to 24	29,821	18,880	7,062	395	3,484
Aged 25 to 34	39,987	20,889	10,532	611	7,955
Aged 35 to 44	43,410	21,083	13,067	692	8,569
Aged 45 to 54	43,925	22,275	14,527	669	6,455
Aged 55 or older	70,570	34,715	26,422	808	8,624

PERCENT DISTRIBUTION BY PLACE OF BIRTH

Total people	**100.0%**	**58.9%**	**27.3%**	**1.3%**	**12.6%**
Under age 18	100.0	80.7	14.4	0.8	4.0
Aged 18 to 24	100.0	63.3	23.7	1.3	11.7
Aged 25 to 34	100.0	52.2	26.3	1.5	19.9
Aged 35 to 44	100.0	48.6	30.1	1.6	19.7
Aged 45 to 54	100.0	50.7	33.1	1.5	14.7
Aged 55 or older	100.0	49.2	37.4	1.1	12.2

PERCENT DISTRIBUTION BY AGE

Total people	**100.0%**	**100.0%**	**100.0%**	**100.0%**	**100.0%**
Under age 18	24.5	33.6	12.9	16.4	7.8
Aged 18 to 24	9.9	10.6	8.6	10.4	9.2
Aged 25 to 34	13.3	11.8	12.8	16.1	20.9
Aged 35 to 44	14.4	11.9	15.9	18.2	22.5
Aged 45 to 54	14.6	12.5	17.7	17.6	17.0
Aged 55 or older	23.4	19.6	32.1	21.3	22.7

Source: Bureau of the Census, 2007 American Community Survey, Internet site http://factfinder.census.gov/home/saff/main .html?_lang=en; calculations by New Strategist

Table 8.9 Foreign-Born Population by Age and World Region of Birth, 2007

(number and percent distribution of foreign-born by age and world region of birth, 2007; numbers in thousands)

	total	Asia	Europe	Latin America total	Mexico
Total people	**38,060**	**10,185**	**4,990**	**20,410**	**11,739**
Under age 18	2,973	713	329	1,694	1,103
Aged 18 to 24	3,484	744	284	2,225	1,456
Aged 25 to 44	16,524	4,308	1,382	9,858	6,104
Aged 45 to 54	6,455	1,915	808	3,286	1,655
Aged 55 or older	8,624	2,506	2,181	3,368	1,409
Median age (years)	40.2	42.0	50.8	37.4	35.1
PERCENT DISTRIBUTION OF FOREIGN-BORN BY REGION OF BIRTH					
Total people	**100.0%**	**26.8%**	**13.1%**	**53.6%**	**30.8%**
Under age 18	100.0	24.0	11.1	57.0	37.1
Aged 18 to 24	100.0	21.3	8.2	63.9	41.8
Aged 25 to 44	100.0	26.1	8.4	59.7	36.9
Aged 45 to 54	100.0	29.7	12.5	50.9	25.6
Aged 55 or older	100.0	29.1	25.3	39.0	16.3
PERCENT DISTRIBUTION BY AGE					
Total people	**100.0%**	**100.0%**	**100.0%**	**100.0%**	**100.0%**
Under age 18	7.8	7.0	6.6	8.3	9.4
Aged 18 to 24	9.2	7.3	5.7	10.9	12.4
Aged 25 to 44	43.4	42.3	27.7	48.3	52.0
Aged 45 to 54	17.0	18.8	16.2	16.1	14.1
Aged 55 or older	22.7	24.6	43.7	16.5	12.0

Note: Numbers do not add to total because "other" is not shown.
*Source: Bureau of the Census, 2007 American Community Survey, Internet site http://factfinder.census.gov/home/saff/main
.html?_lang=en; calculations by New Strategist*

Many Immigrants Are Generation Xers

Nearly one in three immigrants admitted in 2008 was aged 30 to 44.

The number of legal immigrants admitted to the United States in 2008 was over 1 million. More than 350,000 were aged 30 to 44, accounting for 32 percent of the total.

Thirteen percent of immigrants to the United Stated in 2008 were aged 30-to-34—the largest share of any five-year age group. Another 11 percent were aged 35 to 39. The figure declines with age. Just 5 percent of immigrants admitted in 2008 were aged 65 or older.

■ Because most immigrants are young adults, immigration has a much greater impact on the diversity of younger Americans than on the middle-aged or older population.

Immigrants aged 30 to 44 account for 32 percent of the total

(percent distribution of immigrants admitted in 2008, by age)

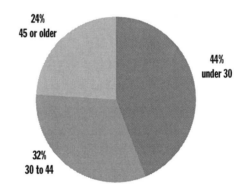

24%
45 or older

44%
under 30

32%
30 to 44

Table 8.10 Newly Arrived Immigrants by Age, 2008

(number and percent distribution of immigrants admitted in 2008, by age)

	number	percent distribution
Total immigrants	**1,107,126**	**100.0%**
Under age 1	8,280	0.7
Aged 1 to 4	29,998	2.7
Aged 5 to 9	52,993	4.8
Aged 10 to 14	74,608	6.7
Aged 15 to 19	94,697	8.6
Aged 20 to 24	104,332	9.4
Aged 25 to 29	121,416	11.0
Aged 30 to 44	357,100	32.3
Aged 30 to 34	140,132	12.7
Aged 35 to 39	124,341	11.2
Aged 40 to 44	92,627	8.4
Aged 45 to 49	69,868	6.3
Aged 50 to 54	53,848	4.9
Aged 55 to 59	43,789	4.0
Aged 60 to 64	35,586	3.2
Aged 65 or older	60,604	5.5

Note: Immigrants are those granted legal permanent residence in the United States. They either arrive in the United States with immigrant visas issued abroad or adjust their status in the United States from temporary to permanent residence. Numbers may not sum to total because "age not stated" is not shown.
Source: Department of Homeland Security, 2008 Yearbook of Immigration Statistics, Internet site http://www.uscis.gov/graphics/shared/statistics/yearbook/index.htm

Many Working-Age Adults Do Not Speak English at Home

Most are Spanish speakers, and most have trouble speaking English.

Fifty-five million residents of the United States speak a language other than English at home, according to the Census Bureau's 2007 American Community Survey—20 percent of the population aged 5 or older. The 62 percent majority of those who do not speak English at home are Spanish speakers.

Among working-age adults (aged 18 to 64), 21 percent do not speak English at home, and 62 percent of those who do not speak English at home are Spanish speakers. Among the Spanish speakers, 53 percent say they speak English less than "very well."

■ The language barrier is a problem for many working-age adults.

Most adults who speak Spanish at home cannot speak English very well

(percent of people aged 18 to 64 who speak a language other than English at home who speak English less than "very well," by language spoken at home, 2007)

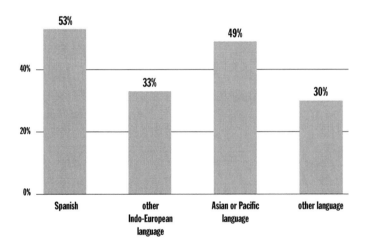

Table 8.11 Language Spoken at Home by People Aged 18 to 64, 2007

(number and percent distribution of people aged 5 or older and aged 18 to 64 who speak a language other than English at home by language spoken at home and ability to speak English very well, by age, 2007; numbers in thousands)

	total		aged 18 to 64	
	number	percent distribution	number	percent distribution
Total, aged 5 or older	**280,950**	**100.0%**	**189,873**	**100.0%**
Speak only English at home	225,506	80.3	150,635	79.3
Speak a language other than English at home	55,444	19.7	39,238	20.7
Speak English less than very well	24,469	8.7	18,624	9.8
Total who speak a language other than English at home	**55,444**	**100.0**	**39,238**	**100.0**
Speak Spanish at home	34,547	62.3	24,333	62.0
Speak other Indo-European language at home	10,321	18.6	7,034	17.9
Speak Asian or Pacific Island language at home	8,316	15.0	6,202	15.8
Speak other language at home	2,260	4.1	1,669	4.3
Speak Spanish at home	34,547	100.0	24,333	100.0
Speak English less than very well	16,368	47.4	12,791	52.6
Speak other Indo-European language at home	10,321	100.0	7,034	100.0
Speak English less than very well	3,384	32.8	2,291	32.6
Speak Asian or Pacific Island language at home	8,316	100.0	6,202	100.0
Speak English less than very well	4,042	48.6	3,034	48.9
Speak other language at home	2,260	100.0	1,669	100.0
Speak English less than very well	676	29.9	508	30.4

Source: Bureau of the Census, 2007 American Community Survey, Internet site http://factfinder.census.gov/servlet/ DatasetMainPageServlet?_program=ACS&_submenuId=&_lang=en&_ts=; calculations by New Strategist

The Largest Share of Generation Xers Lives in the South

More than one-third of Gen Xers in the South are black or Hispanic.

The South is home to the largest share of the population, and consequently to the largest share of Generation X. Thirty-seven percent of Gen Xers live in the South, where the generation accounts for 16 percent of the population.

The diversity of Generation X varies greatly by region. In the West, only 51 percent of 30-to-44-year-olds were non-Hispanic white in 2008 (Gen Xers were aged 32 to 43 in that year). In the Midwest, non-Hispanic whites were a much larger 77 percent of the region's 30-to-44-year-olds.

By state, Generation X accounts for 14 to 18 percent of the population. Gen Xers are only 14 percent of the population of North Dakota, South Dakota, and Montana. They are 18 percent of the population of Nevada and Georgia.

■ Gen Xers outnumber older Americans (aged 63 or older) in most states.

In the West, minorities account for nearly half of Gen Xers

(percent distribution of people aged 30 to 44 by race and Hispanic origin in the West, 2008)

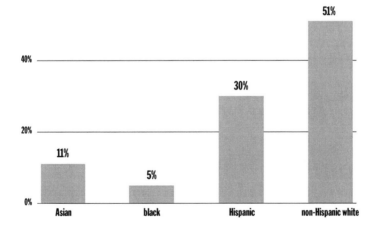

Table 8.12 Population by Age and Region, 2008

(number and percent distribution of people by age and region, 2008; numbers in thousands)

	total	Northeast	Midwest	South	West
Total people	**304,060**	**54,925**	**66,561**	**111,719**	**70,855**
Under age 30	125,033	21,230	27,197	46,233	30,372
Aged 30 to 44	62,099	11,226	13,156	22,881	14,836
Aged 30 to 34	19,598	3,354	4,126	7,261	4,857
Aged 35 to 39	20,994	3,767	4,416	7,776	5,035
Aged 40 to 44	21,507	4,105	4,614	7,844	4,944
Aged 45 to 54	44,372	8,468	9,989	15,940	9,975
Aged 55 or older	72,556	14,001	16,220	26,664	15,671
PERCENT DISTRIBUTION BY AGE					
Total people	**100.0%**	**100.0%**	**100.0%**	**100.0%**	**100.0%**
Under age 30	41.1	38.7	40.9	41.4	42.9
Aged 30 to 44	20.4	20.4	19.8	20.5	20.9
Aged 30 to 34	6.4	6.1	6.2	6.5	6.9
Aged 35 to 39	6.9	6.9	6.6	7.0	7.1
Aged 40 to 44	7.1	7.5	6.9	7.0	7.0
Aged 45 to 54	14.6	15.4	15.0	14.3	14.1
Aged 55 or older	23.9	25.5	24.4	23.9	22.1
PERCENT DISTRIBUTION BY REGION					
Total people	**100.0%**	**18.1%**	**21.9%**	**36.7%**	**23.3%**
Under age 30	100.0	17.0	21.8	37.0	24.3
Aged 30 to 44	100.0	18.1	21.2	36.8	23.9
Aged 30 to 34	100.0	17.1	21.1	37.0	24.8
Aged 35 to 39	100.0	17.9	21.0	37.0	24.0
Aged 40 to 44	100.0	19.1	21.5	36.5	23.0
Aged 45 to 54	100.0	19.1	22.5	35.9	22.5
Aged 55 or older	100.0	19.3	22.4	36.7	21.6

Source: Bureau of the Census, State Population Estimates, Internet site http://www.census.gov/popest/states/asrh/; calculations by New Strategist

Table 8.13 Population by Generation and Region, 2008

(number and percent distribution of people by generation and region, 2008; numbers in thousands)

	total	Northeast	Midwest	South	West
Total people	**304,060**	**54,925**	**66,561**	**111,719**	**70,855**
iGeneration (under age 14)	57,115	9,422	12,350	21,429	13,914
Millennial (aged 14 to 31)	75,757	13,150	16,497	27,709	18,401
Generation X (aged 32 to 43)	49,958	9,063	10,583	18,408	11,905
Baby Boom (aged 44 to 62)	76,319	14,522	17,078	27,612	17,106
Older Americans (aged 63 or older)	44,911	8,768	10,054	16,560	9,529

PERCENT DISTRIBUTION BY GENERATION

	total	Northeast	Midwest	South	West
Total people	**100.0%**	**100.0%**	**100.0%**	**100.0%**	**100.0%**
iGeneration (under age 14)	18.8	17.2	18.6	19.2	19.6
Millennial (aged 14 to 31)	24.9	23.9	24.8	24.8	26.0
Generation X (aged 32 to 43)	16.4	16.5	15.9	16.5	16.8
Baby Boom (aged 44 to 62)	25.1	26.4	25.7	24.7	24.1
Older Americans (aged 63 or older)	14.8	16.0	15.1	14.8	13.4

PERCENT DISTRIBUTION BY REGION

	total	Northeast	Midwest	South	West
Total people	**100.0%**	**18.1%**	**21.9%**	**36.7%**	**23.3%**
iGeneration (under age 14)	100.0	16.5	21.6	37.5	24.4
Millennial (aged 14 to 31)	100.0	17.4	21.8	36.6	24.3
Generation X (aged 32 to 43)	100.0	18.1	21.2	36.8	23.8
Baby Boom (aged 44 to 62)	100.0	19.0	22.4	36.2	22.4
Older Americans (aged 63 or older)	100.0	19.5	22.4	36.9	21.2

Source: Bureau of the Census, State Population Estimates, Internet site http://www.census.gov/popest/states/asrh/; calculations by New Strategist

Table 8.14 Generation X by Region, Race, and Hispanic Origin, 2007

(number and percent distribution of people aged 30 to 44 by region, race, and Hispanic origin, 2007; numbers in thousands)

	total 30 to 44	Asian	black	Hispanic	non-Hispanic white
United States	**62,774**	**3,607**	**7,896**	**10,840**	**39,190**
Northeast	11,433	794	1,352	1,516	7,647
Midwest	13,369	445	1,375	996	10,339
South	23,059	800	4,452	3,835	13,618
West	14,912	1,567	717	4,492	7,586
PERCENT DISTRIBUTION BY RACE AND HISPANIC ORIGIN					
United States	**100.0%**	**5.7%**	**12.6%**	**17.3%**	**62.4%**
Northeast	100.0	6.9	11.8	13.3	66.9
Midwest	100.0	3.3	10.3	7.5	77.3
South	100.0	3.5	19.3	16.6	59.1
West	100.0	10.5	4.8	30.1	50.9
PERCENT DISTRIBUTION BY REGION					
United States	**100.0%**	**100.0%**	**100.0%**	**100.0%**	**100.0%**
Northeast	18.2	22.0	17.1	14.0	19.5
Midwest	21.3	12.3	17.4	9.2	26.4
South	36.7	22.2	56.4	35.4	34.7
West	23.8	43.5	9.1	41.4	19.4

Note: Numbers do not add to total because Asians and blacks are only those who identified themselves as being of the race alone and because Hispanics may be of any race. Non-Hispanic whites are only those who identified themselves as being white alone and not Hispanic.
Source: Bureau of the Census, 2007 American Community Survey, Internet site http://factfinder.census.gov/home/saff/main .html?_lang=en; calculations by New Strategist

Table 8.15 State Populations by Age, 2008

(total number of people and number aged 30 to 44 by state, 2008; numbers in thousands)

| | total population | aged 30 to 44 | | | |
		total	30 to 34	35 to 39	40 to 44
United States	**304,060**	**62,099**	**19,598**	**20,994**	**21,507**
Alabama	4,662	910	287	308	315
Alaska	686	141	47	47	48
Arizona	6,500	1,316	445	444	427
Arkansas	2,855	552	179	185	188
California	36,757	7,891	2,541	2,687	2,663
Colorado	4,939	1,077	356	368	353
Connecticut	3,501	712	200	239	273
Delaware	873	174	53	59	63
District of Columbia	592	133	48	44	40
Florida	18,328	3,580	1,094	1,208	1,279
Georgia	9,686	2,131	669	737	725
Hawaii	1,288	259	85	88	86
Idaho	1,524	291	98	98	96
Illinois	12,902	2,677	868	901	908
Indiana	6,377	1,280	409	430	441
Iowa	3,003	556	175	185	196
Kansas	2,802	531	171	179	181
Kentucky	4,269	870	277	292	301
Louisiana	4,411	833	265	276	292
Maine	1,316	255	73	86	97
Maryland	5,634	1,177	351	393	432
Massachusetts	6,498	1,354	404	452	499
Michigan	10,003	1,979	595	671	712
Minnesota	5,220	1,048	328	347	373
Mississippi	2,939	559	180	189	191
Missouri	5,912	1,149	362	385	402
Montana	967	170	54	56	60
Nebraska	1,783	333	108	112	113
Nevada	2,600	570	188	194	188
New Hampshire	1,316	267	73	91	103
New Jersey	8,683	1,857	545	628	684
New Mexico	1,984	373	123	123	126
New York	19,490	4,046	1,251	1,351	1,444
North Carolina	9,222	1,956	615	676	665
North Dakota	641	109	35	36	38
Ohio	11,486	2,245	689	759	796
Oklahoma	3,642	683	224	229	230
Oregon	3,790	766	256	259	251
Pennsylvania	12,448	2,404	711	810	883
Rhode Island	1,051	211	63	70	77
South Carolina	4,480	891	279	303	309

	total population	aged 30 to 44			
		total	30 to 34	35 to 39	40 to 44
South Dakota	804	142	46	46	50
Tennessee	6,215	1,277	403	434	441
Texas	24,327	5,149	1,710	1,762	1,677
Utah	2,736	521	195	173	154
Vermont	621	119	34	40	45
Virginia	7,769	1,652	513	563	577
Washington	6,549	1,363	438	464	461
West Virginia	1,814	352	113	119	121
Wisconsin	5,628	1,107	339	365	403
Wyoming	533	98	32	33	33

Source: Bureau of the Census, State Population Estimates, Internet site http://www.census.gov/popest/states/asrh/; calculations by New Strategist

Table 8.16 Distribution of State Populations by Age, 2008

(percent distribution of people by state and age, 2008)

	total population	aged 30 to 44			
		total	30 to 34	35 to 39	40 to 44
United States	**100.0%**	**20.4%**	**6.4%**	**6.9%**	**7.1%**
Alabama	100.0	19.5	6.2	6.6	6.8
Alaska	100.0	20.6	6.8	6.9	6.9
Arizona	100.0	20.3	6.8	6.8	6.6
Arkansas	100.0	19.3	6.3	6.5	6.6
California	100.0	21.5	6.9	7.3	7.2
Colorado	100.0	21.8	7.2	7.4	7.1
Connecticut	100.0	20.3	5.7	6.8	7.8
Delaware	100.0	19.9	6.0	6.7	7.2
District of Columbia	100.0	22.5	8.2	7.5	6.8
Florida	100.0	19.5	6.0	6.6	7.0
Georgia	100.0	22.0	6.9	7.6	7.5
Hawaii	100.0	20.1	6.6	6.9	6.7
Idaho	100.0	19.1	6.4	6.4	6.3
Illinois	100.0	20.7	6.7	7.0	7.0
Indiana	100.0	20.1	6.4	6.7	6.9
Iowa	100.0	18.5	5.8	6.2	6.5
Kansas	100.0	18.9	6.1	6.4	6.5
Kentucky	100.0	20.4	6.5	6.8	7.0
Louisiana	100.0	18.9	6.0	6.3	6.6
Maine	100.0	19.4	5.5	6.5	7.4
Maryland	100.0	20.9	6.2	7.0	7.7
Massachusetts	100.0	20.8	6.2	7.0	7.7
Michigan	100.0	19.8	6.0	6.7	7.1
Minnesota	100.0	20.1	6.3	6.6	7.1
Mississippi	100.0	19.0	6.1	6.4	6.5
Missouri	100.0	19.4	6.1	6.5	6.8
Montana	100.0	17.6	5.5	5.8	6.2
Nebraska	100.0	18.7	6.1	6.3	6.3
Nevada	100.0	21.9	7.2	7.5	7.2
New Hampshire	100.0	20.3	5.5	6.9	7.8
New Jersey	100.0	21.4	6.3	7.2	7.9
New Mexico	100.0	18.8	6.2	6.2	6.4
New York	100.0	20.8	6.4	6.9	7.4
North Carolina	100.0	21.2	6.7	7.3	7.2
North Dakota	100.0	17.0	5.4	5.7	5.9
Ohio	100.0	19.5	6.0	6.6	6.9
Oklahoma	100.0	18.7	6.2	6.3	6.3
Oregon	100.0	20.2	6.8	6.8	6.6
Pennsylvania	100.0	19.3	5.7	6.5	7.1
Rhode Island	100.0	20.1	6.0	6.7	7.4
South Carolina	100.0	19.9	6.2	6.8	6.9

	total population	aged 30 to 44			
		total	30 to 34	35 to 39	40 to 44
South Dakota	100.0%	17.7%	5.7%	5.8%	6.2%
Tennessee	100.0	20.6	6.5	7.0	7.1
Texas	100.0	21.2	7.0	7.2	6.9
Utah	100.0	19.0	7.1	6.3	5.6
Vermont	100.0	19.1	5.5	6.4	7.3
Virginia	100.0	21.3	6.6	7.2	7.4
Washington	100.0	20.8	6.7	7.1	7.0
West Virginia	100.0	19.4	6.2	6.5	6.7
Wisconsin	100.0	19.7	6.0	6.5	7.2
Wyoming	100.0	18.3	6.0	6.2	6.1

Source: Bureau of the Census, State Population Estimates, Internet site http://www.census.gov/popest/states/asrh/; calculations by New Strategist

Table 8.17 State Populations by Generation, 2008

(number of people aged 30 to 44 by state and generation, 2008; numbers in thousands)

	total population	iGeneration (under 14)	Millennial (14 to 31)	Generation X (32 to 43)	Baby Boom (44 to 62)	Older Americans (63 or older)
United States	**304,060**	**57,115**	**75,757**	**49,958**	**76,319**	**44,911**
Alabama	4,662	864	1,145	732	1,180	741
Alaska	686	138	192	113	181	62
Arizona	6,500	1,344	1,631	1,053	1,484	988
Arkansas	2,855	545	695	443	703	469
California	36,757	7,224	9,724	6,342	8,706	4,760
Colorado	4,939	946	1,258	863	1,266	606
Connecticut	3,501	617	806	577	949	552
Delaware	873	159	209	140	224	141
District of Columbia	592	87	180	106	137	82
Florida	18,328	3,087	4,164	2,887	4,597	3,593
Georgia	9,686	1,993	2,459	1,719	2,353	1,162
Hawaii	1,288	222	319	208	321	218
Idaho	1,524	323	391	233	364	212
Illinois	12,902	2,458	3,300	2,148	3,180	1,816
Indiana	6,377	1,225	1,574	1,028	1,610	940
Iowa	3,003	548	735	447	767	505
Kansas	2,802	545	714	426	696	421
Kentucky	4,269	779	1,031	699	1,104	656
Louisiana	4,411	855	1,160	669	1,100	627
Maine	1,316	206	287	207	385	231
Maryland	5,634	1,026	1,378	950	1,486	793
Massachusetts	6,498	1,088	1,595	1,093	1,717	1,006
Michigan	10,003	1,810	2,442	1,598	2,641	1,511
Minnesota	5,220	967	1,294	842	1,366	751
Mississippi	2,939	593	756	449	710	429
Missouri	5,912	1,092	1,455	924	1,513	927
Montana	967	168	235	137	268	159
Nebraska	1,783	348	453	267	441	275
Nevada	2,600	525	631	457	637	351
New Hampshire	1,316	220	299	218	379	200
New Jersey	8,683	1,572	1,985	1,502	2,296	1,327
New Mexico	1,984	391	509	298	487	300
New York	19,490	3,360	4,857	3,257	5,013	3,004
North Carolina	9,222	1,752	2,241	1,577	2,320	1,333
North Dakota	641	110	176	88	162	107
Ohio	11,486	2,088	2,774	1,810	3,008	1,806
Oklahoma	3,642	706	934	547	890	565
Oregon	3,790	668	918	614	1,002	589
Pennsylvania	12,448	2,091	2,913	1,943	3,324	2,177
Rhode Island	1,051	173	262	170	276	169
South Carolina	4,480	822	1,096	717	1,147	697

	total population	iGeneration (under 14)	Millennial (14 to 31)	Generation X (32 to 43)	Baby Boom (44 to 62)	Older Americans (63 or older)
South Dakota	804	153	201	114	204	132
Tennessee	6,215	1,143	1,489	1,028	1,600	954
Texas	24,327	5,307	6,426	4,130	5,575	2,890
Utah	2,736	680	828	413	530	286
Vermont	621	96	145	96	183	102
Virginia	7,769	1,413	1,935	1,332	1,990	1,099
Washington	6,549	1,185	1,630	1,096	1,718	921
West Virginia	1,814	296	412	283	496	328
Wisconsin	5,628	1,005	1,379	891	1,490	863
Wyoming	533	99	136	78	143	77

Source: Bureau of the Census, State Population Estimates, Internet site http://www.census.gov/popest/states/asrh/; calculations by New Strategist

Table 8.18 Distribution of State Populations by Generation, 2008

(percent distribution of people by state and generation, 2008)

	total population	iGeneration (under 14)	Millennial (14 to 31)	Generation X (32 to 43)	Baby Boom (44 to 62)	Older Americans (63 or older)
United States	**100.0%**	**18.8%**	**24.9%**	**16.4%**	**25.1%**	**14.8%**
Alabama	100.0	18.5	24.6	15.7	25.3	15.9
Alaska	100.0	20.1	28.0	16.5	26.3	9.1
Arizona	100.0	20.7	25.1	16.2	22.8	15.2
Arkansas	100.0	19.1	24.4	15.5	24.6	16.4
California	100.0	19.7	26.5	17.3	23.7	12.9
Colorado	100.0	19.2	25.5	17.5	25.6	12.3
Connecticut	100.0	17.6	23.0	16.5	27.1	15.8
Delaware	100.0	18.2	23.9	16.1	25.6	16.1
District of Columbia	100.0	14.7	30.4	17.8	23.1	13.9
Florida	100.0	16.8	22.7	15.8	25.1	19.6
Georgia	100.0	20.6	25.4	17.7	24.3	12.0
Hawaii	100.0	17.2	24.8	16.1	25.0	16.9
Idaho	100.0	21.2	25.7	15.3	23.9	13.9
Illinois	100.0	19.0	25.6	16.6	24.7	14.1
Indiana	100.0	19.2	24.7	16.1	25.3	14.7
Iowa	100.0	18.3	24.5	14.9	25.5	16.8
Kansas	100.0	19.5	25.5	15.2	24.8	15.0
Kentucky	100.0	18.2	24.1	16.4	25.9	15.4
Louisiana	100.0	19.4	26.3	15.2	24.9	14.2
Maine	100.0	15.6	21.8	15.7	29.3	17.6
Maryland	100.0	18.2	24.5	16.9	26.4	14.1
Massachusetts	100.0	16.7	24.5	16.8	26.4	15.5
Michigan	100.0	18.1	24.4	16.0	26.4	15.1
Minnesota	100.0	18.5	24.8	16.1	26.2	14.4
Mississippi	100.0	20.2	25.7	15.3	24.2	14.6
Missouri	100.0	18.5	24.6	15.6	25.6	15.7
Montana	100.0	17.3	24.3	14.1	27.7	16.5
Nebraska	100.0	19.5	25.4	15.0	24.7	15.4
Nevada	100.0	20.2	24.2	17.6	24.5	13.5
New Hampshire	100.0	16.7	22.7	16.5	28.8	15.2
New Jersey	100.0	18.1	22.9	17.3	26.4	15.3
New Mexico	100.0	19.7	25.6	15.0	24.5	15.1
New York	100.0	17.2	24.9	16.7	25.7	15.4
North Carolina	100.0	19.0	24.3	17.1	25.2	14.5
North Dakota	100.0	17.1	27.4	13.7	25.2	16.6
Ohio	100.0	18.2	24.1	15.8	26.2	15.7
Oklahoma	100.0	19.4	25.6	15.0	24.4	15.5
Oregon	100.0	17.6	24.2	16.2	26.4	15.5
Pennsylvania	100.0	16.8	23.4	15.6	26.7	17.5
Rhode Island	100.0	16.5	25.0	16.2	26.3	16.1
South Carolina	100.0	18.4	24.5	16.0	25.6	15.6

	total population	iGeneration (under 14)	Millennial (14 to 31)	Generation X (32 to 43)	Baby Boom (44 to 62)	Older Americans (63 or older)
South Dakota	100.0%	19.1%	25.0%	14.1%	25.3%	16.5%
Tennessee	100.0	18.4	24.0	16.5	25.7	15.4
Texas	100.0	21.8	26.4	17.0	22.9	11.9
Utah	100.0	24.9	30.2	15.1	19.4	10.4
Vermont	100.0	15.4	23.4	15.5	29.4	16.4
Virginia	100.0	18.2	24.9	17.1	25.6	14.1
Washington	100.0	18.1	24.9	16.7	26.2	14.1
West Virginia	100.0	16.3	22.7	15.6	27.3	18.1
Wisconsin	100.0	17.9	24.5	15.8	26.5	15.3
Wyoming	100.0	18.7	25.5	14.7	26.8	14.4

Source: Bureau of the Census, State Population Estimates, Internet site http://www.census.gov/popest/states/asrh/; calculations by New Strategist

9

Spending

■ The average household boosted its spending by 8 between 2000 and 2007, after adjusting for inflation. The spending of householders aged 35 to 44 grew by the same percentage, but the spending of householders aged 25 to 34 grew by just 1 percent during those years. (Generation X was aged 31 to 42 in 2007.)

■ The spending of households headed by people aged 25 to 34 almost matches spending by the average household. In 2007, householders aged 25 to 34 spent $47,510, slightly less than the $49,638 spent by the average household.

■ Households headed by people aged 35 to 44 spent 19 percent more than the average household in 2007—or $58,934 and more than any other age group. Householders aged 35 to 44 spend significantly more than average on items commonly purchased by parents with children under age 18. They also spend more on mortgage interest.

Spending of Householders Aged 25 to 34 Is Flat

Householders aged 35 to 44 increased their spending by an average amount between 2000 and 2007.

The spending of householders aged 25 to 34 increased by just 1 percent between 2000 and 2007, after adjusting for inflation. Householders aged 35 to 44 boosted their spending by a much larger 8 percent, a figure that mirrors the national average. (Generation X was aged 31 to 42 in 2007.)

Householders aged 25 to 34 spent $47,510 in 2007, slightly less than the $49,638 spent by the average household in 2007. The 2000-to-2007 spending trends for this age group are mixed, with significant declines in spending on a variety of items such as new and used cars and trucks, all categories of apparel except infants' clothes, and reading material. They boosted their spending on gasoline, health care, and audio and visual equipment and services—a category that includes high–definition television sets.

Householders aged 35 to 44—the age group now filling with Generation X—spent an average of $58,934 in 2007, more than any other age group. One factor that accounts for the increased spending of householders aged 35 to 44 is their oversized mortgage payments. Many bought homes during the housing bubble, which explains why no other age group spends as much on mortgage interest—$6,239 in 2007. This is 20 percent more than the age group spent on mortgage interest in 2000. As the cost of necessities increased, householders aged 35 to 44 have had to cut or limit their spending on discretionary items such as alcoholic beverages. Out-of-pocket health insurance expenses for the age group rose by 24 percent between 2000 and 2007. Their spending on electricity rose 22 percent, property taxes climbed 30 percent, and vehicle insurance increased 10 percent.

■ The economic slowdown of the past few years has forced many young and middle-aged adults to devote more of their household budget to necessities.

Generation Xers have cut back on many, but not all, discretionary items

(percent change in spending by householders aged 35 to 44 on selected items, 2000 to 2007; in 2007 dollars)

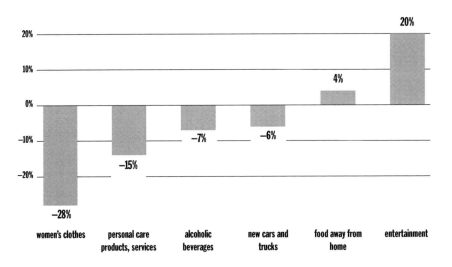

Table 9.1 Average Spending of Total Households, 2000 and 2007

(average annual spending of consumer units, 2000 and 2007; percent change, 2000–07; in 2007 dollars)

	2007	2000	percent change 2000–07
Number of consumer units (in 000s)	120,171	109,367	9.9%
Average annual spending	$49,638	$45,809	8.4
FOOD	**6,133**	**6,211**	**–1.2**
Food at home	**3,465**	**3,638**	**–4.7**
Cereals and bakery products	460	545	–15.7
Cereals and cereal products	143	188	–23.9
Bakery products	317	358	–11.4
Meats, poultry, fish, and eggs	777	957	–18.8
Beef	216	287	–24.6
Pork	150	201	–25.4
Other meats	104	122	–14.5
Poultry	142	175	–18.7
Fish and seafood	122	132	–7.9
Eggs	43	41	5.0
Dairy products	387	391	–1.1
Fresh milk and cream	154	158	–2.4
Other dairy products	234	232	0.7
Fruits and vegetables	600	627	–4.4
Fresh fruits	202	196	2.9
Fresh vegetables	190	191	–0.8
Processed fruits	112	138	–19.1
Processed vegetables	96	101	–5.1
Other food at home	1,241	1,116	11.2
Sugar and other sweets	124	141	–12.0
Fats and oils	91	100	–8.9
Miscellaneous foods	650	526	23.5
Nonalcoholic beverages	333	301	10.6
Food prepared by household on trips	43	48	–10.7
Food away from home	**2,668**	**2,573**	**3.7**
ALCOHOLIC BEVERAGES	**457**	**448**	**2.0**
HOUSING	**16,920**	**14,833**	**14.1**
Shelter	**10,023**	**8,566**	**17.0**
Owned dwellings	6,730	5,541	21.5
Mortgage interest and charges	3,890	3,178	22.4
Property taxes	1,709	1,371	24.6
Maintenance, repairs, insurance, other expenses	1,131	993	13.9
Rented dwellings	2,602	2,449	6.2
Other lodging	691	576	20.1

	2007	2000	percent change 2000–07
Utilities, fuels, public services	**$3,477**	**$2,997**	**16.0%**
Natural gas	480	370	29.9
Electricity	1,303	1,097	18.8
Fuel oil and other fuels	151	117	29.3
Telephone services	1,110	1,056	5.1
Water and other public services	434	356	21.8
Household services	**984**	**824**	**19.5**
Personal services	415	393	5.7
Other household services	569	431	32.0
Housekeeping supplies	**639**	**580**	**10.1**
Laundry and cleaning supplies	140	158	−11.2
Other household products	347	272	27.5
Postage and stationery	152	152	0.2
Household furnishings and equipment	**1,797**	**1,865**	**−3.7**
Household textiles	133	128	4.2
Furniture	446	471	−5.3
Floor coverings	46	53	−13.2
Major appliances	231	228	1.5
Small appliances, miscellaneous housewares	101	105	−3.6
Miscellaneous household equipment	840	880	−4.6
APPAREL AND SERVICES	**1,881**	**2,235**	**−15.8**
Men and boys	**435**	**530**	**−17.9**
Men, aged 16 or older	351	414	−15.3
Boys, aged 2 to 15	84	116	−27.3
Women and girls	**749**	**873**	**−14.2**
Women, aged 16 or older	627	731	−14.2
Girls, aged 2 to 15	122	142	−14.1
Children under age 2	**93**	**99**	**−5.8**
Footwear	**327**	**413**	**−20.8**
Other apparel products and services	**276**	**320**	**−13.8**
TRANSPORTATION	**8,758**	**8,931**	**−1.9**
Vehicle purchases	**3,244**	**4,116**	**−21.2**
Cars and trucks, new	1,572	1,933	−18.7
Cars and trucks, used	1,567	2,131	−26.5
Other vehicles	105	52	102.8
Gasoline and motor oil	**2,384**	**1,554**	**53.4**
Other vehicle expenses	2,592	2,746	−5.6
Vehicle finance charges	305	395	−22.8
Maintenance and repairs	738	751	−1.8
Vehicle insurance	1,071	937	14.3
Vehicle rental, leases, licenses, other charges	478	663	−28.0
Public transportation	**538**	**514**	**4.6**

	2007	2000	percent change 2000–07
HEALTH CARE	**$2,853**	**$2,488**	**14.7%**
Health insurance	1,545	1,184	30.5
Medical services	709	684	3.7
Drugs	481	501	–4.0
Medical supplies	118	119	–1.0
ENTERTAINMENT	**2,698**	**2,243**	**20.3**
Fees and admissions	658	620	6.1
Audio and visual equipment and services	987	749	31.8
Pets, toys, hobbies, and playground equipment	560	402	39.2
Other entertainment supplies, services	493	473	4.2
PERSONAL CARE PRODUCTS, SERVICES	**588**	**679**	**–13.4**
READING	**118**	**176**	**–32.9**
EDUCATION	**945**	**761**	**24.2**
TOBACCO PRODUCTS, SMOKING SUPPLIES	**323**	**384**	**–15.9**
MISCELLANEOUS	**808**	**934**	**–13.5**
CASH CONTRIBUTIONS	**1,821**	**1,435**	**26.9**
PERSONAL INSURANCE AND PENSIONS	**5,336**	**4,052**	**31.7**
Life and other personal insurance	309	480	–35.7
Pensions and Social Security	5,027	–	–
PERSONAL TAXES	**2,233**	**3,753**	**–40.5**
Federal income taxes	1,569	2,901	–45.9
State and local income taxes	468	677	–30.8
Other taxes	196	176	11.5
GIFTS FOR PEOPLE IN OTHER HOUSEHOLDS	**1,198**	**1,304**	**–8.1**

Note: The Bureau of Labor Statistics uses consumer unit rather than household as the sampling unit in the Consumer Expenditure Survey. For the definition of consumer unit, see the glossary. Spending on gifts is also included in the preceding product and service categories. Average spending is rounded to the nearest dollar, but the percent change calculation is based on unrounded figures. "–" means comparable data are not available.
Source: Bureau of Labor Statistics, 2000 and 2007 Consumer Expenditure Survey, Internet site http://www.bls.gov/cex/; calculations by New Strategist

Table 9.2 Average Spending of Householders Aged 25 to 34, 2000 and 2007

(average annual spending of consumer units headed by people aged 25 to 34, 2000 and 2007; percent change, 2000–07; in 2007 dollars)

	2007	2000	percent change 2000–07
Number of consumer units (in 000s)	20,499	18,887	8.5%
Average annual spending	$47,510	$46,893	1.3
FOOD	6,000	6,333	–5.3
Food at home	3,210	3,553	–9.7
Cereals and bakery products	427	517	–17.3
Cereals and cereal products	144	201	–28.4
Bakery products	282	317	–10.9
Meats, poultry, fish, and eggs	692	927	–25.4
Beef	197	288	–31.5
Pork	127	187	–32.0
Other meats	89	118	–24.6
Poultry	138	175	–21.0
Fish and seafood	99	123	–19.4
Eggs	41	36	13.5
Dairy products	368	382	–3.6
Fresh milk and cream	157	161	–2.7
Other dairy products	211	220	–4.2
Fruits and vegetables	529	588	–10.0
Fresh fruits	168	176	–4.4
Fresh vegetables	163	178	–8.5
Processed fruits	111	136	–18.4
Processed vegetables	87	99	–11.9
Other food at home	1,194	1,139	4.8
Sugar and other sweets	100	126	–20.9
Fats and oils	76	93	–18.0
Miscellaneous foods	683	584	17.0
Nonalcoholic beverages	305	297	2.6
Food prepared by household on trips	30	37	–19.6
Food away from home	2,790	2,780	0.4
ALCOHOLIC BEVERAGES	514	519	–1.0
HOUSING	17,329	15,713	10.3
Shelter	10,536	9,518	10.7
Owned dwellings	5,985	4,987	20.0
Mortgage interest and charges	4,286	3,477	23.3
Property taxes	1,076	909	18.4
Maintenance, repairs, insurance, other expenses	623	601	3.7
Rented dwellings	4,288	4,231	1.3
Other lodging	263	299	–11.9

	2007	2000	percent change 2000–07
Utilities, fuels, public services	**$3,063**	**$2,819**	**8.7%**
Natural gas	379	329	15.3
Electricity	1,148	995	15.4
Fuel oil and other fuels	85	70	21.7
Telephone services	1,094	1,144	–4.4
Water and other public services	357	282	26.7
Household services	**1,175**	**1,049**	**12.0**
Personal services	780	772	1.1
Other household services	394	277	42.3
Housekeeping supplies	**522**	**526**	**–0.8**
Laundry and cleaning supplies	129	151	–14.3
Other household products	265	242	9.5
Postage and stationery	127	135	–5.8
Household furnishings and equipment	**2,034**	**1,800**	**13.0**
Household textiles	120	144	–16.9
Furniture	537	550	–2.4
Floor coverings	48	51	–5.1
Major appliances	213	218	–2.3
Small appliances, miscellaneous housewares	103	94	9.7
Miscellaneous household equipment	1,013	743	36.4
APPAREL AND SERVICES	**2,106**	**2,479**	**–15.1**
Men and boys	**508**	**615**	**–17.4**
Men, aged 16 or older	396	443	–10.6
Boys, aged 2 to 15	112	172	–35.0
Women and girls	**729**	**848**	**–14.0**
Women, aged 16 or older	570	675	–15.6
Girls, aged 2 to 15	158	173	–8.9
Children under age 2	**206**	**199**	**3.7**
Footwear	**383**	**474**	**–19.3**
Other apparel products and services	**281**	**343**	**–18.1**
TRANSPORTATION	**9,065**	**10,062**	**–9.9**
Vehicle purchases	**3,930**	**4,984**	**–21.1**
Cars and trucks, new	1,541	2,222	–30.6
Cars and trucks, used	2,256	2,669	–15.5
Other vehicles	133	93	43.5
Gasoline and motor oil	**2,446**	**1,615**	**51.5**
Other vehicle expenses	**2,293**	**2,989**	**–23.3**
Vehicle finance charges	384	525	–26.9
Maintenance and repairs	609	686	–11.3
Vehicle insurance	802	932	–13.9
Vehicle rental, leases, licenses, other charges	498	844	–41.0
Public transportation	**396**	**476**	**–16.7**

	2007	2000	percent change 2000–07
HEALTH CARE	**$1,740**	**$1,512**	**15.1%**
Health insurance	918	771	19.1
Medical services	556	442	25.8
Drugs	203	218	–6.9
Medical supplies	64	83	–23.0
ENTERTAINMENT	**2,462**	**2,259**	**9.0**
Fees and admissions	500	554	–9.7
Audio and visual equipment and services	1,034	819	26.3
Pets, toys, hobbies, and playground equipment	480	423	13.6
Other entertainment supplies, services	448	464	–3.4
PERSONAL CARE PRODUCTS, SERVICES	**512**	**694**	**–26.2**
READING	**72**	**142**	**–49.3**
EDUCATION	**604**	**704**	**–14.3**
TOBACCO PRODUCTS, SMOKING SUPPLIES	**331**	**373**	**–11.3**
MISCELLANEOUS	**589**	**968**	**–39.2**
CASH CONTRIBUTIONS	**1,027**	**780**	**31.6**
PERSONAL INSURANCE AND PENSIONS	**5,159**	**4,352**	**18.6**
Life and other personal insurance	164	291	–43.7
Pensions and Social Security	4,995	–	–
PERSONAL TAXES	**1,491**	**3,411**	**–56.3**
Federal income taxes	982	2,655	–63.0
State and local income taxes	413	686	–39.8
Other taxes	96	70	37.5
GIFTS FOR PEOPLE IN OTHER HOUSEHOLDS	**582**	**862**	**–32.5**

Note: The Bureau of Labor Statistics uses consumer unit rather than household as the sampling unit in the Consumer Expenditure Survey. For the definition of consumer unit, see the glossary. Spending on gifts is also included in the preceding product and service categories. Average spending is rounded to the nearest dollar, but the percent change calculation is based on unrounded figures. "–" means comparable data are not available.
Source: Bureau of Labor Statistics, 2000 and 2007 Consumer Expenditure Survey, Internet site http://www.bls.gov/cex/; calculations by New Strategist

Table 9.3 Average Spending of Householders Aged 35 to 44, 2000 and 2007

(average annual spending of consumer units headed by people aged 35 to 44, 2000 and 2007; percent change, 2000–07; in 2007 dollars)

	2007	2000	percent change 2000–07
Number of consumer units (in 000s)	23,416	23,983	–2.4%
Average annual spending	$58,934	$54,363	8.4
FOOD	7,393	7,335	0.8
Food at home	4,125	4,195	–1.7
Cereals and bakery products	548	639	–14.3
Cereals and cereal products	177	229	–22.6
Bakery products	371	411	–9.6
Meats, poultry, fish, and eggs	976	1,105	–11.7
Beef	284	325	–12.6
Pork	185	224	–17.4
Other meats	127	144	–12.1
Poultry	179	214	–16.5
Fish and seafood	152	152	0.2
Eggs	49	45	10.0
Dairy products	459	461	–0.5
Fresh milk and cream	187	189	–1.1
Other dairy products	271	272	–0.4
Fruits and vegetables	677	665	1.9
Fresh fruits	227	203	11.6
Fresh vegetables	220	197	11.4
Processed fruits	125	151	–16.9
Processed vegetables	105	111	–5.2
Other food at home	1,465	1,326	10.5
Sugar and other sweets	151	177	–14.7
Fats and oils	101	108	–6.8
Miscellaneous foods	781	624	25.2
Nonalcoholic beverages	382	361	5.8
Food prepared by household on trips	50	55	–9.7
Food away from home	3,268	3,139	4.1
ALCOHOLIC BEVERAGES	469	506	–7.3
HOUSING	20,952	18,195	15.2
Shelter	12,758	10,752	18.7
Owned dwellings	9,232	7,746	19.2
Mortgage interest and charges	6,239	5,180	20.4
Property taxes	1,950	1,500	30.0
Maintenance, repairs, insurance, other expenses	1,043	1,064	–2.0
Rented dwellings	2,849	2,489	14.5
Other lodging	677	518	30.8

	2007	2000	percent change 2000–07
Utilities, fuels, public services	**$3,928**	**$3,383**	**16.1%**
Natural gas	534	421	26.7
Electricity	1,479	1,215	21.7
Fuel oil and other fuels	132	117	13.0
Telephone services	1,295	1,226	5.6
Water and other public services	487	405	20.4
Household services	**1,422**	**1,079**	**31.8**
Personal services	844	653	29.3
Other household services	579	426	35.8
Housekeeping supplies	**646**	**686**	**–5.9**
Laundry and cleaning supplies	178	189	–5.8
Other household products	343	337	1.7
Postage and stationery	125	160	–21.9
Household furnishings and equipment	**2,198**	**2,295**	**–4.2**
Household textiles	169	149	13.2
Furniture	625	601	4.0
Floor coverings	50	64	–21.6
Major appliances	251	255	–1.7
Small appliances, miscellaneous housewares	110	112	–1.8
Miscellaneous household equipment	993	1,115	–10.9
APPAREL AND SERVICES	**2,335**	**2,797**	**–16.5**
Men and boys	**582**	**663**	**–12.3**
Men, aged 16 or older	403	442	–8.8
Boys, aged 2 to 15	178	222	–19.7
Women and girls	**855**	**1,126**	**–24.1**
Women, aged 16 or older	604	833	–27.5
Girls, aged 2 to 15	251	291	–13.9
Children under age 2	**119**	**126**	**–5.9**
Footwear	**399**	**483**	**–17.4**
Other apparel products and services	**381**	**399**	**–4.4**
TRANSPORTATION	**10,558**	**10,478**	**0.8**
Vehicle purchases	**4,183**	**4,811**	**–13.1**
Cars and trucks, new	1,955	2,076	–5.8
Cars and trucks, used	2,106	2,647	–20.4
Other vehicles	122	89	36.9
Gasoline and motor oil	**2,870**	**1,899**	**51.1**
Other vehicle expenses	**2,966**	**3,223**	**–8.0**
Vehicle finance charges	400	489	–18.2
Maintenance and repairs	809	852	–5.1
Vehicle insurance	1,173	1,064	10.2
Vehicle rental, leases, licenses, other charges	584	819	–28.7
Public transportation	**540**	**543**	**–0.6**

	2007	2000	percent change 2000–07
HEALTH CARE	**$2,315**	**$2,136**	**8.4%**
Health insurance	1,269	1,023	24.0
Medical services	651	668	–2.6
Drugs	303	342	–11.4
Medical supplies	93	102	–9.1
ENTERTAINMENT	**3,551**	**2,967**	**19.7**
Fees and admissions	967	861	12.3
Audio and visual equipment and services	1,196	950	25.9
Pets, toys, hobbies, and playground equipment	730	543	34.4
Other entertainment supplies, services	658	613	7.4
PERSONAL CARE PRODUCTS, SERVICES	**662**	**775**	**–14.6**
READING	**107**	**182**	**–41.1**
EDUCATION	**819**	**741**	**10.6**
TOBACCO PRODUCTS, SMOKING SUPPLIES	**379**	**514**	**–26.3**
MISCELLANEOUS	**845**	**1,026**	**–17.6**
CASH CONTRIBUTIONS	**1,569**	**1,208**	**29.9**
PERSONAL INSURANCE AND PENSIONS	**6,980**	**5,503**	**26.8**
Life and other personal insurance	286	496	–42.3
Pensions and Social Security	6,694	–	–
PERSONAL TAXES	**2,489**	**4,665**	**–46.6**
Federal income taxes	1,741	3,629	–52.0
State and local income taxes	561	884	–36.5
Other taxes	188	152	23.9
GIFTS FOR PEOPLE IN OTHER HOUSEHOLDS	**806**	**1,205**	**–33.1**

Note: The Bureau of Labor Statistics uses consumer unit rather than household as the sampling unit in the Consumer Expenditure Survey. For the definition of consumer unit, see the glossary. Spending on gifts is also included in the preceding product and service categories. Average spending is rounded to the nearest dollar, but the percent change calculation is based on unrounded figures. "–" means comparable data are not available.
Source: Bureau of Labor Statistics, 2000 and 2007 Consumer Expenditure Survey, Internet site http://www.bls.gov/cex/; calculations by New Strategist

Householders Aged 25 to 34 Are Average Spenders

They spend more than average on the products and services typical of young adults.

The spending of households headed by people aged 25 to 34 almost matches spending by the average household. In 2007, the average householder aged 25 to 34 spent $47,510, slightly less than the $49,638 national average.

The lifestyle of young adults is readily discernable in the spending statistics. In 2007, householders aged 25 to 34 spent 44 percent more than average on used cars and trucks and 26 percent more than average on vehicle finance charges. Householders aged 25 to 34 devoted $514 to alcohol in 2007—or 12 percent more than the average household. Most in the age group cannot yet afford to buy a home. Consequently, their spending on rent is 65 percent more than average.

What is most clearly reflected in the spending data for 25-to-34-year-olds is their status as parents. The spending of these households far exceeds the average for products and services needed by young children. They spend more than twice as much as the average household on clothing for infants and 88 percent more than average on household personal services (mostly day care).

■ The incomes of young adults do not leave much room for extravagance, and the need to buy for children limits them further.

Young adults spent 12 percent more than average on alcoholic beverages

(indexed spending of householders aged 25 to 34 on selected items, 2007)

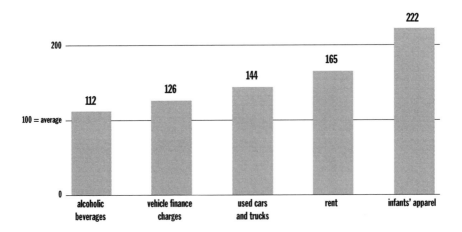

Table 9.4 Average, Indexed, and Market Share of Spending by Householders Aged 25 to 34, 2007

(average annual spending of total consumer units and average annual, indexed, and market share of spending by consumer units headed by 25-to-34-year-olds, 2007)

	total consumer units	consumer units headed by 25-to-34-year-olds		
		average spending	indexed spending	market share
Number of consumer units (in 000s)	120,171	20,499	–	17.1%
Average annual spending	$49,638	$47,510	96	16.3
FOOD	**6,133**	**6,000**	**98**	**16.7**
Food at home	**3,465**	**3,210**	**93**	**15.8**
Cereals and bakery products	460	427	93	15.8
Cereals and cereal products	143	144	101	17.2
Bakery products	317	282	89	15.2
Meats, poultry, fish, and eggs	777	692	89	15.2
Beef	216	197	91	15.6
Pork	150	127	85	14.4
Other meats	104	89	86	14.6
Poultry	142	138	97	16.6
Fish and seafood	122	99	81	13.8
Eggs	43	41	95	16.3
Dairy products	387	368	95	16.2
Fresh milk and cream	154	157	102	17.4
Other dairy products	234	211	90	15.4
Fruits and vegetables	600	529	88	15.0
Fresh fruits	202	168	83	14.2
Fresh vegetables	190	163	86	14.6
Processed fruits	112	111	99	16.9
Processed vegetables	96	87	91	15.5
Other food at home	1,241	1,194	96	16.4
Sugar and other sweets	124	100	81	13.8
Fats and oils	91	76	84	14.2
Miscellaneous foods	650	683	105	17.9
Nonalcoholic beverages	333	305	92	15.6
Food prepared by household on trips	43	30	70	11.9
Food away from home	**2,668**	**2,790**	**105**	**17.8**
ALCOHOLIC BEVERAGES	**457**	**514**	**112**	**19.2**
HOUSING	**16,920**	**17,329**	**102**	**17.5**
Shelter	**10,023**	**10,536**	**105**	**17.9**
Owned dwellings	6,730	5,985	89	15.2
Mortgage interest and charges	3,890	4,286	110	18.8
Property taxes	1,709	1,076	63	10.7
Maintenance, repairs, insurance, other expenses	1,131	623	55	9.4
Rented dwellings	2,602	4,288	165	28.1
Other lodging	691	263	38	6.5

	total consumer units	consumer units headed by 25-to-34-year-olds		
		average spending	indexed spending	market share
Utilities, fuels, public services	**$3,477**	**$3,063**	**88**	**15.0%**
Natural gas	480	379	79	13.5
Electricity	1,303	1,148	88	15.0
Fuel oil and other fuels	151	85	56	9.6
Telephone services	1,110	1,094	99	16.8
Water and other public services	434	357	82	14.0
Household services	**984**	**1,175**	**119**	**20.4**
Personal services	415	780	188	32.1
Other household services	569	394	69	11.8
Housekeeping supplies	**639**	**522**	**82**	**13.9**
Laundry and cleaning supplies	140	129	92	15.7
Other household products	347	265	76	13.0
Postage and stationery	152	127	84	14.3
Household furnishings and equipment	**1,797**	**2,034**	**113**	**19.3**
Household textiles	133	120	90	15.4
Furniture	446	537	120	20.5
Floor coverings	46	48	104	17.8
Major appliances	231	213	92	15.7
Small appliances, miscellaneous housewares	101	103	102	17.4
Miscellaneous household equipment	840	1,013	121	20.6
APPAREL AND SERVICES	**1,881**	**2,106**	**112**	**19.1**
Men and boys	**435**	**508**	**117**	**19.9**
Men, aged 16 or older	351	396	113	19.2
Boys, aged 2 to 15	84	112	133	22.7
Women and girls	**749**	**729**	**97**	**16.6**
Women, aged 16 or older	627	570	91	15.5
Girls, aged 2 to 15	122	158	130	22.1
Children under age 2	**93**	**206**	**222**	**37.8**
Footwear	**327**	**383**	**117**	**20.0**
Other apparel products and services	**276**	**281**	**102**	**17.4**
TRANSPORTATION	**8,758**	**9,065**	**104**	**17.7**
Vehicle purchases	**3,244**	**3,930**	**121**	**20.7**
Cars and trucks, new	1,572	1,541	98	16.7
Cars and trucks, used	1,567	2,256	144	24.6
Other vehicles	105	133	127	21.6
Gasoline and motor oil	**2,384**	**2,446**	**103**	**17.5**
Other vehicle expenses	**2,592**	**2,293**	**88**	**15.1**
Vehicle finance charges	305	384	126	21.5
Maintenance and repairs	738	609	83	14.1
Vehicle insurance	1,071	802	75	12.8
Vehicle rental, leases, licenses, other charges	478	498	104	17.8
Public transportation	**538**	**396**	**74**	**12.6**

	total consumer units	consumer units headed by 25-to-34-year-olds		
		average spending	indexed spending	market share
HEALTH CARE	**$2,853**	**$1,740**	**61**	**10.4%**
Health insurance	1,545	918	59	10.1
Medical services	709	556	78	13.4
Drugs	481	203	42	7.2
Medical supplies	118	64	54	9.3
ENTERTAINMENT	**2,698**	**2,462**	**91**	**15.6**
Fees and admissions	658	500	76	13.0
Audio and visual equipment and services	987	1,034	105	17.9
Pets, toys, hobbies, and playground equipment	560	480	86	14.6
Other entertainment supplies, services	493	448	91	15.5
PERSONAL CARE PRODUCTS, SERVICES	**588**	**512**	**87**	**14.9**
READING	**118**	**72**	**61**	**10.4**
EDUCATION	**945**	**604**	**64**	**10.9**
TOBACCO PRODUCTS, SMOKING SUPPLIES	**323**	**331**	**102**	**17.5**
MISCELLANEOUS	**808**	**589**	**73**	**12.4**
CASH CONTRIBUTIONS	**1,821**	**1,027**	**56**	**9.6**
PERSONAL INSURANCE AND PENSIONS	**5,336**	**5,159**	**97**	**16.5**
Life and other personal insurance	309	164	53	9.1
Pensions and Social Security	5,027	4,995	99	16.9
PERSONAL TAXES	**2,233**	**1,491**	**67**	**11.4**
Federal income taxes	1,569	982	63	10.7
State and local income taxes	468	413	88	15.1
Other taxes	196	96	49	8.4
GIFTS FOR PEOPLE IN OTHER HOUSEHOLDS	**1,198**	**582**	**49**	**8.3**

Note: The Bureau of Labor Statistics uses consumer unit rather than household as the sampling unit in the Consumer Expenditure Survey. For the definition of consumer unit, see the glossary. Spending on gifts is also included in the preceding product and service categories. "–" means not applicable.
Source: Bureau of Labor Statistics, 2007 Consumer Expenditure Survey, Internet site http://www.bls.gov/cex/; calculations by New Strategist

Householders Aged 35 to 44 Spend More than Average

Most households in the age group include children, which accounts for their above-average spending.

Householders aged 35 to 44 spend more than any other age group—$58,934 in 2007 and 19 percent more than the average household. The age group controls 23 percent of household spending. Householders aged 35 to 44 spend significantly more than average on items commonly purchased by parents with children under age 18. They spend 21 percent more than the average household on milk and about twice the average on children's clothing. Many in this age group bought homes during the housing bubble, which explains why their mortgage interest payments are 60 percent above average.

Householders aged 35 to 44 spend less than average on some surprising items. They spend 4 percent less than average on women's clothing, 18 percent less on out-of-pocket health insurance expenses, and 33 percent less on gifts for people in other households.

■ The spending of householders aged 35 to 44 is determined by children, which reduces their spending on other items.

Householders aged 35 to 44 spend 24 percent more than the average household on cereal

(indexed spending of householders aged 35 to 44 on selected items, 2007)

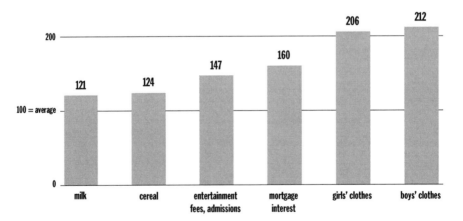

Table 9.5 Average, Indexed, and Market Share of Spending by Householders Aged 35 to 44, 2007

(average annual spending of total consumer units and average annual, indexed, and market share of spending by consumer units headed by 35-to-44-year-olds, 2007)

	total consumer units	consumer units headed by 35-to-44-year-olds		
		average spending	indexed spending	market share
Number of consumer units (in 000s)	120,171	23,416	–	19.5%
Average annual spending	$49,638	$58,934	119	23.1
FOOD	**6,133**	**7,393**	**121**	**23.5**
Food at home	**3,465**	**4,125**	**119**	**23.2**
Cereals and bakery products	460	548	119	23.2
Cereals and cereal products	143	177	124	24.1
Bakery products	317	371	117	22.8
Meats, poultry, fish, and eggs	777	976	126	24.5
Beef	216	284	131	25.6
Pork	150	185	123	24.0
Other meats	104	127	122	23.8
Poultry	142	179	126	24.6
Fish and seafood	122	152	125	24.3
Eggs	43	49	114	22.2
Dairy products	387	459	119	23.1
Fresh milk and cream	154	187	121	23.7
Other dairy products	234	271	116	22.6
Fruits and vegetables	600	677	113	22.0
Fresh fruits	202	227	112	21.9
Fresh vegetables	190	220	116	22.6
Processed fruits	112	125	112	21.7
Processed vegetables	96	105	109	21.3
Other food at home	1,241	1,465	118	23.0
Sugar and other sweets	124	151	122	23.7
Fats and oils	91	101	111	21.6
Miscellaneous foods	650	781	120	23.4
Nonalcoholic beverages	333	382	115	22.4
Food prepared by household on trips	43	50	116	22.7
Food away from home	**2,668**	**3,268**	**122**	**23.9**
ALCOHOLIC BEVERAGES	**457**	**469**	**103**	**20.0**
HOUSING	**16,920**	**20,952**	**124**	**24.1**
Shelter	**10,023**	**12,758**	**127**	**24.8**
Owned dwellings	6,730	9,232	137	26.7
Mortgage interest and charges	3,890	6,239	160	31.3
Property taxes	1,709	1,950	114	22.2
Maintenance, repairs, insurance, other expenses	1,131	1,043	92	18.0
Rented dwellings	2,602	2,849	109	21.3
Other lodging	691	677	98	19.1

	total consumer units	consumer units headed by 35-to-44-year-olds		
		average spending	indexed spending	market share
Utilities, fuels, public services	**$3,477**	**$3,928**	**113**	**22.0%**
Natural gas	480	534	111	21.7
Electricity	1,303	1,479	114	22.1
Fuel oil and other fuels	151	132	87	17.0
Telephone services	1,110	1,295	117	22.7
Water and other public services	434	487	112	21.9
Household services	**984**	**1,422**	**145**	**28.2**
Personal services	415	844	203	39.6
Other household services	569	579	102	19.8
Housekeeping supplies	**639**	**646**	**101**	**19.7**
Laundry and cleaning supplies	140	178	127	24.8
Other household products	347	343	99	19.3
Postage and stationery	152	125	82	16.0
Household furnishings and equipment	**1,797**	**2,198**	**122**	**23.8**
Household textiles	133	169	127	24.8
Furniture	446	625	140	27.3
Floor coverings	46	50	109	21.2
Major appliances	231	251	109	21.2
Small appliances, miscellaneous housewares	101	110	109	21.2
Miscellaneous household equipment	840	993	118	23.0
APPAREL AND SERVICES	**1,881**	**2,335**	**124**	**24.2**
Men and boys	**435**	**582**	**134**	**26.1**
Men, aged 16 or older	351	403	115	22.4
Boys, aged 2 to 15	84	178	212	41.3
Women and girls	**749**	**855**	**114**	**22.2**
Women, aged 16 or older	627	604	96	18.8
Girls, aged 2 to 15	122	251	206	40.1
Children under age 2	**93**	**119**	**128**	**24.9**
Footwear	**327**	**399**	**122**	**23.8**
Other apparel products and services	**276**	**381**	**138**	**26.9**
TRANSPORTATION	**8,758**	**10,558**	**121**	**23.5**
Vehicle purchases	**3,244**	**4,183**	**129**	**25.1**
Cars and trucks, new	1,572	1,955	124	24.2
Cars and trucks, used	1,567	2,106	134	26.2
Other vehicles	105	122	116	22.6
Gasoline and motor oil	**2,384**	**2,870**	**120**	**23.5**
Other vehicle expenses	**2,592**	**2,966**	**114**	**22.3**
Vehicle finance charges	305	400	131	25.6
Maintenance and repairs	738	809	110	21.4
Vehicle insurance	1,071	1,173	110	21.3
Vehicle rental, leases, licenses, other charges	478	584	122	23.8
Public transportation	**538**	**540**	**100**	**19.6**

	total consumer units	consumer units headed by 35-to-44-year-olds		
		average spending	indexed spending	market share
HEALTH CARE	**$2,853**	**$2,315**	**81**	**15.8%**
Health insurance	1,545	1,269	82	16.0
Medical services	709	651	92	17.9
Drugs	481	303	63	12.3
Medical supplies	118	93	79	15.4
ENTERTAINMENT	**2,698**	**3,551**	**132**	**25.6**
Fees and admissions	658	967	147	28.6
Audio and visual equipment and services	987	1,196	121	23.6
Pets, toys, hobbies, and playground equipment	560	730	130	25.4
Other entertainment supplies, services	493	658	133	26.0
PERSONAL CARE PRODUCTS, SERVICES	**588**	**662**	**113**	**21.9**
READING	**118**	**107**	**91**	**17.7**
EDUCATION	**945**	**819**	**87**	**16.9**
TOBACCO PRODUCTS, SMOKING SUPPLIES	**323**	**379**	**117**	**22.9**
MISCELLANEOUS	**808**	**845**	**105**	**20.4**
CASH CONTRIBUTIONS	**1,821**	**1,569**	**86**	**16.8**
PERSONAL INSURANCE AND PENSIONS	**5,336**	**6,980**	**131**	**25.5**
Life and other personal insurance	309	286	93	18.0
Pensions and Social Security	5,027	6,694	133	25.9
PERSONAL TAXES	**2,233**	**2,489**	**111**	**21.7**
Federal income taxes	1,569	1,741	111	21.6
State and local income taxes	468	561	120	23.4
Other taxes	196	188	96	18.7
GIFTS FOR PEOPLE IN OTHER HOUSEHOLDS	**1,198**	**806**	**67**	**13.1**

Note: The Bureau of Labor Statistics uses consumer unit rather than household as the sampling unit in the Consumer Expenditure Survey. For the definition of consumer unit, see the glossary. Spending on gifts is also included in the preceding product and service categories. "–" means not applicable.
Source: Bureau of Labor Statistics, 2007 Consumer Expenditure Survey, Internet site http://www.bls.gov/cex/; calculations by New Strategist

Time Use

■ People aged 35 to 44 have the least amount of leisure time because most are juggling work and family responsibilities.

■ The middle aged spend the most time at work. Men aged 35 to 44 spend 5.43 hours per day at work versus the 4.16 hours per day spent at work by the average man.

■ Women aged 35 to 44 spend twice as much time as the average woman caring for household children. They spend 27 percent more time than the average woman at work.

■ Women aged 35 to 44 have 21 percent less leisure time than the average woman. Men aged 35 to 44 have 15 percent less leisure time than the average man.

Generation X Spends More Time at Work than at Play

People aged 35 to 44 spend 29 percent more time than the average person at work.

Time use varies sharply by age. The middle aged are the ones who spend the most time at work and the least time at play, according to the Bureau of Labor Statistics' American Time Use Survey. Men aged 35 to 44 spend 5.43 hours per day at work versus the 4.16 hours per day spent at work by the average man. Women aged 35 to 44 spend 27 percent more time than the average woman at work.

People aged 35 to 44 have the least amount of leisure time because most are juggling both work and family responsibilities. Women aged 35 to 44 have 21 percent less leisure time than the average woman. Men in the age group have 15 percent less leisure time than the average man.

■ As their children grow up, Gen Xers will have more leisure time.

Time at work peaks in middle age

(average number of hours per day spent working, by age, 2007)

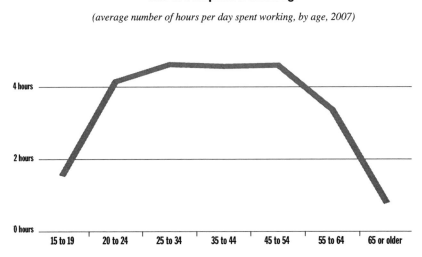

Table 10.1 Detailed Time Use of People Aged 35 to 44, 2007

(hours per day spent in primary activities by total people aged 15 or older and people aged 35 to 44, and index of age group to total, 2007)

	hours per day for total people	hours per day for people aged 35 to 44	index, 35 to 44 to total
TOTAL, ALL ACTIVITIES	**24.00**	**24.00**	**100**
Personal care activities	**9.31**	**9.04**	**97**
Sleeping	8.57	8.35	97
Grooming	0.67	0.63	94
Health-related self-care	0.07	0.06	86
Household activities	**1.87**	**1.89**	**101**
Housework	0.64	0.68	106
Food preparation and cleanup	0.52	0.60	115
Lawn, garden, and houseplants	0.21	0.17	81
Animals and pets	0.09	0.08	89
Vehicles	0.04	0.03	75
Household management	0.22	0.18	82
Household and personal mail and messages (except email)	0.02	0.01	50
Household and personal email and messages	0.05	0.03	60
Caring for and helping household members	**0.45**	**0.92**	**204**
Caring for and helping household children	0.38	0.79	208
Caring for household adults	0.03	0.02	67
Helping household adults	0.01	0.01	100
Caring for and helping people in other households	**0.14**	**0.10**	**71**
Caring for and helping children in other households	0.06	0.03	50
Caring for adults in other households	0.01	0.01	100
Helping adults in other households	0.06	0.06	100
Working and work-related activities	**3.53**	**4.57**	**129**
Working	3.47	4.50	130
Educational activities	**0.40**	**0.11**	**28**
Attending class	0.26	0.06	23
Homework and research	0.14	0.05	36
Consumer purchases	**0.39**	**0.39**	**100**
Shopping (store, telephone, Internet)	0.39	0.39	100
Grocery shopping	0.10	0.08	80
Shopping (except groceries, food, and gas)	0.27	0.28	104
Professional and personal care services	**0.09**	**0.06**	**67**
Medical and care services	0.05	0.04	80
Eating and drinking	**1.11**	**1.06**	**95**
Socializing, relaxing, and leisure	**4.52**	**3.72**	**82**
Socializing and communicating	0.64	0.59	92
Attending or hosting social events	0.09	0.09	100
Relaxing and leisure	3.70	2.95	80
Television and movies	2.62	2.18	83
Playing games	0.19	0.13	68
Computer use for leisure (except games)	0.14	0.12	86
Reading for personal interest	0.35	0.19	54
Arts and entertainment (other than sports)	0.09	0.09	100
Attending movies	0.03	0.02	67

	hours per day for total people	hours per day for people aged 35 to 44	index, 35 to 44 to total
Sports, exercise, and recreation	**0.35**	**0.30**	**86**
Participating in sports, exercise, and recreation	0.32	0.27	84
Attending sporting or recreational events	0.03	0.02	67
Religious and spiritual activities	**0.15**	**0.12**	**80**
Volunteer activities	**0.16**	**0.13**	**81**
Telephone calls	**0.11**	**0.07**	**64**
Traveling	**1.23**	**1.33**	**108**

Note: Primary activities are those respondents identified as their main activity. Other activities done simultaneously are not included. Travel related to activities is reported separately. Numbers do not sum to total because not all activities are shown. The index is calculated by dividing time spent by age group by time spent by average person and multiplying by 100.
Source: Bureau of Labor Statistics, unpublished tables from the 2007 American Time Use Survey, Internet site http://www.bls .gov/tus/home.htm

Table 10.2 Detailed Time Use of Men Aged 35 to 44, 2007

(hours per day spent in primary activities by total men aged 15 or older and men aged 35 to 44, and index of age group to total, 2007)

	hours per day for total men	hours per day for men aged 35 to 44	index, 35 to 44 to total
TOTAL, ALL ACTIVITIES	24.00	24.00	100
Personal care activities	**9.12**	**8.83**	**97**
Sleeping	8.52	8.28	97
Grooming	0.54	0.53	98
Health-related self-care	0.05	0.02	40
Household activities	**1.45**	**1.34**	**92**
Housework	0.29	0.31	107
Food preparation and cleanup	0.28	0.30	107
Lawn, garden, and houseplants	0.30	0.24	80
Animals and pets	0.09	0.06	67
Vehicles	0.07	0.06	86
Household management	0.19	0.16	84
Household and personal mail and messages (except email)	0.02	0.01	50
Household and personal email and messages	0.05	0.03	60
Caring for and helping household members	**0.27**	**0.58**	**215**
Caring for and helping household children	0.22	0.53	241
Caring for household adults	0.02	–	–
Helping household adults	0.01	0.01	100
Caring for and helping people in other households	**0.11**	**0.01**	**9**
Caring for and helping children in other households	0.04	0.01	25
Caring for adults in other households	0.01	0.01	100
Helping adults in other households	0.06	0.07	117
Working and work-related activities	**4.16**	**5.43**	**131**
Working	4.09	5.33	130
Educational activities	**0.38**	**0.08**	**21**
Attending class	0.26	0.05	19
Homework and research	0.12	0.03	25
Consumer purchases	**0.31**	**0.28**	**90**
Shopping (store, telephone, Internet)	0.31	0.28	90
Grocery shopping	0.07	0.06	86
Shopping (except groceries, food, and gas)	0.21	0.20	95
Professional and personal care services	**0.06**	**0.03**	**50**
Medical and care services	0.04	0.02	50
Eating and drinking	**1.14**	**1.08**	**95**
Socializing, relaxing, and leisure	**4.77**	**4.04**	**85**
Socializing and communicating	0.59	0.60	102
Attending or hosting social events	0.08	0.07	88
Relaxing and leisure	4.02	3.27	81
Television and movies	2.88	2.37	82
Playing games	0.24	0.20	83
Computer use for leisure (except games)	0.17	0.13	76
Reading for personal interest	0.28	0.16	57
Arts and entertainment (other than sports)	0.09	0.09	100
Attending movies	0.03	0.03	100

	hours per day for total men	hours per day for men aged 35 to 44	index, 35 to 44 to total
Sports, exercise, and recreation	**0.45**	**0.36**	**80**
Participating in sports, exercise, and recreation	0.42	0.34	81
Attending sporting or recreational events	0.03	0.02	67
Religious and spiritual activities	**0.11**	**0.11**	**100**
Volunteer activities	**0.13**	**0.11**	**85**
Telephone calls	**0.06**	**0.03**	**50**
Traveling	**1.28**	**1.43**	**112**

Note: Primary activities are those respondents identified as their main activity. Other activities done simultaneously are not included. Travel related to activities is reported separately. Numbers do not sum to total because not all activities are shown. The index is calculated by dividing time spent by age group by time spent by average man and multiplying by 100. "–" means sample is too small to make a reliable estimate.
Source: Bureau of Labor Statistics, unpublished tables from the 2007 American Time Use Survey, Internet site http://www.bls .gov/tus/home.htm

Table 10.3 Detailed Time Use of Women Aged 35 to 44, 2007

(hours per day spent in primary activities by total women aged 15 or older and women aged 35 to 44, and index of age group to total, 2007)

	hours per day for total women	hours per day for women aged 35 to 44	index, 35 to 44 to total
TOTAL, ALL ACTIVITIES	**24.00**	**24.00**	**100**
Personal care activities	**9.50**	**9.25**	**97**
Sleeping	8.63	8.41	97
Grooming	0.79	0.74	94
Health-related self-care	0.08	0.09	113
Household activities	**2.27**	**2.43**	**107**
Housework	0.97	1.04	107
Food preparation and cleanup	0.74	0.89	120
Lawn, garden, and houseplants	0.12	0.11	92
Animals and pets	0.10	0.10	100
Vehicles	0.01	–	–
Household management	0.24	0.20	83
Household and personal mail and messages (except email)	0.03	0.01	33
Household and personal email and messages	0.05	0.03	60
Caring for and helping household members	**0.62**	**1.26**	**203**
Caring for and helping household children	0.52	1.05	202
Caring for household adults	0.03	0.03	100
Helping household adults	0.01	0.01	100
Caring for and helping people in other households	**0.16**	**0.10**	**63**
Caring for and helping children in other households	0.09	0.04	44
Caring for adults in other households	0.02	0.01	50
Helping adults in other households	0.05	0.05	100
Working and work-related activities	**2.93**	**3.73**	**127**
Working	2.89	3.70	128
Educational activities	**0.42**	**0.14**	**33**
Attending class	0.25	0.06	24
Homework and research	0.15	0.08	53
Consumer purchases	**0.48**	**0.49**	**102**
Shopping (store, telephone, Internet)	0.48	0.48	100
Grocery shopping	0.12	0.10	83
Shopping (except groceries, food, and gas)	0.33	0.02	6
Professional and personal care services	**0.12**	**0.09**	**75**
Medical and care services	0.06	0.05	83
Eating and drinking	**1.09**	**1.04**	**95**
Socializing, relaxing, and leisure	**4.29**	**3.41**	**79**
Socializing and communicating	0.69	0.59	86
Attending or hosting social events	0.10	0.11	110
Relaxing and leisure	3.40	2.63	77
Television and movies	2.38	2.00	84
Playing games	0.14	0.07	50
Computer use for leisure (except games)	0.11	0.10	91
Reading for personal interest	0.42	0.22	52
Arts and entertainment (other than sports)	0.10	0.08	80
Attending movies	0.03	0.02	67

	hours per day for total women	hours per day for women aged 35 to 44	index, 35 to 44 to total
Sports, exercise, and recreation	**0.25**	**0.23**	**92**
Participating in sports, exercise, and recreation	0.22	0.21	95
Attending sporting or recreational events	0.03	0.02	67
Religious and spiritual activities	**0.18**	**0.14**	**78**
Volunteer activities	**0.18**	**0.14**	**78**
Telephone calls	**0.15**	**0.11**	**73**
Traveling	**1.18**	**1.24**	**105**

Note: Primary activities are those respondents identified as their main activity. Other activities done simultaneously are not included. Travel related to activities is reported separately. Numbers do not sum to total because not all activities are shown. The index is calculated by dividing time spent by age group by time spent by average woman and multiplying by 100. "–" means sample is too small to make a reliable estimate.
Source: Bureau of Labor Statistics, unpublished tables from the 2007 American Time Use Survey, Internet site http://www.bls.gov/tus/home.htm

Wealth

■ Riding the housing bubble, the median net worth of householders aged 35 to 44 rose 14 percent between 2004 and 2007 (Generation Xers were aged 31 to 42 in 2007). According to Federal Reserve Board estimates, household net worth has fallen below 2004 levels since then.

■ The median financial assets of householders aged 35 to 44 grew by a substantial 23 percent (to $25,800) between 2004 and 2007, after adjusting for inflation. Their financial assets are worth much less today.

■ The median value of the nonfinancial assets owned by householders aged 35 to 44 climbed 10 percent between 2004 and 2007 as housing prices inflated.

■ Householders aged 35 to 44 who had debt owed a median of $135,300 in home-secured debt in 2007. They also owed a median of $13,500 in installment loan debt (such as car loans).

■ Generation Xers are worried about retirement. In 2009, only 12 percent of workers aged 35 to 44 were "very confident" they would have enough money to live comfortably throughout retirement, down from 20 percent in 1999.

During the Housing Bubble, Gen Xers Saw Their Net Worth Increase

Before the financial meltdown of 2008–09, the net worth of Generation Xers was growing.

Net worth is one of the most important measures of wealth. It is the amount that remains after a household's debts are subtracted from its assets. During this decade's housing bubble, housing values rose faster than mortgage debt. Consequently, net worth grew substantially—up 18 percent for the average household between 2004 and 2007, after adjusting for inflation. The gain did not last, however. The Federal Reserve Board estimates that by October 2008, median net worth for the average household had fallen to $99,000—3 percent less than in 2004.

The net worth of householders aged 35 to 44 (Generation Xers were aged 31 to 42 in 2007) grew 14 percent between 2004 and 2007, to $86,600. The net worth of this age group is certainly lower today because of the ongoing decline in housing values and stock prices.

■ Inflated housing values boosted the net worth of 35-to-44-year-olds between 2004 and 2007. With housing values likely to remain well below their peak, Generation Xers will find it a struggle to build wealth.

Net worth of householders aged 35 to 44 grew between 2004 and 2007

(percent change in net worth of households by age of householder, 2004 to 2007; in 2007 dollars)

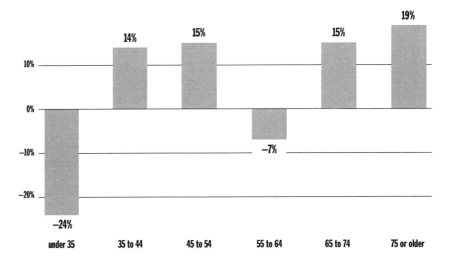

Table 11.1 Net Worth of Households by Age of Householder, 2004 to 2007

(median net worth of households by age of householder, 2004 to 2007; percent change, 2004-07; in 2007 dollars)

	2007	2004	percent change 2004–07
Total households	**$120,300**	**$102,200**	**17.7%**
Under age 35	11,800	15,600	−24.4
Aged 35 to 44	86,600	76,200	13.6
Aged 45 to 54	182,500	158,900	14.9
Aged 55 to 64	253,700	273,100	−7.1
Aged 65 to 74	239,400	208,800	14.7
Aged 75 or older	213,500	179,100	19.2

Source: Federal Reserve Board, Changes in U.S. Family Finances from 2004 to 2007: Evidence from the Survey of Consumer Finances, Federal Reserve Bulletin, February 2009, Internet site http://www.federalreserve.gov/pubs/oss/oss2/2007/scf2007home.html; calculations by New Strategist

Gen Xers Were Doing Well in the Stock Market

The value of their financial assets increased between 2004 and 2007.

Between 2004 and 2007, the value of the financial assets of the average American household rose 14 percent after adjusting for inflation—to a median of $28,800, according to the Federal Reserve Board's Survey of Consumer Finances. The median value of the financial assets owned by householders aged 35 to 44 grew by an even larger 23 percent during those years (to $25,800).

Slightly more than half of all households (51 percent) owned stocks directly or indirectly in 2007, up a shade from the 50 percent of 2004. Stock ownership among householders aged 35 to 44 fell by 1 percentage point (to 53.5 percent). The median value of stocks held by 35-to-44-year-olds rose by 18 percent, making them the only age group that saw their stock holdings appreciate in value between 2004 and 2007.

Only 53 percent of households owned a retirement account in 2007, but among householders aged 35 to 44 the figure was 57 percent. The median value of the retirement accounts owned by householders aged 35 to 44 was $36,000.

■ The value of financial assets owned by Generation Xers has plunged since these figures were collected by the Survey of Consumer Finances.

Value of financial assets owned by Generation Xers was modest in 2007

(median value of financial assets of households, by age of householder, 2007)

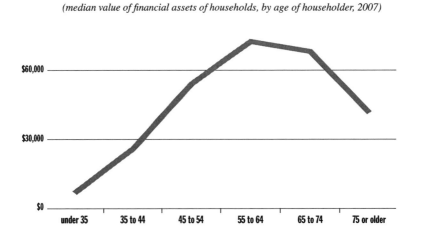

Table 11.2 Financial Assets of Households by Age of Householder, 2004 and 2007

(percentage of households owning financial assets and median value of assets for owners, by age of householder, 2004 and 2007; percentage point change in ownership and percent change in value of asset, 2004–07; in 2007 dollars)

	2007	2004	percentage point change
PERCENT OWNING ANY FINANCIAL ASSET			
Total households	**93.9%**	**93.8%**	**0.1**
Under age 35	89.2	90.1	–0.9
Aged 35 to 44	93.1	93.6	–0.5
Aged 45 to 54	93.3	93.6	–0.3
Aged 55 to 64	97.8	95.2	2.6
Aged 65 to 74	96.1	96.5	–0.4
Aged 75 or older	97.4	97.6	–0.2

	2007	2004	percent change
MEDIAN VALUE OF FINANCIAL ASSETS			
Total households	**$28,800**	**$25,300**	**13.8%**
Under age 35	6,800	5,700	19.3
Aged 35 to 44	25,800	20,900	23.4
Aged 45 to 54	54,000	42,400	27.4
Aged 55 to 64	72,400	85,700	–15.5
Aged 65 to 74	68,100	39,600	72.0
Aged 75 or older	41,500	42,600	–2.6

Source: Federal Reserve Board, Changes in U.S. Family Finances from 2004 to 2007: Evidence from the Survey of Consumer Finances, Federal Reserve Bulletin, February 2009, Internet site http://www.federalreserve.gov/pubs/oss/oss2/2007/ scf2007home.html; calculations by New Strategist

Table 11.3 Financial Assets of Households by Type of Asset and Age of Householder, 2007

(percentage of households owning financial assets, and median value of asset for owners, by type of asset and age of householder, 2007)

	total	under 35	35 to 44	45 to 54	55 to 64	65 to 74	75 or older
PERCENT OWNING ASSET							
Any financial asset	**93.9%**	**89.2%**	**93.1%**	**93.3%**	**97.8%**	**96.1%**	**97.4%**
Transaction accounts	92.1	87.3	91.2	91.7	96.4	94.6	95.3
Certificates of deposit	16.1	6.7	9.0	14.3	20.5	24.2	37.0
Savings bonds	14.9	13.7	16.8	19.0	16.2	10.3	7.9
Bonds	1.6	–	0.7	1.1	2.1	4.2	3.5
Stocks	17.9	13.7	17.0	18.6	21.3	19.1	30.2
Pooled investment funds	11.4	5.3	11.6	12.6	14.3	14.6	13.2
Retirement accounts	52.6	41.6	57.5	64.7	60.9	51.7	30.0
Cash value life insurance	23.0	11.4	17.5	22.3	35.2	34.3	27.6
Other managed assets	5.8	–	2.2	5.1	7.7	13.2	14.0
Other financial assets	9.3	10.0	9.6	10.5	9.2	9.4	5.3
MEDIAN VALUE OF ASSET							
Any financial asset	**$28,800**	**$6,800**	**$25,800**	**$54,000**	**$72,400**	**$68,100**	**$41,500**
Transaction accounts	4,000	2,400	3,400	5,000	5,200	7,700	6,100
Certificates of deposit	20,000	5,000	5,000	15,000	23,000	23,200	30,000
Savings bonds	1,000	700	1,000	1,000	1,900	1,000	20,000
Bonds	80,000	–	9,700	200,000	90,800	50,000	100,000
Stocks	17,000	3,000	15,000	18,500	24,000	38,000	40,000
Pooled investment funds	56,000	18,000	22,500	50,000	112,000	86,000	75,000
Retirement accounts	45,000	10,000	36,000	67,000	98,000	77,000	35,000
Cash value life insurance	8,000	2,800	8,300	10,000	10,000	10,000	5,000
Other managed assets	70,000	–	24,000	45,000	59,000	70,000	100,000
Other financial assets	6,000	1,500	8,000	6,000	20,000	10,000	15,000

Note: "–" means sample is too small to make a reliable estimate.
Source: Federal Reserve Board, Changes in U.S. Family Finances from 2004 to 2007: Evidence from the Survey of Consumer Finances, Federal Reserve Bulletin, February 2009, Internet site http://www.federalreserve.gov/pubs/oss/oss2/2007/scf2007home.html; calculations by New Strategist

Table 11.4 Stock Ownership of Households by Age of Householder, 2004 and 2007

(percentage of households owning stock directly or indirectly, median value of stock for owners, and share of total household financial assets accounted for by stock holdings, by age of householder, 2004 and 2007; percent and percentage point change, 2004–07; in 2007 dollars)

	2007	2004	percentage point change
PERCENT OWNING STOCK			
Total households	**51.1%**	**50.2%**	**0.9**
Under age 35	38.6	40.8	−2.2
Aged 35 to 44	53.5	54.5	−1.0
Aged 45 to 54	60.4	56.5	3.9
Aged 55 to 64	58.9	62.8	−3.9
Aged 65 to 74	52.1	46.9	5.2
Aged 75 or older	40.1	34.8	5.3

	2007	2004	percent change
MEDIAN VALUE OF STOCK			
Total households	**$35,000**	**$35,700**	**−2.0%**
Under age 35	7,000	8,800	−20.5
Aged 35 to 44	26,000	22,000	18.2
Aged 45 to 54	45,000	54,900	−18.0
Aged 55 to 64	78,000	78,000	0.0
Aged 65 to 74	57,000	76,900	−25.9
Aged 75 or older	41,000	94,300	−56.5

	2007	2004	percentage point change
STOCK AS SHARE OF FINANCIAL ASSETS			
Total households	**53.3%**	**51.3%**	**2.0**
Under age 35	44.3	40.3	4.0
Aged 35 to 44	53.7	53.5	0.2
Aged 45 to 54	53.0	53.8	−0.8
Aged 55 to 64	55.0	55.0	0.0
Aged 65 to 74	55.3	51.5	3.8
Aged 75 or older	48.1	39.3	8.8

Source: Federal Reserve Board, Changes in U.S. Family Finances from 2004 to 2007: Evidence from the Survey of Consumer Finances, Federal Reserve Bulletin, February 2009, Internet site http://www.federalreserve.gov/pubs/oss/oss2/2007/scf2007home.html; calculations by New Strategist

Nonfinancial Assets of Gen Xers Grew between 2004 and 2007

Their homeownership rate declined slightly during those years, however.

The median value of the nonfinancial assets owned by the average American household stood at $177,400 in 2007—9 percent more than in 2004, after adjusting for inflation. Paralleling that growth, the median value of nonfinancial assets owned by householders aged 35 to 44 climbed 10 percent during these years.

Because housing equity accounts for the largest share of nonfinancial assets, the rise in home values was the biggest contributor to gains in this category. Among homeowners aged 35 to 44, median home value rose to $205,000 in 2007, a 17 percent gain over 2004, after adjusting for inflation. But perhaps foreshadowing the financial turmoil to come, the rate of homeownership in the age group fell by over 2 percentage points during those years as a growing share of Gen Xers found housing prices too high.

Since 2007, housing values have plunged and the decline is ongoing. The Federal Reserve Board has estimated that the median value of the average home fell from $200,000 in 2007 to $181,600 in October 2008—a 9 percent decline. Housing values have continued to fall since then and are likely lower today than they were in 2004, after adjusting for inflation.

■ The drop in housing values since 2007 has greatly reduced household net worth.

A nostalgic look at median housing values in 2007

(median value of the primary residence among homeowners, by age of householder, 2007)

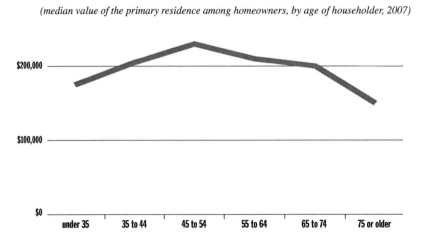

Table 11.5 Nonfinancial Assets of Households by Age of Householder, 2004 and 2007

(percentage of households owning nonfinancial assets and median value of assets for owners, by age of house-holder, 2004 and 2007; percentage point change in ownership and percent change in value of asset, 2004–07; in 2007 dollars)

	2007	2004	percentage point change
PERCENT OWNING ANY NONFINANCIAL ASSET			
Total households	**92.0%**	**92.5%**	**−0.5**
Under age 35	88.2	88.6	−0.4
Aged 35 to 44	91.3	93.0	−1.7
Aged 45 to 54	95.0	94.7	0.3
Aged 55 to 64	95.6	92.6	3.0
Aged 65 to 74	94.5	95.6	−1.1
Aged 75 or older	87.3	92.5	−5.2

	2007	2004	percent change
MEDIAN VALUE OF NONFINANCIAL ASSETS			
Total households	**$177,400**	**$162,300**	**9.3%**
Under age 35	30,900	35,500	−13.0
Aged 35 to 44	182,600	166,200	9.9
Aged 45 to 54	224,900	202,600	11.0
Aged 55 to 64	233,100	248,600	−6.2
Aged 65 to 74	212,200	177,000	19.9
Aged 75 or older	157,100	150,600	4.3

Source: Federal Reserve Board, Changes in U.S. Family Finances from 2004 to 2007: Evidence from the Survey of Consumer Finances, Federal Reserve Bulletin, February 2009, Internet site http://www.federalreserve.gov/pubs/oss/oss2/2007/scf2007home.html; calculations by New Strategist

Table 11.6 Nonfinancial Assets of Households by Type of Asset and Age of Householder, 2007

(percentage of households owning nonfinancial assets, and median value of asset for owners, by type of asset and age of householder, 2007)

	total	under 35	35 to 44	45 to 54	55 to 64	65 to 74	75 or older
PERCENT OWNING ASSET							
Any nonfinancial asset	**92.0%**	**88.2%**	**91.3%**	**95.0%**	**95.6%**	**94.5%**	**87.3%**
Vehicles	87.0	85.4	87.5	90.3	92.2	90.6	71.5
Primary residence	68.6	40.7	66.1	77.3	81.0	85.5	77.0
Other residential property	13.7	5.6	12.0	15.7	20.9	18.9	13.4
Equity in nonresidential property	8.1	3.2	7.5	9.5	11.5	12.3	6.8
Business equity	12.0	6.8	16.0	15.2	16.3	10.1	3.8
Other nonfinancial assets	7.2	5.9	5.5	8.7	8.5	9.1	5.8
MEDIAN VALUE OF ASSET							
Total nonfinancial assets	**$177,400**	**$30,900**	**$182,600**	**$224,900**	**$233,100**	**$212,200**	**$157,100**
Vehicles	15,500	13,300	17,400	18,700	17,400	14,600	9,400
Primary residence	200,000	175,000	205,000	230,000	210,000	200,000	150,000
Other residential property	146,000	85,000	150,000	150,000	157,000	150,000	100,000
Equity in nonresidential property	75,000	50,000	50,000	80,000	90,000	75,000	110,000
Business equity	100,500	59,900	86,000	100,000	116,300	415,000	250,000
Other nonfinancial assets	14,000	8,000	10,000	15,000	20,000	20,000	25,000

Source: Federal Reserve Board, Changes in U.S. Family Finances from 2004 to 2007: Evidence from the Survey of Consumer Finances, Federal Reserve Bulletin, February 2009, Internet site http://www.federalreserve.gov/pubs/oss/oss2/2007/scf2007home.html; calculations by New Strategist

Table 11.7 Household Ownership of Primary Residence by Age of Householder, 2004 and 2007

(percentage of households owning their primary residence, median value of asset for owners, and median value of home-secured debt for owners, by age of householder, 2004 and 2007; percentage point change in ownership and percent change in value of asset, 2004–07; in 2007 dollars)

	2007	2004	percentage point change
PERCENT OWNING PRIMARY RESIDENCE			
Total households	**68.6%**	**69.1%**	**−0.5**
Under age 35	40.7	41.6	−0.9
Aged 35 to 44	66.1	68.3	−2.2
Aged 45 to 54	77.3	77.3	0.0
Aged 55 to 64	81.0	79.1	1.9
Aged 65 to 74	85.5	81.3	4.2
Aged 75 or older	77.0	85.2	−8.2

	2007	2004	percent change
MEDIAN VALUE OF PRIMARY RESIDENCE			
Total households	**$200,000**	**$175,700**	**13.8%**
Under age 35	175,000	148,300	18.0
Aged 35 to 44	205,000	175,700	16.7
Aged 45 to 54	230,000	186,700	23.2
Aged 55 to 64	210,000	218,700	−4.0
Aged 65 to 74	200,000	164,700	21.4
Aged 75 or older	150,000	137,300	9.2

	2007	2004	percent change
MEDIAN VALUE OF HOME-SECURED DEBT			
Total households	**$100,000**	**$95,600**	**4.6%**
Under age 35	78,000	68,600	13.7
Aged 35 to 44	101,600	82,400	23.3
Aged 45 to 54	82,000	95,600	−14.2
Aged 55 to 64	130,000	119,500	8.8
Aged 65 to 74	125,000	109,800	13.8
Aged 75 or older	50,000	42,800	16.8

Source: Federal Reserve Board, Changes in U.S. Family Finances from 2004 to 2007: Evidence from the Survey of Consumer Finances, Federal Reserve Bulletin, February 2009, Internet site http://www.federalreserve.gov/pubs/oss/oss2/2007/scf2007home.html; calculations by New Strategist

Debt Increased for Gen Xers

Householders aged 35 to 44 are the biggest debtors.

The median debt of the average American household grew 11 percent between 2004 and 2007 after adjusting for inflation—to $67,300. Among householders aged 35 to 44, median debt rose 11 percent during those years, to $106,200.

Home-secured debt accounts for the largest share of debt by far. Forty-nine percent of households have debt secured by their primary residence, and they owe a median of $107,000. Naturally such debt declines with age as householders pay off their mortgages, but Generation Xers are at the lifestage when housing debt is largest. Householders aged 35 to 44 who had debt owed a median of $128,000 in home-secured debt in 2007. Slightly more than half the Gen Xers carry a credit card balance, the median balance being $3,500. They also owed a median of $13,500 in installment loan debt (such as car loans).

■ Many Generation Xers owe more in mortgage debt than their home is worth, greatly curtailing future growth in their net worth.

Debt declines with age

(median amount of debt owed by households, by age of householder, 2007)

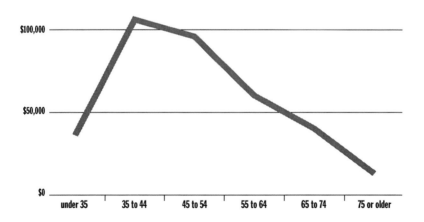

Table 11.8 Debt of Households by Age of Householder, 2004 and 2007

(percentage of households with debt and median amount of debt for debtors, by age of householder, 2004 and 2007; percentage point change in households with debt and percent change in amount of debt, 2004–07; in 2007 dollars)

	2007	2004	percentage point change
PERCENT WITH DEBT			
Total households	**77.0%**	**76.4%**	**0.6**
Under age 35	83.5	79.8	3.7
Aged 35 to 44	86.2	88.6	–2.4
Aged 45 to 54	86.8	88.4	–1.6
Aged 55 to 64	81.8	76.3	5.5
Aged 65 to 74	65.5	58.8	6.7
Aged 75 or older	31.4	40.3	–8.9

	2007	2004	percent change
MEDIAN AMOUNT OF DEBT			
Total households	**$67,300**	**$60,700**	**10.9%**
Under age 35	36,200	36,900	–1.9
Aged 35 to 44	106,200	95,800	10.9
Aged 45 to 54	95,900	91,400	4.9
Aged 55 to 64	60,300	52,700	14.4
Aged 65 to 74	40,100	27,500	45.8
Aged 75 or older	13,000	16,900	–23.1

Source: Federal Reserve Board, Changes in U.S. Family Finances from 2004 to 2007: Evidence from the Survey of Consumer Finances, Federal Reserve Bulletin, February 2009, Internet site http://www.federalreserve.gov/pubs/oss/oss2/2007/scf2007home.html; calculations by New Strategist

Table 11.9 Debt of Households by Type of Debt and Age of Householder, 2007

(percentage of households with debt, and median value of debt for those with debt, by type of debt and age of householder, 2007)

	total	under 35	35 to 44	45 to 54	55 to 64	65 to 74	75 or older
PERCENT WITH DEBT							
Any debt	**77.0%**	**83.5%**	**86.2%**	**86.8%**	**81.8%**	**65.5%**	**31.4%**
Secured by residential property							
Primary residence	48.7	37.3	59.5	65.5	55.3	42.9	13.9
Other	5.5	3.3	6.5	8.0	7.8	5.0	0.6
Lines of credit not secured by residential property	1.7	2.1	2.2	1.9	1.2	1.5	–
Installment loans	46.9	65.2	56.2	51.9	44.6	26.1	7.0
Credit card balances	46.1	48.5	51.7	53.6	49.9	37.0	18.8
Other debt	6.8	5.9	7.5	9.8	8.7	4.4	1.3
MEDIAN AMOUNT OF DEBT							
Any debt	**$67,300**	**$36,200**	**$106,200**	**$95,900**	**$60,300**	**$40,100**	**$13,000**
Secured by residential property							
Primary residence	107,000	135,300	128,000	110,000	85,000	69,000	40,000
Other	100,000	78,000	101,600	82,000	130,000	125,000	50,000
Lines of credit not secured by residential property	3,800	1,000	4,600	6,000	10,000	30,000	–
Installment loans	13,000	15,000	13,500	12,900	10,900	10,300	8,000
Credit card balances	3,000	1,800	3,500	3,600	3,600	3,000	800
Other debt	5,000	4,500	5,000	4,500	6,000	5,000	4,500

Note: "–" means sample is too small to make a reliable estimate.
Source: Federal Reserve Board, Changes in U.S. Family Finances from 2004 to 2007: Evidence from the Survey of Consumer Finances, Federal Reserve Bulletin, February 2009, Internet site http://www.federalreserve.gov/pubs/oss/oss2/2007/scf2007home.html; calculations by New Strategist

Fewer than Half of Gen Xers Have a Retirement Plan

Many worry about their economic security in retirement.

Only 42 percent of American workers participated in an employer's retirement plan in 2007, according to an analysis of government statistics by the Employee Benefit Research Institute (EBRI). Retirement plan participation among workers aged 35 to 44 was higher than average, at 47.5 percent. Yet there is still room for improvement, since 56 percent of workers in the age group were eligible for participation. Those employed in the private sector were much less likely to participate than public-sector workers, 45 versus 78 percent.

Another EBRI study shows that only 47 percent of workers aged 35 to 44 owned an IRA or participated in a 401(k)-type (defined-contribution) retirement plan in 2007. Among 35-to-44-year-old participants in 401(k)-type plans, only 8 percent made the maximum contribution in 2007.

With little savings, it is no surprise that Gen Xers are worried about retirement. The financial meltdown of 2008–09 added to their worries. Only 12 percent of workers aged 35 to 44 were "very confident" in 2009 that they would have enough money to live comfortably throughout retirement. Ten years earlier the figure had been 20 percent.

■ The substitution of defined-contribution for defined-benefit pension plans puts the burden of retirement savings on workers rather than employers. With Gen Xers finding it hard to save, their retirement lifestyle may be Spartan.

Fewer than half of workers aged 35 to 44 participate in an employer-sponsored retirement plan

(percent of workers who participate in an employer-sponsored retirement plan, by age, 2007)

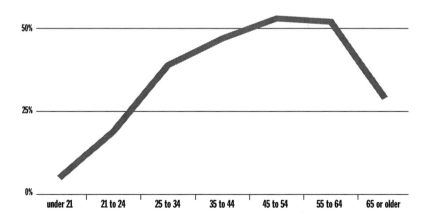

Table 11.10 Retirement Plan Coverage by Age, 2007

(total number of workers, percent whose employer offers a retirement plan, and percent participating in plan, by type of employment and age of worker, 2007; numbers in thousands)

	number of workers	percent with an employer who sponsors a retirement plan	percent participating in employer's retirement plan
Total workers	**158,099**	**51.8%**	**41.5%**
Under age 21	10,450	24.0	4.9
Aged 21 to 24	12,695	38.5	19.3
Aged 25 to 34	33,485	51.1	38.7
Aged 35 to 44	35,299	55.8	47.5
Aged 45 to 54	36,139	59.3	52.6
Aged 55 to 64	22,782	59.2	52.0
Aged 65 or older	7,249	39.1	28.7
PRIVATE WAGE AND SALARY WORKERS AGED 21 TO 64			
Total workers	**110,148**	**52.7**	**42.0**
Aged 21 to 24	11,397	37.3	17.9
Aged 25 to 34	27,816	48.9	35.7
Aged 35 to 44	27,788	54.5	45.3
Aged 45 to 54	27,068	58.1	50.7
Aged 55 to 64	16,079	57.7	49.9
PUBLIC WAGE AND SALARY WORKERS AGED 21 TO 64			
Total workers	**21,106**	**83.3**	**75.4**
Aged 21 to 24	1,035	58.5	38.9
Aged 25 to 34	4,250	80.1	69.5
Aged 35 to 44	5,183	84.3	77.7
Aged 45 to 54	6,179	85.7	79.9
Aged 55 to 64	4,459	87.9	80.7

Source: Employee Benefit Research Institute, Employment-Based Retirement Plan Participation: Geographic Differences and Trends, 2007, Issue Brief 322, October 2008, Internet site http://www.ebri.org/publications/ib/index.cfm?fa=ibDisp&content_ id=3989

Table 11.11 Ownership of IRAs and 401(k)s by Age, 2005

(percentage of workers aged 21 to 64 owning IRAs and/or participating in a 401(k)-type plan, by age, 2005)

	IRA and/or 401(k)-type plan	IRA only	401(k)-type plan only	both IRA and 401(k)-type plan	neither IRA nor 401(k)-type plan
Total workers	**43.8%**	**10.7%**	**20.9%**	**12.2%**	**56.2%**
Aged 21 to 24	11.4	2.1	8.3	1.0	88.6
Aged 25 to 34	35.4	6.6	20.4	8.4	64.6
Aged 35 to 44	47.4	10.2	24.4	12.8	52.6
Aged 45 to 54	51.2	12.4	22.7	16.1	48.8
Aged 55 to 64	52.1	18.5	18.2	15.4	47.9

Source: Employee Benefit Research Institute, Ownership of Individual Retirement Accounts (IRAs) and 401(k)-Type Plans, by Craig Copeland, Notes, Vol. 29, No. 5, May 2008, Internet site http://www.ebri.org/publications/notes/index.cfm?fa=main&doc_type=2

Table 11.12 Participation in IRAs and 401(k)s by Age, 2005

(percent of workers aged 21 to 64 owning an IRA or participating in 401(k)-type plan, percent making a contribution to the IRA, and mean amount contributed and percent making maximum contribution among contributors, by age, 2005)

	has IRA in own name	made tax-deductible contribution to IRA	among IRA contributors	
			mean contribution	percent making maximum contribution
Total workers	**22.9%**	**6.2%**	**$2,540**	**26.8%**
Aged 21 to 24	3.2	0.6	1,149	0.0
Aged 25 to 34	15.0	4.3	2,089	20.5
Aged 35 to 44	23.0	6.4	2,497	31.3
Aged 45 to 54	28.5	7.4	2,527	25.0
Aged 55 to 64	33.9	9.2	2,943	29.3

	percent participating in 401(k)	among 401(k) contributors	
		mean contribution	percent making maximum contribution
Total workers	**33.1%**	**$4,274**	**8.9%**
Aged 21 to 24	9.3	1,597	0.0
Aged 25 to 34	28.8	3,353	5.0
Aged 35 to 44	37.2	4,226	8.4
Aged 45 to 54	38.8	1,695	10.3
Aged 55 to 64	33.5	4,993	13.2

Source: Employee Benefit Research Institute, Ownership of Individual Retirement Accounts (IRAs) and 401(k)-Type Plans, by Craig Copeland, Notes, Vol. 29, No. 5, May 2008, Internet site http://www.ebri.org/publications/notes/index.cfm?fa=main&doc_type=2

Table 11.13 Retirement Planning by Age, 2009

(percentage of workers aged 25 or older responding by age, 2009)

	total	25 to 34	35 to 44	45 to 54	55 or older
Very confident in having enough money to live comfortably throughout retirement	13%	18%	12%	10%	13%
Very confident in having enough money to take care of medical expenses in retirement	13	16	13	11	14
Worker and/or spouse have saved for retirement	75	66	78	78	79
Worker and/or spouse are currently saving for retirement	65	57	68	68	66
Contribute to a workplace retirement savings plan	64	52	72	65	64
Expected retirement age					
Before age 60	9	17	8	9	1
Aged 60 to 64	17	14	16	17	22
Aged 65	23	29	29	18	15
Aged 66 or older	31	22	33	35	34
Never retire	10	9	6	13	11
Don't know/refused	7	8	3	6	12
Total savings and investments (not including value of primary residence)					
Less than $25,000	53	73	53	43	36
$25,000 to $49,999	11	12	8	11	13
$50,000 to $99,999	12	9	14	14	10
$100,000 to $249,999	12	5	16	15	15
$250,000 or more	12	2	9	17	26

Source: Employee Benefit Research Institute, Retirement Confidence Surveys, Internet site http://www.ebri.org/surveys/rcs/2009/

Table 11.14 Changes in Retirement Confidence by Age, 1999 and 2009

(percentage of workers aged 25 or older responding by age, 1999 and 2009)

	total	25 to 34	35 to 44	45 to 54	55 or older
Very confident in having enough money to live comfortably throughout retirement					
2009	13%	18%	12%	10%	13%
1999	22	27	20	21	18
Very confident in having enough money to take care of medical expenses in retirement					
2009	13	16	13	11	14
1999	16	16	15	13	22
Say they are doing a good job of peparing financially for retirement					
2009	20	23	21	18	16
1999	23	22	22	24	29

Source: Employee Benefit Research Institute, Retirement Confidence Surveys, Internet site http://www.ebri.org/surveys/rcs/2009/

Glossary

adjusted for inflation Income or a change in income that has been adjusted for the rise in the cost of living, or the consumer price index (CPI-U-RS).

age Classification by age is based on the age of the person at his/her last birthday.

American Housing Survey The AHS collects national and metropolitan-level data on the nation's housing, including apartments, single-family homes, and mobile homes. The nationally representative survey, with a sample of 55,000 homes, is conducted by the Census Bureau for the Department of Housing and Urban Development every other year.

American Indians In this book, American Indians include Alaska Natives (Eskimos and Aleuts) unless those groups are shown separately.

American Time Use Survey Under contract with the Bureau of Labor Statistics, the Census Bureau collects ATUS information, which reveals how people spend their time. The ATUS sample is drawn from U.S. households that have completed their final month of interviews for the Current Population Survey. One individual from each selected household is chosen to participate in the ATUS. Respondents are interviewed by telephone only once about their time use on the previous day.

Asian Includes Native Hawaiians and other Pacific Islanders unless those groups are shown separately.

Baby Boom Americans born between 1946 and 1964.

Baby Bust Americans born between 1965 and 1976, also known as Generation X.

Behavioral Risk Factor Surveillance System A collaborative project of the Centers for Disease Control and Prevention and U.S. states and territories. It is an ongoing data collection program designed to measure behavioral risk factors in the adult population aged 18 or older. All 50 states, three territories, and the District of Columbia take part in the survey, making the BRFSS the primary source of information on the health-related behaviors of Americans.

black A racial category that includes those who identified themselves as "black" or "African American."

central cities The largest city in a metropolitan area. The balance of the metropolitan area outside the central city is regarded as the "suburbs."

Consumer Expenditure Survey An ongoing study of the day-to-day spending of American households administered by the Bureau of Labor Statistics. The CEX includes an interview survey and a diary survey. The average spending figures shown in this book are the integrated data from both the diary and interview components of the survey. Two separate, nationally representative samples are used for the interview and diary surveys. For the interview survey, about 7,500 consumer units are interviewed on a rotating panel basis each quarter for five consecutive quarters. For the diary survey, 7,500 consumer units keep weekly diaries of spending for two consecutive weeks.

consumer unit *(on spending tables only)* For convenience, the term consumer unit and households are used interchangeably in the spending section of this book, although consumer units are somewhat different from the Census Bureau's households. Consumer units are all related members of a household, or financially independent members of a household. A household may include more than one consumer unit.

Current Population Survey A nationally representative survey of the civilian noninstitutional population aged 15 or older. It is taken monthly by the Census Bureau for the Bureau of Labor Statistics, collecting information from more than 50,000 households on employment and unemployment. In March of each year, the survey includes the Annual Social and Economic Supplement (formerly called the Annual Demographic Survey), which is the source of most national data on the characteristics of Americans, such as educational attainment, living arrangements, and incomes.

disability As defined by the National Health Interview Survey, respondents aged 18 or older are asked whether they have difficulty in physical functioning, probing whether respondents can perform nine activities by themselves without using special equipment. The categories are walking a quarter mile; standing for two hours; sitting for two hours; walking up 10 steps without resting; stooping, bending, kneeling; reaching over one's head; grasping or handling small objects; carrying a 10-pound object; and pushing/pulling a large object. Adults who report that any of these activities is very difficult or they cannot do it at all are defined as having physical difficulties.

dual-earner couple A married couple in which both the householder and the householder's spouse are in the labor force.

earnings The amount of money a person receives from his or her job. *See also* Income.

employed All civilians who did any work as a paid employee or farmer/self-employed worker, or who worked 15 hours or more as an unpaid farm worker or in a family-owned business, during the reference period. All those who have jobs but who are temporarily absent from their jobs due to illness, bad weather, vacation, labor management dispute, or personal reasons are considered employed.

expenditure The transaction cost including excise and sales taxes of goods and services acquired during the survey period. The full cost of each purchase is recorded even though full payment may not have been made at the date of purchase. Average expenditure figures may be artificially low for infrequently purchased items such as cars because figures are calculated using all consumer units within a demographic segment rather than just purchasers. Expenditure estimates include money spent on gifts for others.

family A group of two or more people (one of whom is the householder) related by birth, marriage, or adoption and living in the same household.

family household A household maintained by a householder who lives with one or more people related to him or her by blood, marriage, or adoption.

female/male householder A woman or man who maintains a household without a spouse present. May head family or nonfamily households.

foreign-born population People who are not U.S. citizens at birth.

full-time employment Thirty-five or more hours of work per week during a majority of the weeks worked.

full-time, year-round Fifty or more weeks of full-time employment during the previous calendar year.

Generation X Americans born between 1965 and 1976, also known as the baby-bust generation.

Hispanic Because Hispanic is an ethnic origin rather than a race, Hispanics may be of any race. While most Hispanics are white, there are black, Asian, and American Indian Hispanics.

household All the persons who occupy a housing unit. A household includes the related family members and all the unrelated persons, if any, such as lodgers, foster children, wards, or employees who share the housing unit. A person living alone is counted as a household. A group of unrelated people who share a housing unit as roommates or unmarried partners is also counted as a household. Households do not include group quarters such as college dormitories, prisons, or nursing homes.

household, race/ethnicity of Households are categorized according to the race or ethnicity of the householder only.

householder The person (or one of the persons) in whose name the housing unit is owned or rented or, if there is no such person, any adult member. With married couples, the householder may be either the husband or wife. The householder is the reference person for the household.

householder, age of The age of the householder is used to categorize households into age groups such as those used in this book. Married couples, for example, are classified according to the age of either the husband or wife, depending on which one identified him or herself as the householder.

housing unit A house, an apartment, a group of rooms, or a single room occupied or intended for occupancy as separate living quarters. Separate living quarters are those in which the occupants do not live and eat with any other persons in the structure and that have direct access from the outside of the building or through a common hall that is used or intended for use by the occupants of another unit or by the general public. The occupants may be a single family, one person living alone, two or more families living together, or any other group of related or unrelated persons who share living arrangements.

Housing Vacancy Survey A supplement to the Current Population Survey, which provides quarterly and annual data on rental and homeowner vacancy rates, characteristics of units available for occupancy, and homeownership rates by age, household type, region, state, and metropolitan area. The Current Population Survey sample includes 51,000 occupied housing units and 9,000 vacant units.

housing value The respondent's estimate of how much his or her house and lot would sell for if it were for sale.

iGeneration Americans born from 1995 to the present.

immigration The relatively permanent movement (change of residence) of people into the country of reference.

income Money received in the preceding calendar year by each person aged 15 or older from each of the following sources: (1) earnings from longest job (or self-employment), (2) earnings from jobs other than longest job, (3) unemployment compensation, (4) workers' compensation, (5) Social Security, (6) Supplemental Security income, (7) public assistance, (8) veterans' payments, (9) survivor benefits, (10) disability benefits, (11) retirement pensions, (12) interest, (13) dividends, (14) rents and royalties or estates and trusts, (15) educational assistance, (16) alimony, (17) child support, (18) financial assistance from outside the household, and other periodic income. Income is reported in several ways in this book. Household income is the combined income of all household members. Income of persons is all income accruing to a person from all sources. Earnings are the money a person receives from his or her job.

industry The industry in which a person worked longest in the preceding calendar year.

job tenure The length of time a person has been employed continuously by the same employer.

labor force The labor force tables in this book show the civilian labor force only. The labor force includes both the employed and the unemployed (people who are looking for work). People are counted as in the labor force if they were working or looking for work during the reference week in which the Census Bureau fields the Current Population Survey.

labor force participation rate The percent of the civilian noninstitutional population that is in the civilian labor force, which includes both the employed and the unemployed.

married couples with or without children under age 18 Refers to married couples with or without own children under age 18 living in the same household. Couples without children under age 18 may be parents of grown children who live elsewhere, or they could be childless couples.

median The amount that divides the population or households into two equal portions: one below and one above the median. Medians can be calculated for income, age, and many other characteristics.

median income The amount that divides the income distribution into two equal groups, half having incomes above the median, half having incomes below the median. The medians for households or families are based on all households or families. The median for persons are based on all persons aged 15 or older with income.

Medical Expenditure Panel Survey A nationally representative survey that collects detailed information on the health status, access to care, health care use and expenses and health insurance coverage of the civilian noninstitutionalized population of the U.S. and nursing home residents. MEPS comprises four component surveys: the Household Component, the Medical Provider Component, the Insurance Component, and the Nursing Home Component. The Household Component is the core survey, is conducted each year, and includes 15,000 households and 37,000 people.

metropolitan statistical area A city with 50,000 or more inhabitants, or a Census Bureau-defined urbanized area of at least 50,000 inhabitants and a total metropolitan population of at least 100,000 (75,000 in New England). The county (or counties) that contains the largest city becomes the "central county" (counties), along with any adjacent counties that have at least 50 percent of their population in the urbanized area surrounding the largest city. Additional "outlying counties" are included in the MSA if they meet specified requirements of commuting to the central counties and other selected requirements of metropolitan character (such as population density and percent urban). In New England, MSAs are defined in terms of cities and towns rather than counties. For this reason, the concept of NECMA is used to define metropolitan areas in the New England division.

Millennial generation Americans born between 1977 and 1994.

mobility status People are classified according to their mobility status on the basis of a comparison between their place of residence at the time of the March Current Population Survey and their place of residence in March of the previous year. Nonmovers are people living in the same house at the end of the period as at the beginning of the period. Movers are people living in a different house at the end of the period than at the beginning of the period. Movers from abroad are either citizens or aliens whose place of residence is outside the United States at the beginning of the period, that is, in an outlying area under the jurisdiction of the United States or in a foreign country. The mobility status for children is fully allocated from the mother if she is in the household; otherwise it is allocated from the householder.

National Ambulatory Medical Care Survey An annual survey of visits to nonfederally employed office-based physicians who are primarily engaged in direct patient care. Data are collected from physicians rather than patients, with each physician assigned a one-week reporting period. During that week, a systematic random sample of visit characteristics are recorded by the physician or office staff.

National Health and Nutrition Examination Survey A continuous survey of a representative sample of the U.S. civilian noninstitutionalized population. Respondents are interviewed at home about their health and nutrition, and the interview is followed up by a physical examination that measures such things as height and weight in mobile examination centers.

National Health Interview Survey A continuing nationwide sample survey of the civilian noninstitutional population of the U.S. conducted by the Census

Bureau for the National Center for Health Statistics. Each year, data are collected from more than 100,000 people about their illnesses, injuries, impairments, chronic and acute conditions, activity limitations, and the use of health services.

National Hospital Ambulatory Medical Care Survey The NHAMCS, sponsored by the National Center for Health Statistics, is an annual national probability sample survey of visits to emergency departments and outpatient departments at non-Federal, short stay and general hospitals. Data are collected by hospital staff from patient records.

National Hospital Discharge Survey This survey has been conducted annually since 1965, sponsored by the National Center for Health Statistics, to collect nationally representative information on the characteristics of inpatients discharged from nonfederal, short-stay hospitals in the U.S. The survey collects data from a sample of approximately 270,000 inpatient records acquired from a national sample of about 500 hospitals.

National Household Education Survey The NHES, sponsored by the National Center for Education Statistics, provides descriptive data on the educational activities of the U.S. population, including after-school care and adult education. The NHES is a system of telephone surveys of a representative sample of 45,000 to 60,000 households in the U.S.

National Nursing Home Survey This is a series of national sample surveys of nursing homes, their residents, and staff conducted at various intervals since 1973-74 and sponsored by the National Center for Health Statistics. Data for the survey are obtained through personal interviews with administrators and staff, and occasionally with self-administered questionnaires, in a sample of about 1,500 facilities.

National Survey of Family Growth The 2002 NSFG, sponsored by the National Center for Health Statistics, is a nationally representative survey of the civilian noninstitutional population aged 15 to 44. In-person interviews were completed with 12,571 men and women, collecting data on marriage, divorce, contraception, and infertility. The 2002 survey updates previous NSFG surveys taken in 1973, 1976, 1988, and 1995.

National Survey on Drug Use and Health Formerly called the National Household Survey on Drug Abuse, this survey, sponsored by the Substance Abuse and Mental Health Services Administration, has been conducted since 1971. It is the primary source of information on the use of illegal drugs by the U.S. population. Each year, a nationally representative sample of about 70,000 individuals aged 12 or older are surveyed in the 50 states and the District of Columbia.

net worth The amount of money left over after a household's debts are subtracted from its assets.

nonfamily household A household maintained by a householder who lives alone or who lives with people to whom he or she is not related.

nonfamily householder A householder who lives alone or with nonrelatives.

non-Hispanic People who do not identify themselves as Hispanic are classified as non-Hispanic. Non-Hispanics may be of any race.

non-Hispanic white People who identify their race as white and who do not indicate a Hispanic origin.

nonmetropolitan area Counties that are not classified as metropolitan areas.

occupation Occupational classification is based on the kind of work a person did at his or her job during the previous calendar year. If a person changed jobs during the year, the data refer to the occupation of the job held the longest during that year.

occupied housing units A housing unit is classified as occupied if a person or group of people is living in it or if the occupants are only temporarily absent—on vacation, example. By definition, the count of occupied housing units is the same as the count of households.

outside central city The portion of a metropolitan county or counties that falls outside of the central city or cities; generally regarded as the suburbs.

own children Sons and daughters, including stepchildren and adopted children, of the householder. The totals include never-married children living away from home in college dormitories.

owner occupied A housing unit is "owner occupied" if the owner lives in the unit, even if it is mortgaged or not fully paid for. A cooperative or condominium unit is "owner occupied" only if the owner lives in it. All other occupied units are classified as "renter occupied."

part-time employment Less than 35 hours of work per week in a majority of the weeks worked during the year.

percent change The change (either positive or negative) in a measure that is expressed as a proportion of the starting measure. When median income changes from $20,000 to $25,000, for example, this is a 25 percent increase.

percentage point change The change (either positive or negative) in a value which is already expressed as a percentage. When a labor force participation rate changes from 70 percent of 75 percent, for example, this is a 5 percentage point increase.

poverty level The official income threshold below which families and people are classified as living in poverty. The threshold rises each year with inflation and varies depending on family size and age of householder.

primary activity In the time use tables, those activities that respondents identify as their main activity. Other activities done simultaneously are not included.

proportion or share The value of a part expressed as a percentage of the whole. If there are 4 million people aged 25 and 3 million of them are white, then the white proportion is 75 percent.

race Race is self-reported and can be defined in three ways. The "race alone" population comprises people who identify themselves as only one race. The "race in combination" population comprises people who identify themselves as more than one race, such as white and black. The "race, alone or in combination" population includes both those who identify themselves as one race and those who identify themselves as more than one race.

regions The four major regions and nine census divisions of the United States are the state groupings as shown below:

Northeast:
—New England: Connecticut, Maine, Massachusetts, New Hampshire, Rhode Island, and Vermont
—Middle Atlantic: New Jersey, New York, and Pennsylvania

Midwest:
—East North Central: Illinois, Indiana, Michigan, Ohio, and Wisconsin
—West North Central: Iowa, Kansas, Minnesota, Missouri, Nebraska, North Dakota, and South Dakota

South:
—South Atlantic: Delaware, District of Columbia, Florida, Georgia, Maryland, North Carolina, South Carolina, Virginia, and West Virginia
—East South Central: Alabama, Kentucky, Mississippi, and Tennessee
—West South Central: Arkansas, Louisiana, Oklahoma, and Texas

West:
—Mountain: Arizona, Colorado, Idaho, Montana, Nevada, New Mexico, Utah, and Wyoming
—Pacific: Alaska, California, Hawaii, Oregon, and Washington

renter occupied *See* Owner Occupied.

Retirement Confidence Survey An annual survey, sponsored by the Employee Benefit Research Institute, the American Savings Education Council, and Mathew Greenwald & Associates, of a nationally representative sample of 1,000 people aged 25 or older. Respondents are asked a core set of questions that have been asked since 1996, measuring attitudes and behavior towards retirement.

rounding Percentages are rounded to the nearest tenth of a percent; therefore, the percentages in a distribution do not always add exactly to 100.0 percent. The totals, however, are always shown as 100.0. Moreover, individual figures are rounded to the nearest thousand without being adjusted to group totals, which are independently rounded; percentages are based on the unrounded numbers.

self-employment A person is categorized as self-employed if he or she was self-employed in the job held longest during the reference period. Persons who report self-employment from a second job are excluded, but those who report wage-and-salary income from a second job are included. Unpaid workers in family businesses are excluded. Self-employment statistics include only nonagricultural workers and exclude people who work for themselves in incorporated business.

sex ratio The number of men per 100 women.

suburbs *See* Outside Central City.

Survey of Consumer Finances A triennial survey taken by the Federal Reserve Board. It collects data on the assets, debts, and net worth of American households. For the 2007 survey, the Federal Reserve Board interviewed more than 4,000 households.

unemployed Those who, during the survey period, had no employment but were available and looking for work. Those who were laid off from their jobs and were waiting to be recalled are also classified as unemployed.

white A racial category that includes many Hispanics (who may be of any race) unless the term "non-Hispanic white" is used.

Youth Risk Behavior Surveillance System Created by the Centers for Disease Control to monitor health risks being taken by young people at the national, state, and local level. The national survey is taken every two years based on a nationally representative sample of 16,000 students in 9th through 12th grade in public and private schools.

Bibliography

Agency for Healthcare Research and Quality
    Internet site http://www.ahrq.gov/
    —Medical Expenditure Panel Survey, Internet site http://www.meps.ahrq.gov/mepsweb/ survey_comp/household.jsp

Bureau of Labor Statistics
    Internet site http://www.bls.gov
    —2000 and 2007 Consumer Expenditure Surveys, Internet site http://www.bls.gov/cex/
    —2007 American Time Use Survey, Internet site http://www.bls.gov/tus/home.htm
    —2007 American Time Use Survey, Summary Table 2. Number of persons and average hours per day by detailed activity classification (travel reported separately), 2007 annual averages, unpublished tables received upon special request
    —Characteristics of Minimum Wage Workers, 2008, Internet site http://www.bls.gov/cps/ minwage2008tbls.htm
    —College Enrollment and Work Activity of 2008 High School Graduates, Internet site http://www.bls.gov/news.release/hsgec.toc.htm
    —Contingent and Alternative Employment Arrangements, Internet site http://www.bls .gov/news.release/conemp.toc.htm
    —Economic and Employment Projections, Internet site http://www.bls.gov/news.release/ ecopro.toc.htm
    —Employee Benefits Survey, Internet site http://www.bls.gov/ncs/ebs/benefits/2008/ ownership_civilian.htm
    —Employee Tenure, Internet site http://www.bls.gov/news.release/tenure.toc.htm
    —Employment Characteristics of Families, Internet site http://www.bls.gov/news.release/ famee.toc.htm
    —Labor Force Statistics from the Current Population Survey, Internet site http://www.bls .gov/cps/tables.htm#empstat
    —*Monthly Labor Review*, "Labor Force Projections to 2016: More Workers in Their Golden Years," November 2007, Internet site http://www.bls.gov/opub/mlr/2007/11/contents.htm
    —*Monthly Labor Review*, "Youth enrollment and employment during the school year," February 2008, Internet site http://www.bls.gov/opub/mlr/2008/02/contents.htm
    —Table 15. Employed persons by detailed occupation, sex, and age, Annual Average 2008 (Source: Current Population Survey), unpublished table received upon special request

Bureau of the Census
    Internet site http://www.census.gov
    —2007 American Community Survey, Internet site http://factfinder.census.gov/servlet/ DatasetMainPageServlet?_program=ACS&_submenuId=&_lang=en&_ts=1
    —2008 Current Population Survey Annual Social and Economic Supplement, Internet site http://www.census.gov/hhes/www/income/dinctabs.html

—2008 National Population Projections, Internet site http://www.census.gov/population/ www/projections/2008projections.html

—A Child's Day: 2006 (Selected Indicators of Child Well-Being), Detailed Tables, Internet site http://www.census.gov/population/www/socdemo/2006_detailedtables.html

—American Housing Survey for the United States in 2007, Internet site http://www.census .gov/hhes/www/housing/ahs/ahs07/ahs07.html

—America's Families and Living Arrangements, 2008 Current Population Survey Annual Social and Economic Supplement, Internet site http://www.census.gov/population/www/ socdemo/hh-fam/cps2008.html

—Educational Attainment, Historical Tables, Internet site http://www.census.gov/ population/www/socdemo/educ-attn.html

—Educational Attainment in the United States: 2008, Detailed Tables, Current Population Survey Annual Social and Economic Supplement, Internet site http://www.census.gov/ population/www/socdemo/education/cps2008.html

—Families and Living Arrangements, Historical Time Series, Current Population Survey Annual Social and Economic Supplements, Internet site http://www.census.gov/population/ www/socdemo/hh-fam.html

—Fertility of American Women, Current Population Survey—June 2006, Detailed Tables, Internet site http://www.census.gov/population/www/socdemo/fertility/cps2006.html

—Geographic Mobility: 2007 to 2008, Detailed Tables, Current Population Survey Annual Social and Economic Supplement, Internet site http://www.census.gov/population/www/ socdemo/migrate/cps2008.html

—Geographical Mobility/Migration, Current Population Survey Annual Social and Economic Supplements, Internet site http://www.census.gov/population/www/socdemo/migrate.html

—Health Insurance, Internet site http://pubdb3.census.gov/macro/032008/health/toc.htm

—Historical Health Insurance Tables, Internet site http://www.census.gov/hhes/www/ hlthins/historic/index.html

—Historical Income Tables, Current Population Survey Annual Social and Economic Supplements, Internet site http://www.census.gov/hhes/www/income/histinc/histinctb.html

—Housing Vacancy Surveys, Internet site http://www.census.gov/hhes/www/housing/hvs/ hvs.html

—National Population Estimates, Internet site http://www.census.gov/popest/national/asrh/ NC-EST2008-sa.html

—Number, Timing, and Duration of Marriages and Divorces: 2004, Detailed Tables, Internet site http://www.census.gov/population/www/socdemo/marr-div/2004detailed_tables.html

—School Enrollment, Historical Tables, Internet site http://www.census.gov/population/ www/socdemo/school.html

—School Enrollment—Social and Economic Characteristics of Students: October 2007, detailed tables, Internet site http://www.census.gov/population/www/socdemo/school/cps2007 .html

—State Population Estimates, Internet site http://www.census.gov/popest/states/asrh/

Centers for Disease Control and Prevention

Internet site http://www.cdc.gov

—Behavioral Risk Factor Surveillance System, Prevalence Data, Internet site http://apps
.nccd.cdc.gov/brfss/

—Cases of HIV/AIDS and AIDS, Internet site http://www.cdc.gov/hiv/topics/surveillance/
resources/reports/2006report/table3.htm

—"Youth Risk Behavior Surveillance–United States, 2007," *Mortality and Morbidity Weekly
Report*, Vol. 57/SS-4, June 6, 2008; Internet site http://www.cdc.gov/HealthyYouth/yrbs/
index.htm

Department of Homeland Security

Internet site http://www.dhs.gov/index.shtm

—Immigration, 2008 Yearbook of Immigration Statistics, Internet site http://www.uscis
.gov/graphics/shared/statistics/yearbook/index.htm

Employee Benefit Research Institute

Internet site http://www.ebri.org/

—Retirement Confidence Surveys, Internet site http://www.ebri.org/surveys/rcs/

—"Employment-Based Retirement Plan Participation: Geographic Differences and Trends,
2007," *Issue Brief* 322, October 2008, Internet site http://www.ebri.org/publications/ib/
index.cfm?fa=ibDisp&content_id=3989

—"Ownership of Individual Accounts (IRAs) and 401(k)-Type Plans," by Craig Copeland,
Notes, Vol. 29, No. 5, May 2008; Internet site http://www.ebri.org/publications/notes/index
.cfm?fa=main&doc_type=2

Federal Interagency Forum on Child and Family Statistics

Internet site http://childstats.gov

—America's Children in Brief: Key National Indicators of Well-Being, 2008, Internet site
http://childstats.gov/americaschildren/tables.asp

Federal Reserve Board

Internet site http://www.federalreserve.gov/pubs/oss/oss2/scfindex.html

—"Changes in U.S. Family Finance from 2004 to 2007: Evidence from the Survey of Consumer Finances," *Federal Reserve Bulletin*, February 2009, Internet site http://www
.federalreserve.gov/pubs/oss/oss2/2007/scf2007home.html

National Center for Education Statistics

Internet site http://nces.ed.gov

—The Condition of Education, Internet site http://nces.ed.gov/programs/coe/

—Digest of Education Statistics: 2008, Internet site http://nces.ed.gov/programs/digest/

— National Household Education Surveys Program, Parent and Family Involvement in Education, 2006–07 School Year, Internet site http://nces.ed.gov/pubsearch/pubsinfo
.asp?pubid=2008050

National Center for Health Statistics

Internet site http://www.cdc.gov/nchs

—*2006 National Hospital Discharge Survey,* National Health Statistics Report, No. 5, 2008, Internet site http://www.cdc.gov/nchs/about/major/hdasd/listpubs.htm

—*Ambulatory Medical Care Utilization Estimates for 2006*, National Health Statistics Reports, No. 8, 2008, Internet site http://www.cdc.gov/nchs/about/major/ahcd/adata .htm#CombinedReports

—*Anthropometric Reference Data for Children and Adults: United States, 2003–2006*, National Health Statistics Reports, Number 10, 2008, Internet site http://www.cdc.gov/nchs/ products/pubs/pubd/nhsr/nhsr.htm

—*Births: Final Data for 2006*, National Vital Statistics Reports, Vol. 57, No. 7, 2009, Internet site http://www.cdc.gov/nchs/products/nvsr.htm#57_12

—*Births: Preliminary Data for 2007*, National Vital Statistics Reports, Vol. 57, No. 12, 2009, Internet site http://www.cdc.gov/nchs/products/nvsr.htm#57_12

—*Complementary and Alternative Medicine Use Among Adults and Children: United States, 2007*, National Health Statistics Report, No. 12, 2008, Internet site http://nccam.nih.gov/ news/camstats/2007/index.htm

—*Deaths: Final Data for 2006*, National Vital Statistics Reports, Vol. 57, No. 14, 2009, Internet site http://www.cdc.gov/nchs/products/nvsr.htm#vol57

—*Fertility, Contraception, and Fatherhood: Data on Men and Women from Cycle 6 of the 2002 National Survey of Family Growth*, Vital and Health Statistics, Series 23, No. 26, 2006; Internet site http://www.cdc.gov/nchs/nsfg.htm

—*Fertility, Family Planning, and Reproductive Health of U.S. Women: Data from the 2002 National Survey of Family Growth*, Vital and Health Statistics, Series 23, No. 25, 2005; Internet site http://www.cdc.gov/nchs/nsfg.htm

—*Health Characteristics of Adults 55 Years of Age and Over: United States, 2000-2003, Advance Data, No. 370,* 2006, Internet site http://www.cdc.gov/nchs/nhis.htm

—*National Ambulatory Medical Care Survey: 2006 Summary,* National Health Statistics Report, No. 3, 2008, Internet site http://www.cdc.gov/nchs/about/major/ahcd/adata.htm

—National Center for Chronic Disease Prevention and Health Promotion, Prevalence Data, Internet site http://apps.nccd.cdc.gov/HRQOL/

—*National Hospital Ambulatory Medical Care Survey: 2006 Emergency Department Summary,* National Health Statistics Report, No. 4, 2007, Internet site http://www.cdc.gov/nchs/ about/major/ahcd/adata.htm

—*National Hospital Ambulatory Medical Care Survey: 2006 Outpatient Department Summary,* National Health Statistics Report, No. 4, 2008, Internet site http://www.cdc.gov/nchs/ about/major/ahcd/adata.htm

—*Health United States 2008,* Internet site http://www.cdc.gov/nchs/hus.htm

—*Sexual Behavior and Selected Health Measures: Men and Women 15-44 Years of Age, United States, 2002*, Advance Data, No. 362, 2005; Internet site http://www.cdc.gov/nchs/ nsfg.htm

—Summary Health Statistics for U.S. Adults: National Health Interview Survey, 2007, Series 10, No. 240, 2008, Internet site http://www.cdc.gov/nchs/nhis.htm

—Summary Health Statistics for U.S. Children: National Health Interview Survey, 2007, Series 10, No. 239, 2008, Internet site http://www.cdc.gov/nchs/nhis.htm

—Summary Health Statistics for the U.S. Population: National Health Interview Survey, 2007, Series 10, No. 238, 2008, Internet site http://www.cdc.gov/nchs/nhis.htm

National Sporting Goods Association

Internet site http://www.nsga.org

—Sports Participation, Internet site http://www.nsga.org

Substance Abuse and Mental Health Services Administration

Internet site http://www.samhsa.gov

—National Survey on Drug Use and Health, 2007, Internet site http://www.oas.samhsa.gov/nsduh.htm

Survey Documentation and Analysis, Computer-assisted Survey Methods Program, University of California, Berkeley

Internet site http://sda.berkeley.edu/

—General Social Surveys, 1972-2008 Cumulative Data Files, Internet site http://sda.berkeley.edu/cgi-bin32/hsda?harcsda+gss08

Index